APT Initiativ

ELEMENTARY EXPLANATIONS

for AQA A2
Business Studies Students

Unit 3:
STRATEGIES FOR SUCCESS

written by **Claire Baker**

In-depth, up-to-date, precise information on
The essential theory required by
The unit specification

© APT Initiatives Limited, 2009.

Author

Claire Baker

All rights reserved. No part of this publication may be reproduced, stored in or introduced into a retrieval system, or transmitted, in any form, or by any means (electronic, mechanical, photocopying, recording or otherwise) without the written permission of APT Initiatives Ltd, or under licence from the Copyright Licensing Agency Limited, of 90 Tottenham Court Road, London W1P 9HE. Any person who does any unauthorised act in relation to this publication may be liable to criminal prosecution and civil claims for damages.

A CIP catalogue record for this book is available from the British Library.

ISNB: 978-0-9556408-5-8

Published by

APT Initiatives Limited
Millstone Lodge
Eaton Upon Tern
Market Drayton
Shropshire
TF9 2BX

Tel / Fax: 01952 540877
email:sales@apt-initiatives.com
www.apt-initiatives.com

Colour illustrations including cover ©iStockphoto.com

Licence to use the illustrations has been purchased from iStockphoto.com. The copyright of these illustrations remains with iStockphoto or the original supplier of the content, as the case may be. These illustrations cannot, therefore, be copied, used or adapted for use in other works without the prior permission of iStockphoto.

Printed and bound by Think Ink, Ipswich, Suffolk, UK.

These 'Elementary Explanations' are one of several resources produced by APT Initiatives Ltd to support teachers and their students taking the AQA A2 Unit 3 examination. For further information on these and other resources produced for a wide range of Business Studies and Economics courses refer to APT Initiatives Ltd's website: www.apt-initiatives.com where products can be ordered and paid for on-line.

FOREWORD

This book has been produced for students of AQA GCE AS / A Level Business Studies. It contains highly comprehensive coverage of the essential theory required for the GCE Business Studies Specification for AQA A2 Unit 3: Strategies for Success.

Explanations are sufficiently detailed to enable students to grasp the essential theory required with minimum teacher assistance. Care has been taken to ensure the information provided is accurate, up-to-date and precise and directly matches the specification requirements.

At the beginning of each topic there are learning objectives and definitions of key terms which are then explained in detail throughout each chapter. The learning objectives can later be used as revision questions either at the end of each topic and / or upon completion of the entire unit. The book also contains a detailed index, to enable readers to quickly access the information they require.

The author, Claire Baker, is an experienced teacher, examiner, author and the owner and Managing Director of APT Initiatives Limited. She has taught Business Studies from ages 11 to 19 and has been an examiner, Principal Examiner and Reviser for Business Studies and Business related courses for a leading awarding body.

An 'Essential Revision Pocketbook' has been published by APT Initiatives Ltd to complement this book. It contains condensed versions of the 'Elementary Explanations' as well as comprehensive information on what examiners look for when marking students' answers, and how to demonstrate these skills.

This book concentrates solely on providing students with the essential theory relating to Unit 3. A range of activities to test and develop students' knowledge and understanding of the business studies theory and concepts covered is provided in other resources available from APT Initiatives Ltd.

APT Initiatives Ltd can be contacted directly with any orders, queries or feedback via the website: www.apt-initiatives.com, via email: support@apt-initiatives.com or by phone: 01952 540877.

CONTENTS

	Page No
FUNCTIONAL OBJECTIVES AND STRATEGIES	**1**

1. USING OBJECTIVES AND STRATEGIES — 2

General Introduction to Objectives & Strategies — 3
Functional Objectives and their Relationship with Corporate Objectives — 4
The Relationship between Functional Objectives and Strategies — 7

FINANCIAL STRATEGIES AND ACCOUNTS — 8

1. UNDERSTANDING FINANCIAL OBJECTIVES — 9

Financial Objectives — 10
Assessing Internal and External Influences on Financial Objectives — 13

2. USING FINANCIAL DATA TO MEASURE AND ASSESS PERFORMANCE — 16

Analysing Balance Sheets — 17
Analysing Income Statements — 27
Using Financial Data for Comparisons, Trend Analysis and Decision Making — 33
Assessing Strengths and Weaknesses of Financial Data in Judging Performance — 38

3. INTERPRETING PUBLISHED ACCOUNTS — 42

Conducting Ratio Analysis — 43
The Value and Limitations of Ratio Analysis — 54

4. SELECTING FINANCIAL STRATEGIES — 56

Raising Finance — 57
Implementing Profit Centres — 63
Cost Minimisation — 67
Allocating Capital Expenditure — 74

5. MAKING INVESTMENT DECISIONS — 76

Why Businesses Invest – Helping to Reach Functional Objectives — 77
Conducting Quantitative Investment Appraisal — 79
Investment Criteria — 84
Assessing the Risks and Uncertainties of Investment Decisions — 86
Evaluating Quantitative and Qualitative Influences on Investment Decisions — 90

© APT Initiatives Limited, 2009

MARKETING STRATEGIES 94

1. UNDERSTANDING MARKETING OBJECTIVES — 95

- Marketing Objectives — 96
- Assessing Internal and External Influences on Marketing Objectives — 99

2. ANALYSING MARKETS AND MARKETING — 102

- Reasons for, and the Value of, Market Analysis — 103
- Methods of Analysing Trends — 106
- The Use of Information Technology in Analysing Markets — 115
- Difficulties in Analysing Marketing Data — 118

3. SELECTING MARKETING STRATEGIES — 120

- Porter's Generic Strategies: Low Cost versus Differentiation — 121
- Ansoff's Matrix Marketing Strategies (& Other Strategies) — 127
- Methods, Risks and Benefits in Entering International Markets — 131
- Assessing Effectiveness of Marketing Strategies — 142

4. DEVELOPING AND IMPLEMENTING MARKETING PLANS — 144

- Components of Marketing Plans — 145
- Assessing Internal and External Influences on Marketing Plans — 149
- Issues in Implementing Marketing Plans — 152

OPERATIONAL STRATEGIES 154

1. UNDERSTANDING OPERATIONAL OBJECTIVES — 155

- Operational Objectives — 156
- Assessing Internal and External Influences on Operational Objectives — 161

2. SCALE AND RESOURCE MIX — 165

- Choosing the Right Scale of Production: Economies and Diseconomies of Scale — 166
- Choosing the Optimal Mix of Resources: Capital and Labour Intensity — 171

3. INNOVATION — 175

- Innovation, Research and Development — 176
- Purpose, Costs, Benefits and Risks of Innovation — 181

© APT Initiatives Limited, 2009

4.	**LOCATION**	**184**
	Methods of Making Location Decisions	185
	Benefits of Optimal Location	192
	The Advantages and Disadvantages of Multi-site Locations	193
	Issues Relating to International Location	195
5.	**LEAN PRODUCTION**	**199**
	Introduction to Lean Production	200
	The Effective Management of Time	202
	Assessing the Value of Critical Path Analysis	205
	Effective Management of Other Resources through Methods of Lean Production	212

HUMAN RESOURCE STRATEGIES — 216

1.	**UNDERSTANDING HR OBJECTIVES AND STRATEGIES**	**217**
	HR Objectives	218
	Assessing Internal and External Influences on HR Objectives	220
	HR Strategies	224
2.	**DEVELOPING AND IMPLEMENTING WORKFORCE PLANS**	**229**
	Components of Workforce Plans	230
	Assessing Internal and External Influences on Workforce Plans	234
	Issues in Implementing Workforce Plans	238
	The Value of Using Workforce Plans	240
3.	**COMPETITIVE ORGANISATIONAL STRUCTURES**	**242**
	Types of Organisational Structure and Factors Determining Choice	243
	Adapting Organisational Structures to Improve Competitiveness	249
4.	**EFFECTIVE EMPLOYER / EMPLOYEE RELATIONS**	**258**
	Managing Communications with Employees	259
	Methods of Employee Representation	270
	Methods of Avoiding and Resolving Industrial Disputes	275

INDEX — **281**

© **APT Initiatives Limited**, 2009

1

FUNCTIONAL OBJECTIVES AND STRATEGIES

© APT Initiatives Limited, 2009

1.1
USING OBJECTIVES & STRATEGIES

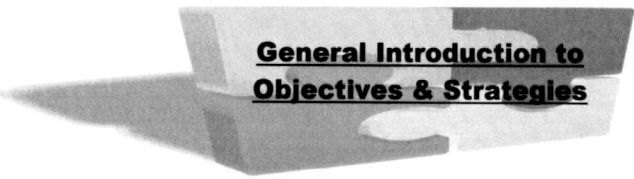

General Introduction to Objectives & Strategies

Objectives

By the end of this introductory topic to Unit 3 you should be able to:

1. Define the terms objectives and strategies.
2. Explain the difference between, and relationship between, objectives and strategies.

Key Terms

Objectives are goals or targets that businesses strive to achieve.
Strategies are plans or courses of action required in order to achieve an objective.

The Nature of, and Relationship Between, Objectives and Strategies

Objectives – *what do we want to achieve?*

As Unit 1 has previously discussed, the key people (owners / directors / managers) involved in a business set objectives ie goals or targets for the business (and individual departments within the business) to achieve, which help to provide direction and a focus for decision making. Objectives are particularly important as a business increases in size because they help to ensure everyone works towards a common goal. They also provide a means of measuring performance and so provide an important means of control. To achieve these benefits, however, objectives should be SMART ie **s**pecific, **m**easurable, **a**greed by the key people involved, **r**ealistic and **t**imescaled.

Strategy – *how are we going to get there?*

Once objectives have been set, decision makers need to decide upon the most appropriate strategy ie course of action to ensure the objective(s) can be achieved. In line with the need to ensure SMART objectives, strategy should also be evaluated in terms of three specific criteria:

1. Is it **suitable** - in achieving the business's objectives and / or addressing specific problems / weaknesses?
2. Is it **acceptable** - to the key stakeholders?
3. Is it **feasible** - in terms of implementation? Eg does the business have the resources eg financial, human, physical? If not, can it obtain the resources required?

Closing Comments

Determining SMART objectives and the most appropriate strategy to achieve these objectives, requires the key decision makers to take into account the internal capabilities of the business ie its strengths and weaknesses, and the external business environment including any opportunities and threats. This is essential to ensure the objectives and strategies decided upon are appropriate in terms of realism, and in maximising the business's potential.

© APT Initiatives Limited, 2009

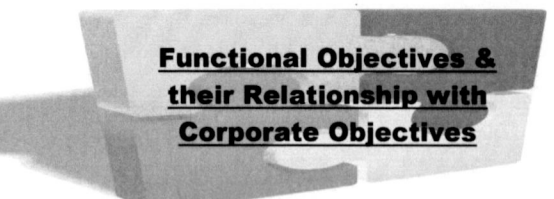

Functional Objectives & their Relationship with Corporate Objectives

Objectives

By the end of this topic you should be able to:

1. Define the terms corporate objectives and functional objectives.
2. List at least 3 potential objectives relating to each of the four main functional areas of business ie Finance, Marketing, Operations and Human Resources.
3. Explain, using examples, how functional objectives contribute to the achievement of corporate objectives.

Key Terms

Corporate objectives are goals or targets that concern the business as a whole and provide the boundaries for setting functional eg marketing objectives.

Functional objectives are goals or targets that must be achieved by the individual functional areas (or departments) into which a business is divided (eg Finance, Marketing, Operations and Human Resources) to ensure that the overall corporate objectives are met.

Corporate Objectives

Corporate objectives are goals or targets that relate to the business as a whole. They are often expressed in financial terms - for example - to make a certain percentage, amount of, or rate of:

- sales
- profit
- return (on investment)
- growth in terms of markets or share valuation.

They are set at the highest level of the organisation, ie owner or chairman / managing director / board level and provide the boundaries for setting functional objectives.

Functional Objectives

As a business increases in size employees are often grouped or sub-divided according to the nature of the work they carry out, that is, they are often grouped into different departments / functional areas which perform a common set of activities. The most common functional areas are Finance, Marketing, Operations and Human Resources. Functional objectives are goals or targets that relate to these individual functional areas (or departments). They will normally be set at the executive level ie below owner or board / director level, but may involve owner or board / director approval or consultation.

Numerous examples of functional objectives are listed below, the majority of which are explained in more detail in subsequent sections of these Elementary Explanations (as required by the AQA A2 specifications).

Marketing objectives, for example, may include targets relating to:

- Product or brand awareness / recognition.
- Sales, customer base, repeat business or brand / customer loyalty.
- Market standing / position (image), market share or leadership.

Financial objectives may include targets relating to:

- Raising finance.
- Cash flow / liquidity.
- Cost minimisation.
- ROCE ie return on capital employed.
- Shareholders' returns on their investment.

Operational objectives may include targets relating to:

- Product or service quality.
- Production costs.
- Production volumes.
- Capacity utilisation.
- New product development / innovation.
- Overall productive efficiency (including time).
- Minimising waste and the impact of the business on the environment.

Human Resources objectives may include targets relating to:

- The recruitment of staff and matching workforce skills, size and location to business needs.
- Making full use of the workforce's potential - training and development.
- Minimising labour costs eg reducing unauthorised absence, minimising labour turnover.
- Maintaining good employer / employee relations.

Other objectives not referred to in the AQA Unit 3 specifications include objectives relating to:

- Profit margins (financial)
- Pricing (marketing)
- Sourcing products (operational)

The latter ie sourcing products, is particularly important within the current UK economy as manufacturing is now the smallest part, following the general move towards 'service' industries. For example, in retailing / distribution buying and selling products without adding actual value is a major operational activity.

The Relationship between Functional and Corporate Objectives

Functional objectives must be achieved by particular functions or departments of a business in order to ensure that the overall corporate objectives are met. They must be consistent with, and supportive of, the overall corporate objectives. For example, a business's overall corporate objective may be to **achieve a 10% increase on profit for the year** and it may set the following functional objectives to ensure this corporate objective is achieved:

- **Marketing:** To increase sales from £45,000 to £50,000 per month.
- **Human Resources:** To reduce total average unauthorised absence from 10 days to 2 days per month.
- **Finance:** To eliminate the need for a bank overdraft (and, thus interest payments) by reducing the average number of days it takes customers to pay from 73 to 56 days within the next 3 months.
- **Production:** To reduce the number of rejects / defective products from 2.5% to 1.5% over the next 6 months.

Closing Comments

The most appropriate corporate objective will depend upon the individual circumstances facing the business - for example - if a business is new or introducing a new product, then it may have survival or breakeven as its overall objective for the first year. If a business is established in the market place, its corporate objective is likely to be more ambitious than merely to survive or breakeven - for example - to make a certain percentage net profit. Whatever the corporate objective decided upon, the functional objective must be supportive of the overall corporate objective, and also consistent with the objectives of other functional areas.

The Relationship between Functional Objectives & Strategies

Objectives

By the end of this topic you should be able to:

1. Define the terms corporate strategies and functional strategies.
2. Explain, using examples, the relationship between functional objectives and strategies.

Key Terms

Corporate strategy concerns the plan or course of action required to achieve a business's corporate objectives.

Functional strategy concerns the plan or course of action required to achieve a business's functional objectives.

The Relationship between Functional Objectives and Strategies

As previously explained above, decision makers within a business decide upon strategies to achieve the business's objectives. Functional strategies may simply be defined as plans of action required to achieve a business's functional objective(s). For example, to achieve the marketing (and overall corporate) objective of increasing market share, a business's marketing strategy could include the following:

Marketing Objective	Marketing Strategy
To increase market share from 12 to 20% ie by 8% by 20XX.	Concentrate on the middle market sector through product differentiation – a business strategy that involves making a firm's product look different from its competitors in the eyes of its customers. This may, for example, be achieved through improvements to product packaging, or persuasive TV advertising emphasising product benefits.

A wide range of functional strategies will be considered in turn in subsequent sections of these Elementary Explanations - as required by the AQA GCE A2 specifications.

Closing Comments

Corporate objectives and strategies are concerned with setting direction on aspects which are of vital importance to the business and its overall success. Functional objectives and strategies are concerned with how the corporate objectives and strategies can be achieved. They must be supportive of the overall corporate objectives and strategies, and be consistent with the objectives and strategies of other functional areas.

One further distinction to appreciate between corporate and functional levels is that if a corporate strategy proved to be wrong, then the ramifications to the business would probably be serious. In contrast, if a functional strategy proved to be wrong, it would probably be easier to correct. Although the rectification may be costly, it would probably not threaten the business's very survival.

2

FINANCIAL STRATEGIES AND ACCOUNTS

2.1
UNDERSTANDING FINANCIAL OBJECTIVES

Financial Objectives

Objectives

By the end of this topic you should be able to:

1. Define the term financial objectives.
2. State at least 3 examples of financial objectives.

Key Terms

Financial objectives may be defined as goals or targets that must be achieved by the finance function in order to achieve the business's overall corporate objective(s) - for example - a target relating to raising a certain amount of finance through borrowing or shares in order to achieve a corporate growth / expansion objective. Financial objectives may, however, also be defined as goals or targets that concern the management of money and other assets, and so might include targets relating to cash flow or return on capital employed in the business (ROCE).

Overview

In keeping with the definitions of other functional objectives of a business (outlined in the previous section), financial objectives should essentially concern goals or targets that must be achieved by the finance function in order to achieve the business's overall corporate objective(s). However, based on the examples of financial objectives cited in the AQA Unit 3 specification, financial objectives may also be defined as goals or targets that concern the management of monetary resources ie resources with a financial value, and so may include targets relating to ROCE and shareholders' returns, which are more commonly cited as examples of corporate objectives.

The AQA Unit 3 specification states that financial objectives should include reference to targets relating to: Cash flow (liquidity); Cost minimisation; ROCE (Return on Capital Employed); and Shareholders' returns. Each of these objectives are considered in more detail below.

Examples of Financial Objectives

Cash Flow and Liquidity

Cash flow (as Unit 1 explained) refers to the movement of money into and out of a business.

Liquidity concerns the amount of cash available in a business to meet the business's daily requirements, in particular, to meet debts as they fall due.

Forecasting and monitoring cash flow and setting and achieving targets relating to liquidity is, as Unit 1 has already highlighted, essential to ensure a business's short-term survival. Without sufficient cash to pay debts as they fall due a business could be forced - by creditors - to close, and sell off business assets in order to settle any debts.

Cash flow / liquidity targets might – for example – concern:

- maintaining a maximum spend per department through the use of departmental budgets.
- reducing the number of customers owing the business money (debtors).
- reducing inventory (stock) levels - to free up cash tied up in stock.
- increasing or reducing the bank overdraft by a certain amount by a certain date.
- increasing the credit period granted by suppliers for purchases.

Remember any targets set should be SMART and state by how much something should be reduced / increased, and by what date.

Ways in which a business might achieve targets relating to cash flow and liquidity are discussed in detail in the section on 'Working Capital' under 'Analysing Balance Sheets' below.

Cost Minimisation

Cost minimisation should be an ongoing objective of any efficient organisation - though not at the expense of quality of product or service levels as this could affect revenues. This is because targets for minimising costs are essential to achieve targets relating to profitability and return on capital employed and shareholders' investment (see below). Cost minimisation may also help to achieve targets relating to marketing. This is because a reduction in costs may enable a firm to lower its selling price and, thus, attract more customers, thereby increasing market share. This is probably why the AQA specifications list cost minimisation both as a financial 'objective' <u>and</u> a financial 'strategy' (ie the action required to achieve an objective).

Targets relating to cost minimisation may concern reducing any one or a mixture of the firm's:

- variable costs eg materials, direct labour (by x amount by x date); and / or
- fixed costs or overheads eg rent, salaries (by x amount by x date).

Ways in which a business might achieve targets to reduce a wide range of costs are considered in detail under the subsequent section on 'Cost Minimisation' as a 'Financial Strategy' below.

ROCE

Return on capital employed concerns the amount of operating profit (ie net profit before interest and tax) a business generates from the total capital employed within the business.

ROCE % = Operating Profit (ie profit before interest and tax) / Capital Employed x 100

The main task of management is to maximise the return on capital invested in a business and so objectives relating to ROCE are very common. If a business is unable to generate more than the rate of interest it may as well close, sell off its assets, and put the money in a bank.

Targets relating to ROCE may concern:

- **Increasing operating profit whilst maintaining the same level of capital investment**, eg by reducing costs whilst maintaining sales revenues or increasing sales revenues whilst maintaining costs, and / or increasing the efficiency of asset use.

- **Maintaining operating profit but reducing the amount of capital it takes to generate this amount of profit** eg by selling off any under-utilised assets to pay off a long-term loan.

ROCE is discussed in more detail in the section on 'Ratio Analysis' under 'Interpreting Published Accounts' below.

Shareholders' Returns

Investing in shares provides two potential rewards / return to shareholders:

- a share in any profits made ie dividends (a percentage of after tax profits).
- any capital gain made on the sale of their shares.

Thus, targets relating to shareholders' returns may concern targets relating to increasing the:

- dividend (or dividend per share and dividend yield).
- share price / the market value of shares.

Shareholder returns are also discussed in more detail in the section on 'Ratio Analysis' under 'Interpreting Published Accounts' below.

Closing Comments

This section of our Elementary Explanations has drawn attention to the following points which are worth emphasising:

1. Targets relating to ROCE and shareholder returns concern the business as a whole and may be regarded and cited as corporate objectives, as opposed to objectives that specifically relate to the finance function that (according to the definition of functional objectives in general) must be achieved for the overall corporate objective(s) to be met.

2. There are a range of other possible financial objectives not listed in the AQA specifications - for example - targets that concern raising a set amount of money through bank borrowing or through selling shares in order to fund the achievement of a corporate growth / expansion objective. Raising finance is, however, listed as a financial 'strategy' in the AQA specifications.

3. Although the AQA specifications initially list cost minimisation as a financial 'objective', the specification later lists cost minimisation as a financial 'strategy' and so we will consider cost minimisation in more detail later - as a strategy for achieving other financial objectives.

It should also be highlighted and appreciated at this stage of these Elementary Explanations, that Marketing and Operations are the prime functions of business which actually control most of the resources – the efficient use of which will determine the achievement of corporate objectives. Finance and HR are, largely, supporting functions which, in themselves, will not achieve main objectives but should improve the two main prime functions through, for example, management advice, management information and training.

Assessing Internal and External Influences on Financial Objectives

Objectives

By the end of this topic you should be able to:

1. Outline at least 4 internal influences on financial objectives.
2. Outline at least 4 external influences on financial objectives.

Key Terms

Internal influences on financial objectives are factors stemming from inside the business that can affect decisions over, or success in achieving, financial objectives – for example – corporate objectives, age, size and structure of the business, and the human resources employed.

External influences on financial objectives are factors stemming from outside the business that can affect decisions over, or success in achieving, financial objectives – for example – a change in political, legal, economic, social and technological factors, or competitor and supplier activities.

Internal Influences on Financial Objectives

Corporate Objectives

The previous section has highlighted how objectives are set for the whole business and that these provide the boundaries for setting functional objectives. Thus, corporate objectives will clearly influence the functional (including financial) objectives of the business. These must be consistent with, and support, the achievement of the business's overall corporate objectives.

Age

Generating a certain amount of reward for the time and money invested in the form of profit and return on capital employed (ROCE) or dividends to shareholders, is a key objective of private sector businesses (in the profit making sector). However, many businesses just starting up may be content to survive and break-even in the short to medium term, due to lack of experience and resources, limited customer awareness, competition from established firms, and / or unexpected costs.

In addition, the more established a business, the more options it has with regard to raising finance and the more likely it will be able to achieve targets relating to raising finance. This is because new businesses have no credit or financial history and are considered to be more of a risk. They will need to do much to convince the financier or investor that their business will be successful, including in depth market research, detailed sales forecasts and cost calculations.

Size

The size of a business may also influence objectives and strategies concerned with raising finance. For instance, small and medium-sized businesses are often considered to be high risk. They tend not to have sufficient assets on which to secure finance or make sufficient profits to attract investors. In addition, as a business grows it becomes more difficult to control and co-ordinate, and many sole traders or partnerships often resort to selling shares and forming limited companies, as a means of minimising the risks involved, because of the protection of personal assets this type of business provides.

Legal Structure

As highlighted above, legal status also affects strategies with regard to raising finance. Unlike sole traders or partnerships, limited companies can sell shares to raise finance. Because companies can raise a large amount of finance in this way, they are usually larger, and have more assets to offer as security for loans.

Financial Position

The financial position of a business will also affect objectives and strategies relating to raising finance. A sound credit history, healthy profitability and liquidity position, and the need for security, may be required in order to secure a loan and interest potential investors. Banks and building societies will be particularly interested in liquidity, ie whether the business is able to meet debts as they fall due. They are also likely to examine key financial ratios such as interest cover, to assess the business's ability to pay its interest payments out of operating or net profit, and gearing, which measures the proportion of capital employed provided by loans. The business is also likely to consider these ratios to assess the risk involved. The higher the gearing, the higher the risk, as the business is committed to paying interest on loans before it can reinvest profits and / or pay dividends to shareholders. On the other hand, shareholders and venture capitalists will be more interested in profitability. (NB Key ratios used to assess profitability, gearing and liquidity are covered later in these Elementary Explanations).

Size and Strength of Worker Representation

Objectives relating to cost minimisation that involve redundancies or significant changes in working practices, may be opposed and resisted by the workforce and be difficult to achieve, particularly if they have the backing of a strong union.

External Influences on Financial Objectives

The Credit Crunch and Availability of Finance

In recent years banks have been reluctant to lend money and business's have found it increasingly difficult to raise finance and, thus, the funds required to support an expansion objective and / or have struggled to achieve objectives relating to cash flow and liquidity.

The State of the Economy – The Business Cycle

In a recession previous targets relating to profits or ROCE and shareholder returns may be unrealistic and a business may be forced to concentrate on cost minimisation and survival - at least in the short term.

Other Aspects Relating to the Economy – Tax and Interest Rates

Changes in corporation tax or VAT may impinge upon objectives relating to shareholder returns.

Changes in income tax and interest rates may reduce demand for a business's product / service, and thus its sales and profit and, ultimately, ROCE objective.

Changes in interest rates may also increase a business's costs and so affect objectives relating to cost minimisation or targets relating to raising finance through borrowing. A steep rise in interest rates may, for example, force a business to choose methods of finance other than loans or leasing agreements as these prove too costly.

Legislation

New legislation may necessitate costly changes in order to comply with the legislation, which cut into a profit or ROCE objective.

Competition

A new competitor may result in reduced demand for a business's product / service and, thus, may restrict targets relating to ROCE and shareholder returns.

The State of the Market

If the market for a business's product or service is growing then a business may be able to set and achieve higher targets for ROCE and shareholder returns. In a saturated or declining market where competition tends to become more aggressive, emphasis may need to be placed on cost minimisation in order to maintain competitiveness on price and / or targets relating to cash flow and liquidity as sales start to fall.

Changes in the Cost of Materials / Inputs

Increases in the cost of materials or other inputs, for example, steep rises in oil prices may increase a business's energy bills, restricting the achievement of objectives relating to ROCE and shareholder returns.

Closing Comments

Internal and external influences on a business's financial objective should be taken into account not only when setting objectives – to ensure the objectives set are both realistic and serve to maximise the business's potential, but also when evaluating a business's financial performance.

Many of the influences discussed in this section clearly not only affect a firm's financial objectives, but also affect decisions relating to, and success in achieving, strategies to achieve these objectives.

2.2

USING FINANCIAL DATA TO MEASURE AND ASSESS PERFORMANCE

Analysing Balance Sheets

Objectives

By the end of this topic you should be able to:

1. Define the term balance sheet and key balance sheet terms including assets, liabilities and capital, non-current assets (fixed assets), current assets, current liabilities, net current assets, long-term liabilities, net assets, shareholder's equity (capital and reserves) and total equity (shareholders' funds).
2. Outline key differences between the balance sheets of public and private limited companies and sole traders.
3. Define and explain the importance of working capital and outline at least 6 ways a business can ensure sufficient working capital to fund day to day operations.
4. Define and explain the importance of depreciation and the effect of depreciation on asset value, profit and cash.
5. Undertake simple analysis of a particular business's balance sheet to help assess the business's performance in a given situation.

Key Terms

A **balance sheet** is a snapshot of a firm's worth / financial position at a particular moment in time. It shows what the business owns (assets) in monetary terms, and from where funds have been obtained to purchase what it owns (capital and liabilities).

Assets are items owned by the business.

Liabilities are what the business owes to other organisations or individuals.

Capital is the money invested or kept within the business by the owners / shareholders.

Non-current assets (or **fixed assets**) are items that usually have a life span of more than a year, and do not get used up in the production or provision of a product or service. They can be tangible (ie they can be seen and touched eg buildings), intangible (eg trademarks) or financial (eg shares in other businesses).

Depreciation is a cost that occurs when a business writes off the net cost of a fixed asset over its useful life.

Current assets are items that are usually held for a relatively short period of time, ie under one year. They typically include inventories (stock), trade and other receivables (debtors) and cash.

Current liabilities are monies owed by the business that must be paid within one year from the balance sheet date. They typically include bank overdrafts and trade and other payables (creditors). They may include dividends payable, corporation tax and accruals (suppliers of services used eg telephone, gas and electricity who have not yet invoiced the firm).

Working capital is the finance available for the day-to-day running of a business. In the balance sheet it is represented as current assets less current liabilities (**net current liabilities**).

Non-current liabilities (long-term liabilities) concern monies owed by a business which do not have to be settled within one year. These typically concern bank or building society loans such as mortgages over 12 months.

Net assets are assets (non-current and current) less liabilities (current and non-current). This figure represents the part of total assets which is funded by shareholders' funds or equity (ie capital put into the business by the owners of the business) and not by short-term liabilities or long-term debt. It, therefore, provides **the net value of what the company owns / is worth** as a going concern (not taking into account any differences in book value and actual value of property and goodwill, or trading conditions).

Shareholders' equity consists of money raised by selling shares to family members and friends (private limited companies) or members of the general public (public limited companies), as well as profit retained within the business (retained earnings) and other funds (reserves) generated from selling shares for more than their nominal value (share premiums), and from selling land or property over the original purchase price (revaluations).

Total equity or shareholders' funds (or capital employed for a sole trader) is the sum of the total amount of money put into the business by owners / shareholders (capital), profit kept within the business (retained earnings) and any other reserves.

Overview including Typical Formats for Different Legal Structures

Overview

A balance sheet is a snapshot of a firm's worth / financial position at a particular moment in time. It shows what the business owns in monetary terms, and from where funds have been obtained, to purchase what it owns, as follows:

- **Assets** are the items owned by the business.
- **Liabilities** are the debts of the business, ie what it owes to other businesses, individuals and institutions.
- **Capital** is the money invested in the business or kept in the business by the business owners / shareholders (owners / equity capital)

The value of assets should always equal capital and liabilities. This is known as the **accounting equation**. This is because the money used to purchase an asset has to come from somewhere – either through owner's capital, ie money put into or kept in the business by the owner(s), or borrowed from others, ie liabilities.

The balance sheet is one of the most important business documents, along with the income statement (profit and loss account). Both these documents are produced to help decision-making and are essentially used, not only by management to assess the financial performance of the business, but potential lenders and investors, to assess the business's stability and ability to repay moneys borrowed, and the likely return on their investment.

In the same way that a business hopes to make a profit each year, it also aims to have assets greater than liabilities. Once profit has been earned, this makes the business worth more than before - representing business growth.

Typical Format

The typical format of a balance sheet and / or terms used on a balance sheet varies slightly according to the legal status of the business. This is mainly because Since 1 January 2005, following a European Union regulation, public limited companies' financial statements must comply with International Financial Reporting Standards (IFRS).

The rule has not yet been extended to private limited companies. As a result there may be differences in the terms used on the balance sheets of public and private limited companies.

Below is a typical format for balance sheets of companies operating in the UK. Terms that may still be used on the balance sheets of private limited companies but are no longer used on the balance sheets of public limited companies are shown in brackets.

Balance Sheet of ABC plc at 31/3/09

	£	£	£
Non-current Assets (Fixed Assets)			
Premises			1,200,000
Fixtures & Fittings			800,000
Machinery & Equipment			1,900,000
Motor Vehicles			100,000
			4,000,000
Current Assets			
Inventories (Stock)	700,000		
Trade and other Receivables (Debtors)	900,000		
Cash and Cash Equivalents (Cash)	100,000		
		1,700,000	
Current Liabilities			
Bank overdraft	120,000		
Trade and other Payables (Creditors)	880,000		
		1,000,000	
Net Current Liabilities (Net Current Assets)			700,000
Total Assets less Current Liabilities			4,700,000
Non-current Liabilities (Long-term Liabilities)			
Long Term Bank Loan			400,000
Net Assets			**4,300,000**
Shareholders' Equity (Capital and Reserves)			
Ordinary share capital		3,000,000	
Reserves and Retained Earnings (Profit&Reserves)		1,300,000	
Total Equity (Shareholders' Funds)			**4,300,000**

To enable easy comparison within and between businesses, assets are usually listed on the balance sheet in the order shown above, with fixed assets listed according to how long they are likely to last, and current assets listed according to how quickly they can be turned into cash, with the least liquid current asset, ie stock, being shown first.

The above balance sheet shows the business to be worth £4.3 million. This essentially means that if all the assets were sold and the money used to pay off the liabilities, then the shareholders would be left with £4.3 million. This is, however, not strictly true. The net worth of the company is basically what the company can be sold for as a going concern with the potential for maintaining profits. If the premises are more valuable than the book value and / or the value of goodwill is high, then the company may be much more valuable than the Balance Sheet figure. Conversely, if the trading conditions were poor, or the company went into liquidation, then many of the assets may not be worth the Balance Sheet figure, for example, some stock and work in progress may only be worth scrap value.

NB The layout and terminology used on sole trader balance sheet is similar to the above. The main difference is that there is a 'Capital Account' not a 'Shareholders' Equity or 'Capital and Reserves' section on the balance sheet.

Explanation of Key Balance Sheet Terms

Non-current Assets (Fixed Assets)

Non-current assets (or fixed assets) are items that usually have a life span of **more than a year**, and do not get used up in the production or provision of a product or service. They can be tangible (ie they can be seen and touched), intangible or financial.

- **Tangible.** For many businesses, these typically include land, buildings, fixtures and fittings, machinery and vehicles. They provide collateral (security) for a loan from the bank. Land is the only item accountants normally accept that can be revalued. Buildings can be freehold (owned forever) or leasehold (owned for a specified period). Other fixed assets are written off by **depreciation** over an agreed period of time. They are shown in the balance sheet at Net Book Value, ie purchase cost less cumulative depreciation, not current market value. (NB Depreciation is discussed in more detail later in this section).

- **Intangible.** These include goodwill, patents, copyrights and trademarks including website domain names. Goodwill is the estimated value placed on regular custom established over the years. It usually only appears when one business takes over another, and is usually the difference between the Net Asset Value and the purchase price of the company. Some companies have begun to put a value on their brands in the balance sheet, but it is difficult to assess their true worth.

- **Financial.** These are investments / shares held by the business in other companies. They are valued at their cost price, or their current market price, whichever is the lower.

Current Assets

Current assets are items that are usually held for a relatively short period of time, ie **under one year**. They are constantly changing and the ultimate aim is to convert them into cash. For the majority of businesses these typically include:

- **Inventories (Stock).** This may be in the form of raw materials and components, work in progress or finished goods. It is valued at the purchase cost or market value, whichever is the lower.

- **Trade and other receivables (Debtors).** These are people or other organisations who owe the business money for goods or services received. Almost all businesses provide their customers with an interest free period of grace in which to pay for their goods or services once received. This is usually 30 days, but in practice nearer 70 days.

- **Prepayments.** These relate to expenses that, by custom or law, have to be paid in advance, eg insurance. At the balance sheet date, part of the amount paid may relate to the next accounting period. (They are usually grouped with debtors).

- **Cash and cash equivalents.** This includes cash in hand and held in bank accounts or money market funds or other investments which mature / can be accessed within 90 days.

Current Liabilities

Current liabilities are **monies owed by the business that must be paid within one year** from the balance sheet date. For the majority of businesses these typically include:

- **Overdrafts.** These are arrangements between a firm and its bank, or building society, to withdraw more money from its account than that which is deposited in it, to an agreed limit. Interest is charged on any amounts overdrawn.
- **Trade and other payables (Creditors).** Individuals or businesses to whom the firm owes money (mostly suppliers of goods received but not yet paid for).
- **Dividends payable.** A percentage of profit to be paid to shareholders.
- **Corporation tax.** A tax based on company profits.
- **Accruals.** Creditors who have not yet invoiced the firm eg phone, gas, electricity or wages of those who have worked for the firm but have not yet received their weekly or monthly pay. The amount likely to be owed up to the point of the balance sheet is estimated (and included as an expense on the income statement / profit & loss account).

Net Current Liabilities (Net Current Assets)

Balance sheets group current assets with current liabilities and show the net difference, ie current assets less current liabilities as net current liabilities (or assets). This tells a business **how much capital is available to fund day to day operations in the short term.** The more working capital a business has the more funds a business has available to pay for new stock, wages and other bills. In general, if current liabilities are **greater** than current assets, a firm may struggle to meet debts as they fall due. NB The importance of working capital is discussed in more detail later in this section).

Total Assets less Current Liabilities

This figure represents all assets owned by the business less its current liabilities. It may not always be listed as a separate item on the balance sheet.

Non-current Liabilities (Long-term Liabilities)

This section concerns monies owed by a business which do not have to be settled within one year. These typically concern **bank or building society loans such as mortgages over 12 months.** Non-current (long-term) liabilities may also include **debentures** (sometimes called stocks, bonds or gilts). This is a type of loan, where the money to be raised is divided into smaller units, and members of the public are invited to lend money to the business for a fixed period of time (usually long-term), and at a fixed rate of interest. They are bought and sold on the Stock Exchange.

NB Not all businesses will be funded by medium or long-term loans. In which case, there will be no listing on the balance sheet for creditors falling due after one year.

Net Assets

Net Assets represents all assets (non-current and current) less all liabilities (current and non-current). It represents the part of total assets which is funded not by short-term liabilities or long-term debt but by shareholders' funds or equity (ie capital put into the business by the owners of the business). It provides **the net value of what the company owns / is worth** as a going concern. Although – as previously stated – this is not strictly true as differences in book value and actual value of property, the value of goodwill and / or trading conditions can, for example, increase or decrease the value of the company if it was sold as a going concern.

The net asset figure is **balanced by the 'Shareholders' Equity** (see below).

Shareholders' Equity: Share Capital, Reserves & Retained Earnings

Share capital consists of money raised by selling shares to family members and friends (private limited companies) or members of the general public (public limited companies). Companies are permitted to issue shares up to authorised capital, which reflects the real value of assets owned by the company. Share capital shown is only that issued, and is calculated by multiplying the number of shares issued by the nominal value of the shares. There are two main types of share capital as follows:

- **Ordinary share capital.** 'Ordinary' shareholders receive a variable dividend (a percentage of after tax profits), according to how well the company has performed, and voting rights on important matters, such as the election of directors.

- **Preference share capital.** Preference shareholders have priority over ordinary shareholders with regard to dividends, and usually receive a fixed dividend. For example, the holder of £1,000 worth of 10% preference shares will receive £100 every year. Preference share dividends, therefore, are regarded as a 'safer bet' to ordinary shareholders. However, preference shareholders have no voting rights, and because dividend payments to ordinary shareholders are not fixed, they often receive a lower return than ordinary shareholders.

Reserves mainly consists of:

- **Retained profit.** All the retained profit ever made, including this year's profit extracted from the Profit & Loss Account (not necessarily available to spend).

However, reserves may also include funds generated from the following:

- **Share premiums.** The amount raised by selling shares for more than their nominal value.
- **Revaluation.** This matches any increase in the value of land, or property, held by a business over the original purchase price.

Total Equity (Shareholders' Funds)

Total equity or shareholders' funds (or capital employed for a sole trader) is the sum of the above ie the total amount of money put into the business by owners / shareholders (capital) and profit kept within the business (retained earnings or profit) and any reserves. This is where all the funds have come from to purchase company assets besides borrowed capital and, therefore, total equity or shareholders' funds (or capital employed) should **equal the Net Assets** figure.

NB The specifications state that candidates should understand the importance of working capital and depreciation. Hence, before moving on to examining income statements, these two items are considered in more detail below.

The Importance of Working Capital

What is Working Capital?

Working capital is the finance available for the day-to-day running of a business. As previously highlighted above, it is represented in the balance sheet as current assets less current liabilities. At any one particular moment of time a firm may have: a certain amount of cash at the bank and in hand; customers owing the business money; a stock of finished goods or work in progress. These are its current assets. It may also owe money to suppliers for goods received (creditors), and have a bank overdraft. These are its current liabilities.

In general, if current liabilities are greater than current assets, a firm may struggle to meet debts as they fall due. A business, therefore, needs to pay close attention to the effective management of each of its current asset items and current liabilities.

The efficient management of working capital is something that is frequently overlooked in fast growing businesses because of the need to achieve sales and profit targets. Whereas profit leads to growth, working capital does not. It simply allows a business to achieve growth. Careless attention to working capital, in particular poor cash management, might well lead to liquidity problems and has often resulted in profitable companies going out of business.

The Link Between Working Capital and Liquidity

Liquidity is concerned with *how fast an asset can be converted into cash*. All assets have varying degrees of liquidity. As stated above in the section on current assets, they can be ranked in order of liquidity as follows (with the most liquid asset first):

- **Cash.**

- **Shares in other businesses.** These could be sold one day and the money received the next.

- **Trade and other payables (debtors).** Although debtors are always considered to be the most liquid asset next to cash, this is not necessarily the case. Whether customers are able and willing to pay for goods is outside a business's control.

- **Inventory (stock).** There are various types of stock that can be listed in order of liquidity with finished goods being the most liquid, then work-in-progress, then stocks of raw materials. This does, however depend on the nature of the stock. For example, if the stock concerns gold, the raw material may be easier to sell than a finished product such as an item of jewellery.

- **Non-current assets (fixed assets).** A business may own land, buildings, machinery, vehicles and equipment. Such assets could be sold off to generate cash.

Prudent financial management requires the assets of a business to be 'appropriately liquid' to enable the appropriate amount of cash to be available at any point of time.

The Implications of Poor Liquidity

In the **short-term** if a business has low liquidity, this may lead to some or all of the following:

- **Delaying payments to suppliers.** This could result in a poor reputation, with suppliers refusing credit in the future and inability to take advantage of early settlement discounts.

- **Loss in purchasing economies of scale** as the business is unable to buy the large quantities required to secure discounts for bulk purchases.

- **Loss of potential business** as the business is unable to finance the extra expenditure required.

- **Increased borrowing**, resulting in increased finance (interest) costs (but see below).

- **Difficulty in raising funds through borrowing or increased interest rates.** If a business's liquidity is poor, banks / lenders may refuse to lend money as they lack faith in the business's ability to pay back the loan, or charge high interest rates to cover the extra risk involved.

If the business suffers poor liquidity in the **long-term** this is likely to result in the following:

- **Inability to expand / grow** due to lack of funds.
- **Creditors asking for the business to be declared insolvent and thus the business being forced to close.** NB When this happens sole traders and partnerships are declared bankrupt, and limited companies are forced into liquidation.

Managing Working Capital to Secure Liquidity

Businesses can ensure sufficient working capital is available to fund day to day operations, in the following ways:

- **Regularly monitor and control cash** through the use of **budgets and forecasts** to avoid overspending, and seek timely additional funding as required to meet debts as they fall.
- **Get goods to market in the shortest possible time** through efficient production and distribution. This minimises the cost of holding stocks and speeds up payment.
- **Minimise spending on fixed assets.** Spending large amounts on fixed assets drains resources. A business could consider renting and leasing rather than buying premises, vehicles or machinery. This increases expenses but conserves working capital.
- **Cut costs** - for example - by upgrading machinery and replacing labour with machines. This impacts on short-term capital availability (due to the initial cost of the machinery, any additional training and installation costs, redundancy payments), but reduces working capital requirements over the longer term.
- **Maximise sales and profits** either by increasing revenues without increasing fixed costs eg through more effective (targeted) marketing, or increasing margins by raising prices and / or cutting costs. This increases cash within the firm.
- **Minimise the number of customers owing the business money (debtors).** A great deal of business is now done on credit. One of the dangers is allowing customers too long to pay, thus forcing the supplying firm to borrow money to pay its suppliers / creditors. Offering shorter credit periods, discounts for prompt payment, and / or improved credit control, ie by requesting and obtaining references to check / review credit worthiness and being quick to chase late payments, could do much to improve cash flow. Possible disadvantages of such methods include the fact that business may be lost to suppliers who offer better credit terms. In addition, if discounts are offered, the loss in income arising from customers taking up this incentive may be significant, and firms operating on low profit margins may be unable to afford such an incentive.
- **Obtain the maximum possible credit for purchases.** This allows time to receive money from customers, but may be difficult for new firms. In addition, taking too much might result in higher prices as a result of lost discounts for prompt payments.
- **Reduce inventory (stock) levels.** This reduces the costs involved in holding stocks such as heating and lighting, security, insurance and opportunity cost (ie the loss of interest that could be gained if money held in stocks had been invested in a bank or in the business in some other way). Many firms may find this too risky to implement. It depends upon very good working relationships with suppliers and may result in loss of discounts offered on bulk purchases.
- **Ensure that changes in market conditions are responded to immediately eg reducing the workforce.** This may appear harsh but a company that survives a difficult trading period will at least be employing some personnel. A company that fails will not be employing anyone.

The Importance of Depreciation

What is Depreciation?

As highlighted above depreciation is a cost that occurs when a business writes off the net cost of a fixed asset over its useful life. The net cost of a fixed asset is calculated by subtracting the original cost (ie historic cost) of the asset by its expected value at the end of its useful life (ie its residual value).

Why Do Assets Depreciate?

Assets depreciate for the following reasons:

- **Wear and tear.** This occurs in the daily use of an asset. When a car is used each day, then it becomes subject to wearing of the parts and the bodywork. It loses value year on year and eventually becomes worthless due to use and age.
- **Lack of proper maintenance / servicing.** Sound maintenance and servicing can help to extend the life of an asset (and vice versa).
- **Technological advancement.** New products are invented to replace old ones. For example, computers are frequently up-dated with larger hard disk space and a faster processing speed. This makes present computers obsolescent and reduces their value.
- **Product obsolescence.** Customers' tastes change, resulting in a business having to modify existing products or introduce new products, which may necessitate investment in new fixed assets and make current assets redundant / obsolete.

The Purpose of Depreciation

There are several reasons why a business depreciates its assets.

- **Presenting 'a true and fair view'.** Firstly accountants are legally obliged to present *a true and fair view* of the financial state of affairs of the business. This applies to the 'true' value of an asset, in terms of what it is worth at current 'market' prices.
- **The matching principle.** This is a principle in accounting that states that the revenue earned must be matched with the costs of earning such revenue during the time period it is earned. Let us look at what happens if a business does not depreciate an asset. If an asset was bought for £50,000 and was worth nothing after 10 years, then the business would have two choices:
    1. Write off all £50,000 when the asset was bought.
    2. Write off all £50,000 when the asset was sold / became obsolete.

    The former option would significantly reduce the profit level during the year it writes off the value, and would understate the value of the asset for the rest of its useful life. A fixed asset generates revenues and profit for several years, hence the cost should not be written off in the year it occurred. Similarly, the latter option will understate the profit during the other nine years, because it will have used the asset at no apparent cost.

- **A source of finance / provision for replacement.** As the business writes off a small amount each year, the cash is not actually leaving the business (it left the business when the asset was bought). Hence, in a way it is saving up (in cash terms) for the purchase of the next fixed asset. Efficient firms will set up a separate account in a bank or building society and put the depreciation provision aside in this account each year.

The Implications of Depreciation

- **Effect on Asset Value.** Depreciation will reduce the value of an asset each year and will ultimately mean the asset's net book value at the end of its life will equal the residual value. If there is a difference between the two, the business must make an adjustment in the accounts, according to whether it makes a profit on disposal (net book value is less than residual value) or a loss on disposal (net book value is more than the residual value).

- **Effect on Profit.** Each year the profit figure will be reduced by the depreciation figure. This annual amount appears in operating expenses. Sometimes, governments will allow businesses to write off more than the usual amount as a tax incentive, because as profit falls (due to the depreciation charge rising) the amount payable in taxation will also fall.

- **Effect on Cash.** Despite depreciation being a cost, it is a non-cash cost. An allowance is made for the reduction in the value of the asset, but no cash actually leaves the business. This is why depreciation can be viewed as a source of finance. The cash has already left the business (when it paid for the asset) and, therefore, the cash stays within the business.

Concluding Remarks Regarding Depreciation

Depreciation is a necessity. If the business does not subject its assets to depreciation, then this will not present a true and fair view of the business and will distort asset values and profit during the life of a fixed asset. However, the process of depreciation, by its very nature, can be open to some guesswork. Both the residual value and economic life are subjective assessments based on past information. If either of these is incorrect, there will need to be some adjustment in the accounts. To conclude, whilst a business must take an objective approach to depreciation, some subjectivity is also required.

Closing Comments

This section of the Elementary Explanations has highlighted differences in terms used in the balance sheets of companies ie between private limited companies and public limited companies (and sole traders). For the foreseeable future it is likely that either set of terms may be referred to in the AQA A2 Unit 3 examination papers.

The specification also states that *'no construction of accounts or calculation of depreciation will be required'*. Students can, therefore, only be asked to analyse given balance sheet figures or to comment on the importance of working capital or depreciation in a given scenario.

Analysing Income Statements

Objectives

By the end of this topic you should be able to:

1. Define the term income statement (profit and loss account) and key income statement terms including revenue (turnover), cost of sales, gross profit, expenses, operating profit, finance income (interest received), finance costs (interest paid), profit before tax, taxation and profit for the year.
2. Outline key differences between income statements (profit and loss accounts) of public and private limited companies and sole traders.
3. Define the term profit utilisation and outline at least 4 factors that determine profit utilisation.
4. Define the term profit quality and briefly explain its importance.
5. Undertake simple analysis of a business's income statement (profit and loss account) to help assess the business's performance.

Key Terms

An **income statement (or profit and loss account)** is a statement showing the net income (or profit) of a business within a trading period ie revenue less all its costs / expenses.

Revenue (turnover) is the total value of sales made within a trading period ie year, quarter, month, week, day.

Cost of sales are all the costs **directly** involved in producing the product or service, eg the cost of materials used to produce a business's product and wages paid to production staff (direct labour).

Gross profit is the profit made before overheads (other running costs) are deducted. It is calculated by deducting the cost of sales (direct costs) from revenue (turnover).

Expenses are indirect costs (fixed costs **or overheads**), ie costs **not directly** involved with producing the goods / services, eg wages of office staff, rent, rates, electricity, maintenance and depreciation.

Operating profit (net profit) is the surplus / deficit made by a firm's 'normal' activities. It is calculated by deducting a business's total expenses from the gross profit figure.

Finance income is revenue earned from other activities / interests, eg rent from property owned by the business, interest from cash in bank, dividends from shares held in other companies. On the income statement it is added to the operating profit.

Finance costs is interest payable on any loans and is deducted from the operating profit on the income statement.

Profit before tax is profit after cost of sales, other expenses and interest have been deducted from sales revenue, but before tax.

Corporation tax is a tax levied on the profit of companies, paid as a proportion of profit before tax. It varies according to the size of the profit (before tax) made by the business.

Extraordinary / exceptional items are any items unusual to the day-to-day operations of the business, eg the sale of assets, the purchase of another business, large bad debts, factory closure, windfall profit on shares held.

Profit for the year (profit after tax) is profit for the year after corporation tax has been deducted.

Profit utilisation refers to how profit is used ie whether the business pays out profit to the owners and in the case of limited companies, in the form of dividends to shareholders, or whether profit is re-invested in the business.

Profit quality refers to how sustainable the profit of a particular business is over time.

Overview including Typical Formats for Different Legal Structures

Overview

Profit is the main reason why most businesses exist and the reason why most people set up and / or invest in a business. It is the reward for the risk and / or effort involved in setting up / running and / or investing in a business. As the amount of profit a business makes is of vital importance to the owners / shareholders, measurement of how well a business is performing in relation to profit is essential. Consequently, businesses produce statements showing the net income (profit) received after all costs and expenses have been deducted from revenue in order to help monitor and control performance. It is also a legal requirement as businesses are required to pay tax on any profits made.

The vast majority of a firm's revenue comes from the sale of its products, although occasionally it might invest some money in shares, bonds or perhaps property, and will earn some money from that investment. Its costs are divided into specific sections, which then allow the business to analyse its performance and profitability more accurately.

Typical Format

As with balance sheets, the typical format of a profit and loss account or income statement and / or terms used on the account / statement varies slightly according to the legal status of the business. Below is a typical format of the income statement of a public limited company.

Income Statement for XYZ plc for the year ending 31/08/09

	£	£
Revenue (Turnover)		1,210,000
Cost of Sales		400,000
Gross Profit		**810,000**
Expenses		
Salaries	400,000	
Advertising	80,000	
Rent	20,000	
Heating & Lighting	16,000	
Telephone	10,000	
Depreciation	14,000	
Total Expenses		540,000
Operating Profit (Net Profit)		**270,000**
Finance Income		-
Finance Costs (Interest)		10,000
Profit before Tax		**260,000**
Taxation		54,600
Profit for the Year (Profit after Tax)		**205,400**

Note that the statement is headed 'for the year ending'. This is because the income and costs have been incurred throughout the year.

As the above statement shows, profit is calculated by **subtracting the costs of a business from the income** received from selling its goods / services **(sales revenue)**. The difference is the profit, **unless** the costs are **greater** than the income, in which case a **loss** is made.

Profit / Income statements of private limited companies choosing to retain the traditional profit and loss account format:

- use the term turnover instead of revenue and net profit instead of operating profit.
- refer to finance income as interest on investments and finance costs as interest paid.
- would use the term profit after tax instead of profit for the year.
- have an 'appropriation section' showing any dividend payments and any profit retained within the business. For example, using the above scenario if dividends paid to shareholders amounted to £170,000 then dividends would be listed after the figure for 'Profit after tax' (Profit for the year) and retained profit calculated as £35,400 and listed as the final item on the statement.

The profit and loss account of a sole trader stops at the profit before tax figure. This is the Sole Trader's income / earnings and is, therefore, taxed as such. There is no 'Appropriation Section'. Drawings are not included on a Sole Trader's profit and loss account. Drawings are deducted from the net profit figure once it has been transferred to the balance sheet in the 'Financed By' section, as follows:

FINANCED BY:

Opening capital	20,000
Capital introduced	10,000
Add Net profit	<u>25,000</u>
	55,000
less Drawings	<u>25,000</u>
	30,000

Explanation of Income Statement (Profit and Loss Account) Terms

Revenue (Turnover)

This is the total value of sales made within a trading period ie year, quarter, month, week, day. It is the main source of income for a business and is calculated by multiplying the number of units sold by the selling price per unit.

$$\text{Revenue} = \text{No. of units sold} \times \text{Selling price per unit}$$

Cost of Sales

This includes all the costs **directly** involved in producing the product or service, for example, costs of materials, wages of production staff (direct labour) and is usually the same as variable costs.

Cost of sales, with regard to materials, is cost of materials actually used / sold, not purchased. This is calculated by adding the cost of any purchases to the value of the opening inventories (stock) and then deducting the value of the closing stock (inventories).

GROSS PROFIT

This is the profit made before overheads (other running costs) are deducted. It is sales revenue (or turnover) minus the cost of sales (cost of goods sold).

Expenses

These are indirect / fixed costs / **overheads**, ie costs **not directly** involved with producing the goods / services, eg wages of office staff, rent, rates, electricity, maintenance, **depreciation** - on fixed assets only. As previously explained in the section on Balance Sheets above, the full cost of buying any fixed assets is not included in costs for the period, but spread over the total number of years they are expected to provide benefit to the company, ie estimated useful life.

OPERATING PROFIT (or profit before interest and tax or trading profit).

This is the surplus / deficit made by a firm's 'normal' activities. It is gross profit minus expenses. It does not include income from other investments, nor interest charges. This is the measure most commonly used for assessing management performance.

Finance Income (Non-operating income)

This is revenue the business may earn through other activities / interests, eg rent from property owned by the business, interest from cash in bank, dividends from shares held in other companies. This is added to the operating profit.

Finance Costs (Interest)

This is interest payable on any loans and is deducted from the operating profit.

PROFIT BEFORE TAX (OR NET PROFIT)

This is profit after cost of sales, other expenses and interest have been deducted from sales revenue, but before tax.

Extraordinary / Exceptional items

The income statement may also have a listing for the above (or one-off items). These are any items unusual to the day-to-day operations of the business, eg the sale of assets, the purchase of another business, large bad debts, factory closure, windfall profit on shares held. (Shown here to avoid distorting the Operating Profit figure).

Taxation

This is **corporation tax** ie tax on the profit of companies, paid as a proportion of profit before tax. It varies according to the size of the business.

PROFIT FOR THE YEAR (PROFIT AFTER TAX)

This is profit for the financial year - profit attributable to the company. Simply, profit after Corporation Tax has been deducted. **The income statement of a public limited company ends here with the after tax calculation listed as 'Profit for the year'.**

Profit Utilisation

What is Meant by Profit Utilisation?

This refers to how the profit is used - whether the business pays out profit in dividends, or whether it re-invests. These are briefly explained below. NB The profit and loss accounts of private limited companies will detail this information after the profit for the year figure (profit after tax).

Dividends

These are a percentage of the profit after tax paid to shareholders. They do not legally have to be paid. They can be declared when a business has made a loss, to keep shareholders happy. The business may have built up cash reserves from profit from previous years and can use these to pay.

Retained profit

This is the profit made after cost of sales, other expenses, interest, tax and dividends have been deducted from revenues. Any retained profit the business earns is transferred to the retained profit reserve in the balance sheet. This may be in the form of cash at bank or in hand, or money that has already been used to purchase new machinery or stocks of materials.

Factors that Determine Profit Utilisation

There are several factors that determine the profit utilisation. These include the following:

- **Age and size of business and access to finance.** Younger businesses or small businesses (frequently the two go together) will have restricted sources of finance, based on their size. Younger businesses, in particular, may be unlikely to pay out much in dividends during the first few years of their life, because they are often re-investing profit into financing growth.

- **Competition.** If competitors are paying a similar proportion of their profit in dividends, it becomes difficult to justify a lower proportion to the shareholders, without obvious plans for expansion.

- **State of the market.** If the market is saturated, then growth opportunities are restricted, hence growth in the share price is likely to be limited. Companies such as banks are in a relatively saturated market and, therefore, tend to pay out a significant proportion of their profits in dividends (about half), in order to keep the shareholders interested in the business.

- **The rate of inflation.** If inflation is high, or unstable, or both, investors will require an increase in dividends each year to compensate for this.

- **Exceptional items.** Extra profits resulting from sale of an asset, might lead a business to pay out extra dividends. With a sudden loss, however, a business might still insist on paying out similar dividends to previous years, to show their commitment to investors. Certain companies might simply apply a percentage to their dividends ie pay a fixed percentage of profit after taxation. In the case of a loss, however, no dividends will be paid.

Profit Quality

What is Meant by Profit Quality?

Profit quality refers to how sustainable the profit of a particular business is. When buying shares, an investor would look at the sustainable earnings. Similarly, the level of re-investment would vary according to the variation of profit quality.

Assessing Profit Quality

Refer to the figures provided in the table below. These figures are profit for the year (profit after tax) for a car manufacturing business. Throughout the eight year period, assume the business remained in the same market, with similar resources, ie there was no sudden expansion.

Year	1	2	3	4	5	6	7	8
Profit after tax (£000)	150	180	30	200	190	310	220	235

Clearly, years 3 and 6 stand out as being either much less or much more than expected. There might be several reasons for this:

- In Year 3 either the business had to bear extraordinary costs, or it suffered lower margins. With regard to the former, a new range of cars may have been launched the year before but developed faults several months after the cars had been sold to customers. During year 3 the business may have had to recall all cars sold to rectify the fault. Alternatively, lower margins may have been experienced as a result of a major new competitor entering the market, forcing prices down.

- In Year 6 the business, may have had record car sales as a result of a wide variety of factors, including changes in the economic environment and / or the closure of a competitor. It might have received windfall profits on shares held in other businesses or sold off part of the business.

If the business does have an over-stated profit figure due to 'one-off profits', resulting from the sale of assets or windfall profits received on shares, then investors would view such a profit as lower 'quality' because it is not sustainable.

Closing Comments

As with the previous section on balance sheets, this section of the Elementary Explanations has highlighted differences in terms used in the income statement (profit and loss account) of companies ie between private limited companies and public limited companies (and sole traders). Therefore, as with balance sheet items, for the foreseeable future it is likely that either set of terms may be referred to in AQA A2 Unit 3 examination papers.

Using Financial Data for Comparisons, Trend Analysis and Decision Making

Objectives

By the end of this topic you should be able to:

1. Define the terms comparisons and trend analysis in the context of financial data.
2. Use financial data to make comparisons, analyse trends, and as an aid to decision making.

Key Terms

Comparisons of financial data consist of horizontal analysis, vertical analysis, ratio analysis (covered in the following section), trend analysis, as well as industry comparisons.

Horizontal analysis involves making comparisons between a particular item of financial data for a single business for two or more years. It involves the analyst reading across the page to compare figures on the same line and calculating - for example - the percentage change (increase or decrease) in operating profit from one year to the next.

Vertical analysis involves making comparisons between different items on a single financial statement for a single business in any given year. It involves the analyst reading down the page to compare figures on different lines and calculating component percentages - for example - the percentage gross profit made as a proportion of revenue.

Ratio analysis compares items listed on a single financial statement (vertical analysis) - for example - current assets in relation to current liabilities, or compares items listed on separate financial statements relating to a business in the same financial year - for example - expressing operating profit as a percentage of total capital (long-term debt and equity) employed.

Trend analysis is the examination of a business's financial data over time to determine whether the business's financial situation is improving or worsening.

Industry comparisons involves examining the financial data of a business in relation to similar businesses or industry averages or norms, in order to determine how the business is performing in relation to competitors or similar businesses.

Using Financial Data for Comparisons, Trend Analysis and Decision Making

Overview

Balance sheets and income statements are two of the most important business documents. Both these documents are produced to help decision making and are essentially used, not only by management to assess the financial performance of the business, but potential lenders and investors to assess the business's stability and ability to repay monies borrowed, and likely return on investment. Potential investors / shareholders and lenders, eg banks and building societies, would examine a business's balance sheet and income statement before making a decision to invest or lend a business money.

To help in the decision making process, interested parties will compare items listed on a single financial statement or across two different financial statements in any given financial year, over time and / or between businesses. This sub-section will examine each type of comparison in turn, and will refer to the following financial statements (relating to a UK based home delivery pizza company) to support explanations.

Balance Sheet - Pikka Pizza plc

	At 31/3/2009 £000	At 31/3/2008 £000
Non-current Assets		
Intangible assets	416	238
Property, Plant and Equipment	7,655	4,605
Vehicles	886	875
	8,957	5,718
Current Assets		
Inventories	847	780
Trade and other Receivables	4,550	3,357
Cash and Cash Equivalents	6,200	4,876
	11,597	9,013
Current Liabilities		
Trade and other Payables	(6,841)	(6,062)
Bank overdraft	(1,622)	(2,272)
Current tax liabilities	(876)	(834)
	(9,339)	(9,168)
Net Current Liabilities	2,258	(155)
Non-current Liabilities		
Long Term Bank Loan	(7,303)	(3,127)
Net Assets	3,912	2,436
Shareholders' Equity		
Called up share capital	841	846
Reserves and Retained earnings	3,071	1,590
Total Equity (Shareholders' Funds)	3,912	2,436

Income Statement Pikka Pizza plc

	Year ending 31/3/09 £000	Year ending 31/3/08 £000
Revenue	45,326	38,397
Cost of Sales	(28,384)	(23,579)
Gross Profit	16,942	14,818
Expenses		
Operating Profit	7,509	6,222
Finance Income	195	176
Finance Costs	(321)	(206)
Profit before Tax	7,383	6,192
Taxation	(2,067)	(1,858)
Profit for the Year	5,316	4,334

Horizontal Analysis

Horizontal analysis involves making comparisons between a particular item of financial data for a single business for two or more years. It involves the analyst reading across the page to compare figures on the same line and calculating - for example - the change (increase or decrease) in net assets or in profit for the year from one year to the next.

Profit comparisons with one year and the next will allow managers to assess the success of new strategies in increasing the profitability of the business and / or identify the need for change(s) (in the case of a loss or falling profit situation).

Comparing profit (or loss) and dividends paid from one year to the next will also allow shareholders to determine whether the profit and / or dividend is increasing or decreasing and, ultimately, whether it is worth continuing to invest in the business in the coming year(s) or whether it might be better to sell their shares and invest their money elsewhere.

Percentage changes may be calculated by working out the difference between the two figures and dividing the difference into the original figure and then multiplying by 100 to give a percentage. Refer to the following two examples for Pikka Pizza plc.

- **Percentage change in net assets 2008 to 2009:** £3,912,000 - £2,436,000 = £1,476,000 / £2,436,000 x 100 = + 60.59% (+ 61%).
- **Percentage change in profit for the year 2008 to 2009:** £5,316,000 - £4,334,000 = £982,000 / £4,334,000 x 100 = + 22.66 (+ 23%).

Vertical Analysis

Vertical analysis involves making comparisons between different items on a single financial statement for a single business in any given year. It involves the analyst reading down the page to compare figures on different lines and calculating component percentages. For example, vertical analysis of items on a balance sheet enables potential and existing lenders to assess a business's:

- **liquidity / solvency position**, ie whether it is likely to be able to meet debts as they fall due. This information is obtained by examining the value of a business's current liabilities in relation to its current assets.

- **gearing position**, ie the extent to which the total capital employed by a business is borrowed money. This information is obtained by dividing the capital employed in the business (debt and equity) with the value of any loans held.

NB The liquidity and gearing position of Pikka Pizza plc will be calculated and considered in the section on ratio analysis below.

Banks will also specifically look at the income statement to determine the business's ability to meet interest payments. The higher the 'profit before interest' figure, the greater the feeling of security the banks will have that any money borrowed will be repaid. Ideally, banks like this **'profit before interest' figure to be at least 3 or 4 times the level of interest paid** / payable during the trading period. In the case of Pikka Pizza the bank is likely to be very happy with the operating profit figure as it is over 23 times the finance costs (£7,509,000 / £321).

Vertical analysis of items on an income statement also enables managers to assess **how effectively costs are being managed** within the business by comparing the amount of gross or operating profit made to revenue (gross and net profit margin). Refer to the following examples for Pikka Pizza plc:

- **Gross profit as a proportion of revenue in 2009 (Gross margin):** £16,942,000 / £45,326,000 x 100 = 37.38% (37%).

- **Operating profit as a proportion of revenue in 2009 (Operating margin):** £7,509,000 / £45,326,000 x 100 = 16.57% (17%).

This type of analysis produces financial statements (balance sheets and income statements) that can more easily be compared across the years for a single business or across different businesses (known as common-size financial statements).

Ratio Analysis

Ratio analysis compares items listed on a single financial statement (vertical analysis) - for example - current liabilities in relation to current assets, or compares items listed on separate financial statements relating to a business in the same financial year. With regard to the latter, for example, managers can use the balance sheet and income statement figures, to:

- assess how well they are performing in relation to their main task ie to maximise the **return on capital** invested: by dividing the capital employed in the business (shown on the balance sheet) with the operating profit made (on the income statement).

- assess how well the business is **utilising its assets to generate revenue**: by dividing the total assets employed figure (obtained from the balance sheet) with the revenue (turnover) figure (on the income statement). A lower figure to previous years or similar businesses could be due to: uncompetitive prices, inadequate promotion, problems with new machinery, high stock costs, or delivery problems leading to a stockpile of finished goods.

NB Both these ratios will be calculated and considered for Pikka Pizza plc in the more detailed section on ratio analysis below.

Shareholders are also able to assess the likely **return on investment** using both the balance sheet and income statement figures, as well as records of dividends (ie the percentage of the business's annual profits) paid / proposed.

Ratio analysis is the most common form of financial analysis as it enables comparisons to be made across the years for a single business, or across different businesses. It is covered in much greater detail in a subsequent section below.

Trend Analysis

Trend analysis is the examination of a business's financial data over time to determine whether the business's financial situation is improving or worsening. Directors / managers can, for example, review several year's performance, particularly with regard to profit, and use this as a basis to make future decisions. Trend analysis is particularly useful in highlighting potential problems that need to be addressed.

Inter-year analysis can also allow shareholders and other potential investors to examine the **use of profit**, the **trend of dividend payments** over time, and the **quality of profit** (explained in a previous sub-section above).

Trend analysis may involve choosing the first year of a business, or a past financial year of the business as the base to make comparisons with subsequent years. In which case, items listed on the business's subsequent financial statements may be expressed as a percentage of the matching item listed on the base year, which in percentage terms are represented as 100.

Let us assume, for example, that the year 2007 was chosen as the base year for Pikka Pizza plc and that in this year, operating profit amounted to £3,763,000. This figure would, therefore, represent 100%, and the subsequent years' operating profit made in 2008 and 2009 would be expressed as follows:

Comparison of operating profit made in 2008 and 2009 with the base year (2007)

- £4,334,000 / £3,763,000 x 100 = 115
- £5,316,000 / £3,763,000 x 100 = 141

Trends over time, such as a change in assets, turnover or profit, should obviously be considered along with changes in any external factor affecting the accounts, such as the level of competition, or the state of the economy.

Industry Comparisons

Industry comparisons - as the term suggests - involve examining the financial data of a business in relation to similar businesses or industry averages or norms, in order to determine how the business is performing in relation to competitors or similar businesses. It is useful in highlighting whether there is room for improvement and potential problems / weaknesses that need to be addressed in order to maximise the business's potential.

Closing Comments

The financial accounts of both private and public limited companies have to be submitted to Companies House by a certain date at the end of their financial year. These are available for the public to review for a small fee. Some final accounts are, however, available to obtain free from a variety of organisations on-line. One such service, for example, is the annual report service provided free by an organisation called PrecisionIR for readers of the London Stock Exchange. The service provides quick access to annual reports, quarterly earnings, and other information on select companies.

Assessing Strengths and Weaknesses of Financial Data in Judging Performance

Objectives

By the end of this topic you should be able to:

1. Describe at least 4 ways in which financial data can be used to judge performance.
2. Describe at least 6 limitations of using financial data to judge performance.

Key Terms

Window dressing is the process of deliberately presenting a better picture of the company than is the case, by 'dressing up' the accounts, some of which are illegal, some of which represent a broad interpretation of accounting rules.

Introduction

Ways of assessing the strength and weaknesses of a business from a financial perspective have partially been covered in the previous sections on 'Using Financial Data to Measure and Assess Performance' and will be considered in much greater detail in the subsequent section on 'Ratio Analysis' below. This section of the 'Elementary Explanations, therefore, simply summarises the particular things to look for to assess the strengths (and weaknesses) in financial statements, before focusing in more detail on the limitations of financial data in making judgements about a business's performance.

Strengths of Financial Data in Judging Performance

The Balance Sheet

The balance sheet can be used to assess the following:

- **The net worth of a business.** Although the limitations of financial statements will be discussed later in this section, it is important to emphasise here, that the balance sheet is just a snapshot of the financial state of a business at one particular point in time, and it is difficult to judge strength without looking at trends over time. By examining a series of balance sheets over time incremental growth in net worth would indicate that the business is a viable concern, and doing well.

- **The level of gearing** ie the extent to which the business is dependant on borrowed funds. The more capital raised on borrowed funds, the more highly geared a business is. Existing shareholders might prefer a business to fund growth through borrowing, as opposed to raising funds through additional share capital, as the latter only serves to dilute their return. However, the higher the gearing, the more vulnerable the business is with regard to negative changes in the business environment, particularly interest rates. It is, therefore, important for a business to achieve a balance in this respect.

- **The level of liquidity.** A greater proportion of current assets to current liabilities indicates that the business is likely to be able to meet debts as they fall due. For example, if a business has no cash and a large overdraft this indicates that it may be struggling to pay its bills. A high proportion of stock in relation to cash and debtors might also indicate liquidity problems (depending on the nature of the business and how quickly stock is turned over). Having some cash reserves and a debtors figure greater than creditors, in particular, is an indicator of sound financial management. Alternatively, a business holding too much cash, or seen to be building cash over a period of years, might be perceived as a business unwilling to take risks, or one that cannot find profitable investments.
- **The level and nature of fixed assets.** Fixed assets can be used by a business as collateral on which to secure loans to finance growth. Land and buildings, as opposed to machinery and equipment, could be sold to raise funds in a crisis situation.

The Income Statement (Profit and Loss Account)

The income statement (or profit and loss account) can be used to assess the following:

- **Growth in revenue (turnover).** This is, obviously, a good thing but it must be considered in the context of growth in market size. For example, if the market grows by 10%, but turnover of one particular business grows by 7%, then although such a business has experienced a rise in turnover and probably profit, its market share has fallen.
- **Growth in profit.** The aim of every business is to maximise the profit made in any given year but this should also be viewed not in isolation, but in relation to revenue and, indeed in relation to capital employed. For example, the operating profit may be significantly higher from one year to the next but if the revenue and / or capital employed has also grown and at a much higher rate, then although the business has experienced a rise in profit, the profitability of the business has fallen.

Limitations of Financial Data in Judging Performance

Introduction

Because the balance sheet is meant to be a snapshot, by definition, certain variables will have changed significantly when the accounts are finally published. In addition, despite employing an auditor to ensure the accounts are a 'true and fair view' of the business, such a claim might not always hold true. Certain items might be deliberately over or understated, and such variables might then alter significantly the following day. There are, in fact, several limitations to published accounts. These are considered below.

Historical / Out of Date

As stated in the introduction, the balance sheet is simply a snapshot of a firm's financial situation at one particular moment in time. Viewed on its own, it tells you nothing about a business's past and nothing about its future. It could be, for example, that the day before the balance sheet was produced, the business merged with another business, or the day after a significant part of the company was sold off. Working capital, in particular, changes on a day-to-day basis. Therefore, conclusions about a company's liquidity, based on a snapshot of one particular day in the year, are likely to be inaccurate.

Missing Information – Non-Financial Assets

A business might have a unique selling point, a high degree of customer loyalty, and a highly motivated, highly skilled workforce that gives it a competitive advantage and suggests solid future growth potential...

This is almost impossible to build into the accounts, because it requires some form of subjective judgement on the ability of the workforce and management team.

Missing Information – Trading Conditions

Accounts on their own do not inform the user of the trading conditions in which a business operates. A well-established business may just about break-even in one particular year and this might be considered poor performance. However, it might have taken a major improvement in productivity and performance, just to break-even, due to unfavourable trading conditions. Consequently, the business actually performed well.

Inflation

Inflation distorts values over a period of time. Growth in turnover might suggest growth in output yet the turnover might have grown due to prices rising and not due to an increase in sales volume. Inflation is not usually accounted for in accounts. The user must take inflation into account when interpreting the figures, particularly during periods of high inflation.

Personal Judgement / Estimates

Many of the figures are estimates, especially the value of fixed assets. Imagine trying to value a car plant or 10 acres of land for housing. The value of the fixed asset is only 100% accurate when there is a buyer. In the meantime, the business relies on the value provided by the surveyor, which is subjective and, therefore, may not be accurate.

Businesses also 'estimate' other items in the accounts. For example, whether or not debtors will actually pay their bills, and whether or not all stock will actually be sold, so there is some doubt over those values. Alternatively, the value of cash in current assets is certain.

Different Valuation Methods

Businesses may also value their assets using different methods, eg to value stock or to allow for depreciation, thus making inter-firm comparisons difficult.

Different Accounting Periods

Businesses may have different accounting periods which make comparisons difficult. For example, a toy manufacturing business reporting at the end of October, might have extremely high stock levels on its balance sheet, compared to a similar business reporting at the end of March, but this is entirely normal given that the stock will reduce in the run-up to Christmas.

Window Dressing

Window dressing refers to the process of deliberately presenting a better picture of the company than is the case, by 'dressing up' the accounts. Ways in which companies might 'window dress' their accounts are summarised below, some of which are illegal, some of which represent a broad interpretation of accounting rules.

- **Falsifying dates of costs and revenue:** If a business wishes to increase profit, it might decide to 'postpone' the writing off of costs. For example, if a large invoice is received just before the end of the year, then a business might try to 'hide it' until the start of the next financial year. Similarly, if a business has a contract for products to be made and delivered over the following eighteen months, then it might decide to state the entire value of the contract in one year, even though the revenue (earned when the goods change hands) has not been earned in its entirety.

- **Brand valuations (boosting intangible fixed assets):** A form of fixed assets is known as intangible fixed assets. These might include patents to protect the value of inventions. It might also include brands. In recent years there has been a good deal of discussion amongst accountants on whether to include brands as an ongoing valuation in the balance sheet, and if so, how to make such a valuation. When one company buys a brand, its value is based on future earnings, so it is therefore a highly subjective valuation. To alter such a valuation by 10% either up or down would have a significant effect on the level of net assets represented in a balance sheet. A similar debate has covered the inclusion of football players in the value of a firm's assets. The earning potential of some-one like David Beckham in terms of merchandise might be fairly easy to calculate, but in terms of his earning potential with regard to winning football games, this becomes more of a job for the book makers.

- **Sale and leaseback shortly before the balance sheet date to boost liquidity:** If a business is short of cash, and wishes to portray otherwise, then one way of boosting liquidity is to sell an asset and lease it back, thereby generating a significant increase in cash, yet retaining the assets for its own use. This is very much a short-term measure, because the asset will need to be leased back from the new owner and, therefore, the costs will rise during the following year, reducing profit.

- **Manipulating working capital items:** Stock, debtors, cash, creditors, all change daily as stock is sold, debtors pay, and bills (creditors) are paid. For this reason, it is never easy to make a judgement on the state of working capital. A business might deliberately increase it or reduce it to represent a picture of the business in a particular way.

- **Temporarily suppressing gearing:** Sometimes a business will repay debt temporarily just before the end of the year, after which it takes out another loan, thereby artificially suppressing gearing for the very short term, with the aim of minimising the perceived risk.

Closing Comments

The main limitation in using financial data to assess performance is that, on its own such data only shows *what* has happened from a financial perspective, it does not tell you *why* it has happened. Additional information on the trading conditions, inflation, the quality of human resources, etc is required to enable a full and accurate assessment of the business's performance.

2.3

INTERPRETING PUBLISHED ACCOUNTS

Conducting Ratio Analysis

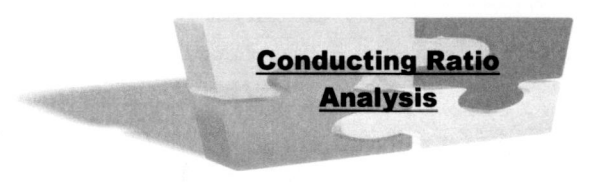

Objectives

By the end of this topic you should be able to: select, calculate and interpret ratios to measure financial performance, including: liquidity (current and acid test ratios), profitability (ROCE), financial efficiency (asset turnover, stock turnover, creditor and debtor days), gearing and shareholder ratios (dividend per share and dividend yield).

Key Terms

Ratio analysis compares items listed on a single financial statement (vertical analysis) - for example - current assets in relation to current liabilities - or compares items listed on separate financial statements relating to a business in the same financial year - for example - expressing operating profit as a percentage of total capital (long-term debt and equity) employed.

Liquidity (or solvency) ratios measure the amount of cash available to meet the business's daily requirements ie they measure the ability of the business to meet debts as they fall due.

The **current ratio** assesses the business's liquidity position by comparing current assets to current liabilities. It measures how many current assets the firm has for every one current liability. It is calculated by dividing current assets by current liabilities and is expressed in the form of a ratio eg 2 to 1.

The **acid test ratio** assesses the business's liquidity position by comparing current assets **excluding inventories (stocks)**, to current liabilities. It is calculated in the same way as the current ratio, ie by dividing current assets less inventories (stock) by current liabilities.

Profitability ratios measure the ability of the business to generate profit.

ROCE which stands for **r**eturn **o**n **c**apital **e**mployed expresses the operating profit of the business as a percentage of the capital invested. It is calculated by dividing operating profit (or net profit before interest and tax) into the total capital employed in the business (total equity + non-current liabilities or owners / shareholders' equity and any long-term loan capital) and multiplying by a hundred.

Financial Efficiency ratios measure the ability of a firm to use or control the use of its assets.

Asset turnover is a measurement of how many pounds worth of sales a business generates from the assets employed within the business. It is calculated by dividing the revenue (turnover) of the business into the figure for net assets and is expressed as number of times.

Inventory (Stock) turnover measures the frequency with which a business sells and replenishes inventory (stock) within a year. It can be expressed as the number of times it takes inventory (stock) to turnover in a year or the number of days (or even weeks or months) inventory (stock) is held within the business. The former is calculated by dividing cost of sales by the average inventory (stock) held in the period. The latter is calculated by dividing the average inventory (stock) held by cost of sales and multiplying by 365 to give the number of days, or 52 to give a figure for the number of weeks, or 12 to give a figure for months.

Payables' (Credit) collection period measures the number of days it takes a business to pay any money owed to its suppliers (ie its creditors). It is calculated by dividing the average figure for payables (creditors) in the period by the value of purchase made on credit during the period (or cost of sales if this figure is not available) and multiplying by 365.

Receivables' (Debt) collection period measures the number of days it takes a business to collect any money owed by its customers (ie its debtors). It is calculated by dividing the average receivables (debtors) over the period by the value of sales made on credit over the period (or figure for revenue if this figure is not available) and multiplying the resultant figure by 365.

Gearing ratios measure the extent to which a business is dependent on borrowed funds. It is most commonly calculated by dividing long-term debt / liabilities (or non-current liabilities) by the total capital employed in a business ie total equity plus non-current liabilities (or owners / shareholders equity + long-term debt finance) and multiplying by 100 to give a percentage.

Shareholder ratios measure the ability of the business to generate a return to shareholders on their investment.

Dividend per share measures the amount of money shareholders receive per share. It is calculated by dividing the total amount of dividends declared (or paid) by directors, with the number of shares issued, and is expressed as amount per share eg X pence per share.

Dividend yield measures the rate of return a shareholder gets by comparing the market value of the shares with the dividend received. It is calculated by dividing the dividend per share paid to ordinary shareholders by the market price per share and multiplying by 100 to give a percentage.

Liquidity Ratios

Current Ratio

The current ratio provides a means of assessing the business's liquidity position by comparing current assets to current liabilities. It measures how many current assets the firm has for every one current liability. It is calculated by dividing current assets by current liabilities and is expressed in the form of a ratio, as follows:

$$\frac{\text{Current assets}}{\text{Current liabilities}} = X : 1$$

For example, if a business's current assets amounted to £389,000 and current liabilities amounted to £243,000, then the current ratio would be 1.6 : 1 (389,000 / 243,000). Let us now calculate the current ratio for Pikka Pizza plc in 2009 and 2008:

Current ratio for Pikka Pizza plc for 2009:
11,597 / 9,339 = 1.24 to 1.

Current ratio for Pikka Pizza plc for 2008:
9,013 / 9,168 = 0.98 to 1.

Accountants suggest that the ideal is 1.5 to 2 : 1. The latter means that for every £2 of short-term assets, the business has £1 of short-term debt. Below this figure there is a danger that the business will not have enough cash to pay off debts as they fall due, particularly if current assets consist of a very high proportion of inventories (stocks). With regard to this, a more accurate measure of a business's liquidity position is the acid test ratio (below).

Acid Test Ratio

The acid test ratio provides a means of assessing the business's liquidity and solvency position by comparing current assets **excluding inventories (stock)**, to current liabilities. Inventory (stock) is left out of the equation as it is the least liquid asset, ie it can take a long time to convert into cash and may become obsolete, and thus unsaleable. The acid test ratio is calculated in the same way as the current ratio, ie by dividing current assets less inventories (stock) by current liabilities, as follows:

$$\frac{\text{Current assets } - \text{ inventories (stock)}}{\text{Current liabilities}} = X : 1$$

For example if a business's current assets less inventories amounted to £96,000 and current liabilities amounted to £87,000, then the acid test ratio would be 1.1 : 1 (96,000 / 87,000). Let us now calculate the acid test ratios for Pikka Pizza plc:

Acid test ratio for Pikka Pizza plc for 2009:
(11,597 – 847) / 9,339 = 1.15 to 1

Acid test ratio for Pikka Pizza plc for 2008:
(9,013 – 780) / 9,168 = 0.90 to 1

Accountants suggest that the ideal is 1:1. This means that for every £1 of short-term assets, the business has £1 of short-term debt. Below this ratio, (for example 0.9:1 in the case of Pikka Pizza plc), there is a danger that the business has insufficient cash to meet its debts as they fall due.

In the worst-case scenario, if a business has insufficient cash to meet debts as they fall due, it could be forced to close as its creditors push to declare the business **insolvent**. It is important, however, to recognise that the term 'current' means receivable or payable within the next twelve months, so a business does not always have to settle all of its current debts within the next week / month. Therefore, one must be careful when interpreting the ratio, not to assume a ratio of say 0.9:1 means the business is insolvent. Certain bills eg tax or dividends in particular, may not need to be paid until 6 months time. Businesses may also have fixed assets that they can sell to generate cash.

Profitability Ratios

ROCE

This ratio relates profit to the size of the business, thus helping to avoid sweeping judgements being made about a profit of, say, £100 million being high and £1,000 being low (which might be highly acceptable if the capital invested was £4,000). It is one of the most useful inter-firm comparisons of operational efficiency and is sometimes referred to as the **'primary efficiency'** ratio. This is because it provides a direct measure of the main task of management, ie to maximise the return on capital invested. It is calculated by dividing operating profit (ie net profit before interest and tax) into total capital employed (total equity plus non-current liabilities) and is expressed as a percentage as follows:

$$\frac{\text{Operating profit (net profit before interest and tax)}}{\text{Capital employed (total equity plus non-current liabilities)}} \times 100 = X\%$$

For example, if a company has an operating profit of £220,000 and capital employed of £1.8 million, then the return on capital is 12.2% (220,000 / 1,800,000 x 100). The ratio should be compared with previous years or similar entities / industry norms. The higher the percentage, the better the business performance.

Return on capital provides the business with a ratio that can help it to decide whether or not it is worth continuing. If a large proportion of the capital invested is via loans then the return on capital should, at the very least, be sufficient to cover interest that firms have to pay on their loans plus inflation. If the business is unable to generate more than the rate of interest it may as well close, sell off its assets, and put the money in a bank. Let us calculate the ROCE for Pikka Pizza plc in 2009 and 2008:

ROCE for Pikka Pizza plc for 2009: 7,509 / 11,215 (ie 3,912 + 7,303) x 100 = 67%
ROCE for Pikka Pizza plc for 2008: 6,222 / 5,563 (ie 2,436 + 3,127) x 100 = 112%

Although the ROCE performance of Pikka Pizza has fallen from 2008 to 2009, the business would appear to be performing exceptionally well in relation to the simple alternative of investing the money in the bank.

As stated in the section on financial objectives, ROCE performance can be improved by:

- **Increasing operating profit whilst maintaining the same level of capital investment**, eg by reducing costs whilst maintaining sales revenues or increasing sales revenues whilst maintaining costs, and / or increasing the efficiency of asset use.
- **Maintaining operating profit but reducing the amount of capital it takes to generate this amount of profit** eg by selling off any under-utilised assets to pay off a long-term loan.

NB Other profitability ratios include gross profit margin and net profit margin percentage calculations. These have, however, already been covered in Unit 2 of our Elementary Explanations in accordance with the AQA specifications.

Financial Efficiency Ratios

Asset Turnover

Asset turnover is a measurement of how many pounds worth of sales a business generates from the assets employed within the business. It is calculated by dividing revenue (turnover) of the business into the net value of the assets employed in the business and is expressed as number of times.

$$\frac{\text{Revenue (Turnover)}}{\text{Net Assets}} = X \text{ times}$$

NB The assets employed figure usually used in the calculation, is the value of fixed assets plus working capital (ie current assets less current liabilities), though fixed assets on their own are sometimes used.

For example, if the revenue (turnover) of a business in a particular year was £1million and the net assets employed (at the time of the balance sheet) amounted to £0.5 million, then the asset turnover figure would be 2 times. This would mean that for every £1 of money invested in assets, £2 of revenue is being generated. Obviously the higher the asset turnover figure, the better the business is performing.

Judgement as to whether the figure is good or bad cannot be made without comparing the figure to previous years or businesses operating within the same industry. The asset turnover for Pikka Pizza plc can be calculated as follows:

Asset turnover for Pikka Pizza plc for 2009: 45,326 / 3,912 = 11.6 times
Asset turnover for Pikka Pizza plc for 2008: 38,397 / 2,436 = 15.8 times

The asset turnover for Pikka Pizza plc has clearly fallen between 2008 and 2009. If the figure is lower than previous years or similar businesses, this could be due to any one or a number of the following:

- uncompetitive prices.
- inadequate promotional activities.
- problems with new machinery.
- high inventory costs.
- delivery problems.

The more revenue a business can generate from its assets, the higher the asset turnover figure. Consequently, the figure can be improved by **anything that could lead to increased sales from existing assets.** For example:

- more effective marketing and distribution.
- better maintenance of machinery (avoids stoppages).
- better trained staff, resulting in increased output.

All of the above may increase costs in the short-run but reduce costs in the long run as the business may benefit from:

- purchasing economies of scale, resulting from increased sales.
- better quality products due to well maintained machinery / well trained staff.

Another way of boosting the asset turnover figure would be to **sell off any assets that are under-utilised.** The sales revenue figure would then be divided by a lower asset total, resulting in a higher asset turnover figure. In this scenario, however, the business must take care to ensure that such assets are no longer required and that their sale will not restrict future flexibility (opportunity cost).

Inventory (Stock) Turnover

Inventory (stock) turnover measures the number of times in a year that a business sells and replenishes its inventory. It can be expressed in terms of the number of times it takes inventory to turnover in a year or in terms of the number of days (or even weeks or months) inventory is held within the business. It can, therefore, be calculated as follows:

$$\frac{{}^1\text{Cost of sales}}{{}^2\text{Inventory}} = \text{X times per year}$$

$$\frac{{}^2\text{Inventory}}{{}^1\text{Cost of sales}} \times {}^3 365 = \text{No. of days}$$

[1] The cost of sales figure (opening inventory + purchases − closing inventory) can be substituted with the revenue figure if the cost of sales figure is not provided / known. This is not as accurate but still useful in highlighting differences over time and / or between businesses in the same industry.

[2] The average inventory figure should ideally be used, ie opening inventory at the beginning of the trading period less closing inventory at the end of the trading period divided by 2.

[3] To calculate how long it takes for inventory to turnover in terms of weeks or months, the 365 would be substituted with 52 or 12 respectively.

For example, if the average inventory held is £5,000 and cost of sales is £120,000, then the number of times inventory turns over in a year is 24 (120,000 / 5,000). Alternatively, the amount of time it takes to sell and replenish inventory is, (rounded up), 16 days (5,000 / 120,000 x 365 = 15.21).

In terms of the 'number of times' calculation, the higher the figure the more efficient the business. In terms of the 'number of days / weeks / months' calculation, the lower the figure, the more efficient the business. This means that less money is being tied up in unproductive assets and this minimises the risk of stock obsolescence (deterioration in the case of food items) and stock holding costs such as heating and lighting, security, insurance and opportunity cost (eg the loss of interest that could be gained if money held in stocks had been invested in a bank or in the business in some other way).

An inventory turnover of 2 would suggest the business has about 6 months of sales in inventory, whereas an inventory turnover of 12 would mean the business only had a month's normal sales in inventory. In most circumstances 6 months would appear to be high. When interpreting the figures, however, comparisons must be made to other firms operating within the same industry (and / or previous figures). Some businesses need high stocks and carry high values eg cars. These are slow moving items that have higher gross profit margins, which compensate for the low stock turn. Supermarkets on the other hand, would have a much higher inventory turnover as many of the items they stock need to be replaced frequently due to the short shelf life.

Given the short shelf-life of food items and, thus, the nature of the inventories help by Pikka Pizza plc, you would also expect a fairly rapid inventory turnover for this particular business. We do not have opening and closing inventory figures for Pikka Pizza plc. However, if we assume that the figure cited for inventory on the balance sheet is close to the average inventory held, then we can calculate inventory turnover as follows:

Inventory turnover for Pikka Pizza plc for 2009:   28,384 / 847 = 33.5 times per year;
                                                    847 / 28,384 x 365 = 10.9 days.
Inventory turnover for Pikka Pizza plc for 2008:   23,579 / 780 = 30.2 times per year;
                                                    780 / 23,579 x 365 = 12.1 days.

Pikka Pizza plc has clearly become more efficient with regard to the management of its inventories.

Reducing the average level of inventory held without losing sales can increase inventory turnover. This can be done by tightening stock control, for example, through improved checking procedures, in order to pick up on any delivery discrepancies, ie short or poor quality deliveries, as well as improved handling procedures in order to minimise the cost of damaged stock. It can also be achieved by implementing a Just-in-time stock control system. The latter involves ordering stock only once a customer has placed an order, as well as despatching goods immediately on completion to the customer. There are, however some potential drawbacks, namely that the business is much more vulnerable to machine breakdowns and changes in supply, increasing the risk of a 'stock out' situation occurring. The costs of this are considerable in that labour is wasted, customers are upset and the business gets a reputation for unreliability. Furthermore, a business may lose out on bulk-buying discounts offered by suppliers, as well as incur greater ordering and handling costs from dealing with a greater number of smaller deliveries. However, the reduction in the holding, financing and opportunity costs associated with carrying stocks, as well as the reduction in waste stemming from increased pressure to get quality right first time (because there is no spare stock to fall back on and less time for checking) should outweigh the above costs.

Another way of increasing inventory turnover is by **increasing the rate of sales without raising levels of stock**. This could be done by extending opening hours (within legal limits), improving service and efficiency and / or more selective advertising.

Payables' (Credit) Collection Period

Payables' (credit) collection period measures the number of days it takes a business to pay any money owed to its suppliers (ie its creditors).

Just as a business may grant customers an interest free period of grace in which to pay for their goods, a business's suppliers (called its creditors) may also grant a business an interest free period of grace in which to pay for supplies received. The following ratio is used to calculate how long a business takes to settle its debts to suppliers:

$$\frac{^1\underline{Payables\ (Creditors)}}{^2 Credit\ purchases} \times 365 = \text{No. of days}$$

[1] Average payables (creditors) should be used ie opening payables (creditors) + closing payables (creditors) divided by 2. Closing payables (creditors) may be used providing this is representative.

[2] Cost of sales can be substituted for the credit purchases figure if the latter is unavailable.

For example, if a business's payables (creditors) at any one time total £140,000 and credit purchases (or cost of sales) amount to £1.7 million, then it takes the business 30 days on average to settle their bills (140,000 / 1,700,000 x 365).

Ideally this figure should be **higher than the receivables (debtor) days figure** – see below. If shorter, this could lead to a cash flow problem. An increase would suggest the firm may be having difficulty in finding cash to pay its debts. Alternatively, suppliers may have extended the credit period. NB Negotiating an extension in credit terms with suppliers could lead to loss of discounts for prompt payment.

In the case of Pikka Pizza plc the payables' collection period can be calculated as follows:

2009: 6,841 / 28,384 x 365 = 88 days.
2008: 6,062 / 23,579 x 365 = 94 days.

The ratios tell us that Pikka Pizza settled its debts more quickly in 2009 than in 2008.

Receivables' (Debt) Collection Period

Receivables' (debt) collection period measures the number of days it takes a business to receive any money owed by its customers (and other debtors).

A great deal of business is now done on credit. Customers granted credit, ie an interest free period of grace in which to pay for their goods (usually 30 days but in practice nearer 70 days), are called debtors. The following ratio is used to calculate how long customers (and other debtors) take to settle their debts:

$$\frac{^1\underline{Receivables\ (Debtors)}}{^2 Credit\ sales} \times 365 = \text{No. of days}$$

[1] Average receivables (debtors) should be used ie opening receivables (debtors) + closing receivables (debtors) divided by 2. Closing receivables (debtors) may be used providing this is representative.

[2] Revenue (turnover) can be substituted for the credit sales figure if the latter is unavailable.

For example, if a business's debtors at any one time total £400,000 and credit sales amount to £2 million, then it takes credit customers 73 days on average to settle their bills (400,000 / 2,000,000 x 365).

The figure should be viewed in relation to previous figures rather than similar businesses, as a higher figure may not indicate inefficiency in collecting debts, just differences in credit terms.

In the case of Pikka Pizza plc the receivables' collection period can be calculated as follows:

2009: 4,550 / 45,326 x 365 = 37 days.
2008: 3,357 / 38,397 x 365 = 32 days.

The ratios tell us that Pikka Pizza is taking more time to collect in money owed by customers in 2009 than in 2008.

Receivables' days should be kept as low as possible to enable funds to be ploughed back into the working capital cycle. If it is too long then, the firm may encounter problems in paying their own debts so much so that they are forced to borrow money in order to settle their debts. Trends upwards might suggest that the company's credit control was beginning to weaken. Increases may also be due to changes in company settlement policy, and / or a new customer base demanding longer settlements.

The receivables' collection period figure may be improved by:

- **reducing the credit period.** The business must take care to ensure that this does not lead to loss of customers to an alternative supplier.

- **offering discounts for prompt payment.** The business must ensure that the loss of income arising from customers taking up this incentive does not outweigh the benefits (eg lower administration costs, discounts and better relationship with suppliers due to prompt payment). NB Firms operating on low profit margins may be unable to afford such an incentive.

- **improving credit control by:** requesting and obtaining references to check / review credit worthiness; being quick to chase late payments, through the use of aged debtor analysis, ie sorting / listing debtors into age with oldest first, in order to identify and target / focus attention on the slowest payers.

Gearing Ratio

Gearing measures the extent to which a business is dependent on borrowed funds and its financial stability. It measures the proportion of total capital employed (ie debt and equity capital) provided from borrowed funds. It is expressed as a percentage and usually only concerns non-current (long-term) liabilities and excludes short-term loans or overdrafts or money owed to suppliers and / or other creditors, as follows:

$$\frac{^1\text{Non-current (long-term) liabilities}}{\text{Total equity + non-current (long-term) liabilities}} \times 100 = X\%.$$

[1] Bank loans + Debentures.

For example, if a company's non-current liabilities amounted to £300,000, share capital amounted to £700,000, and reserves and retained earnings amounted to £200,000 (ie total equity amounted to £900,000), the company's gearing ratio would be 25% (£300,000 / £1,200,000 X 100).

NB There are other ways of calculating gearing, as follows:

$$\frac{\text{Total liabilities}}{\text{Equity plus total liabilities}} \times 100$$

$$\frac{\text{Long-term debt}}{\text{Equity}} \times 100$$

Consequently, when making comparisons between businesses it is important to ensure that the same formula is / has been used.

In general if long-term loans represent more than 50% of total capital employed, then the firm is said to be highly geared.

In the case of Pikka Pizza plc, gearing can be calculated as follows:

Pikka Pizza plc's gearing in 2009: 7,303 / 11,215 (ie 7,303 + 3,912) x 100 = 65%.
Pikka Pizza plc's gearing in 2008: 3,127 / 5,563 (ie 3,127 + 2,436) x 100 = 56%.

Pikka Pizza's gearing has, therefore, increased between 2008 and 2009 and the company could be said to be highly geared.

The **higher the gearing**, the **higher the risk**. This is because:

- the business is committed to meeting interest payments, which has a negative effect on cash flow and net profit.
- loans are often secured on a business's fixed assets and if the business cannot meet the interest payments then the lender has the right to claim the asset on which the loan is secured.
- debtors have priority over owners / shareholders if the business fails.

Before taking out a loan, a business should therefore, be certain that the rate of return on assets / projects financed by borrowing, exceeds the cost of financing (eg through the use of **investment appraisal** techniques).

On the other hand, one could argue that the risk to the individual owner / shareholder is **lower,** and the potential reward is **greater.** This is because it provides an opportunity for a greater return to owners / shareholders without the need to provide a greater amount of capital. In other words they are risking someone else's money. Debt is also normally cheaper than equity because it is tax deductible.

Shareholder Ratios

Dividend Per Share

Dividend per share shows the amount of money shareholders receive per share. It is calculated by dividing the total amount of dividends declared (or paid) by directors, with the number of shares issued, and is expressed as amount per share, as follows:

$$\frac{\text{Total dividends payable or received}}{\text{Number of shares issued}} = \text{X pence}.$$

NB The ratio is usually only applied to ordinary shareholders as preference shareholders receive a fixed dividend, (eg the holder of £1,000 worth of 10% preference shares will receive £100 every year).

Whether the amount of dividend per share is high or low can only be judged in relation to other companies in the same sector of the market and / or previous year's figures. Obviously the higher the amount the better the investment / potential investment. A higher result can be obtained by:

- making greater profits.
- distributing a greater proportion of profit as dividends.
- buying back shares whilst maintaining the level of dividend.

Dividend Yield

Dividend yield shows the rate of return a shareholder gets by comparing the market value of the shares with the dividend received. It is, essentially, a return on capital employed calculation for shareholders and shows how the shares compare as an investment against alternatives.

Dividend yield is calculated by dividing the dividend per share paid to ordinary shareholders by the market price per share. It is expressed as a percentage:

$$\frac{\text{Dividend paid on ordinary shares}}{\text{Market price per share}} \times 100 = X\%$$

As with dividend per share, dividend yield should be judged in relation to other companies in the same sector of the market and previous year's figures. It should also be compared to the interest that could be received in a year if the shares were sold and the money were invested in a bank or building society.

Obviously the higher the amount the better the return shareholders are getting on their investment (at today's prices). A higher result can be obtained by:

- a factor lowering the market price per share.
- distributing a greater proportion of profit as dividends.

Summary of Other Shareholder / Investment Ratios

Dividend Cover

This ratio shows how many times the proposed dividend could have been met from the profits available for distribution to shareholders.

$$\frac{\text{Profit accruing to Ordinary Shareholders}}{\text{Dividends}} \text{(Profit after Tax, Interest and Preference Dividends)} = X \text{ times}$$

When reviewing this ratio it is important to remember that the potential reward shareholders get for their investment in a company consists of dividends as well as any capital gain they get from selling their shares. Therefore, shareholders may accept lower dividends in a particular year (or for several years running), if it is believed that investment is likely to increase the value of the business in the future, and thus the capital gain on selling shares, or lead to a significant increase in profits and future dividends as a result.

Regular, high dividends are, however, important for shareholders who need an annual income to boost their earnings, eg pensioners. Such groups would want a high payout each year. This leads to pressure for short-term profit, which could sacrifice longer-term gain. The reason for this is fairly obvious – the higher the dividend, the less profit retained and reinvested in the business. Thus growth is restricted, along with the potential for higher profits as a result of growth, leading to higher dividends and capital gain on shares sold.

Return on Equity (Owners / Shareholders Investment)

This is almost exactly the same as the ROCE, but excludes long-term loans, to provide the return on shareholders funds. It is calculated as follows:

$$\frac{\text{Profit accruing to Ordinary Shareholders (Profit after Tax, Interest and Preference Dividends)}}{\text{Ordinary Share Capital + Reserves}} \times 100 = X\%$$

The result should be compared to the interest that could be earned if the money was invested in a high interest account (plus inflation).

Earnings Per Share

This ratio measures the pence made on every one share invested in a Company. It is calculated as follows:

$$\frac{\text{Profit accruing to Ordinary Shareholders}}{\text{Number of Ordinary Shares}} = X \text{ pence}$$

The result should be compared to previous performance. Shareholders would also hope that the figure at least increases in line with inflation.

Price Earnings Ratio

This ratio compares the earnings per share and market price per share. It tells us that the market price is X times the earnings and, ultimately, how long it would take to recover the price paid for a share, assuming earnings remain constant.

$$\frac{\text{Market Price}}{\text{Earnings per share}} = X \text{ times}$$

A high ratio means that people are willing to pay a price many times higher than the return currently being produced for shareholders by management and thus, a high ratio indicates a high level of confidence in the company.

The ratio should also be judged in relation to other companies in the same sector or industry.

Closing Comments

The specification states that *'candidates will be given a table of relevant formulae for ratios as part of the examination paper where appropriate'*. Therefore, candidates will not be expected to know from memory the formula for calculating specific ratios. They will be expected to: select the correct data from the text to calculate ratios; interpret and comment on the result; and use calculations to support arguments made.

This section has explained the need to compare performance with previous years and other businesses / industry norms. Up to date information on industry norms can be obtained from companies like Dun and Bradstreet (D&B). The following website also provides a free summary of key business ratios: http://www.creditguru.com/ratios/inr.htm

The Value and Limitations of Ratio Analysis

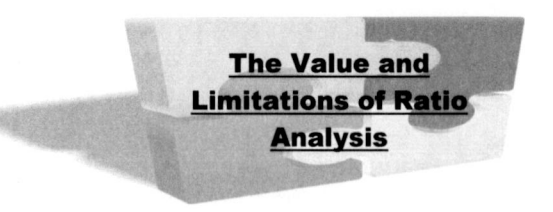

Objectives

By the end of this topic you should be able to:

1. Outline the use and value of ratios to compare performance over time, between firms and in relation to norms that accountants have identified as efficient.
2. Outline at least 9 things that can distort the figures and / or affect the validity of any comparisons made.

The Use and Value of Ratios

Ratios can be used to assess and make decisions over a business's past and its future performance. They can help to answer three key questions relating to business success. These concern:

- the **efficiency of management**.
- the **financial stability** of the business.
- **how well the owners / shareholders are doing**.

Ratios are, however, not very helpful when viewed in isolation. They only really become meaningful when compared with a business's past performance, similar entities and accepted standards of performance laid down by accountants (accountants' norms), as follows:

- **Comparing performance over time.** Ratios can be used to compare performance over time, ie between different trading periods. This identifies trends, which enable judgements to be made as to whether things are improving, worsening or staying the same.

- **Inter-firm comparison.** Ratios can be used to compare the performance of one firm within a particular industry or market with that of another firm operating in the same industry or market. Together with a comparison over time, this enables a more effective assessment to be made of a business's performance / potential performance. For example, a business's net profit margin and return on capital may be increasing every year but, when compared to other firms operating within the same industry, it may still be much lower. This suggests that there is room for improvement and encourages further investigation to identify possible reasons for the lower performance and ways performance can be improved.

- **Accountancy Norms.** Ratios can also be viewed in relation to norms that accountants have identified as efficient. For example, an acid test ratio of 1:1 is generally considered to be the right balance to ensure debts can be paid as they fall due, and a 20% return on capital employed may be regarded as a reasonable return.

To conclude, for management, ratio analysis provides an indication something may not be going well (or vice versa) and thus, where further action may be required. For shareholders, ratios provide key information to help in making decisions over whether or not to invest or to continue investing in a particular business.

Limitations of Ratios

Despite their usefulness, there are several problems with drawing solid conclusions from any given ratio. Any of the following can distort the figures, and / or affect the validity of any comparisons made, many of which have already been considered in a previous section outlining the 'weaknesses of financial data in judging performance'.

1. Changes in the value of money ie **inflation**. For example, an increase in asset turnover might be a result of prices rising and not an increase in sales volume.

2. Changes in the **accounting methods** used within a business.

3. Changes in **a business's activities** from one year to the next.

4. Changes in the **external business environment** / market and trading conditions.

5. Differences in **product mix, cost structure, objectives and strategies** of business – even those operating within the same industry.

6. Differences in **financial year ends**.

7. Differences in **methods used to value assets** eg to value stock, allow for depreciation – particularly relevant when examining accounts of firms operating in different countries.

8. Reliance on **personal judgement** eg information such as bad debts is estimated.

9. The practice of **window dressing**, eg by keeping stock levels artificially low, or chasing debtors just before the financial year end and preparation of accounts.

10. **Outdated information** – published accounts on which the ratios are based may be several months old.

11. **Missing published financial information** eg sales revenue = sales volume x selling price – useful in explaining certain results.

12. **Missing other vital business information** vital in assessing performance and potential, eg quality of product, quality of human resources.

NB: Points 1-4 are particularly relevant for comparisons over time, points 5-8 (inter-firm comparisons) and point 5 are particularly relevant for comparisons of accounting norms.

To conclude, ratios can be useful for assessing performance and can highlight potential weaknesses / problem areas, but they do not provide the answers. Further investigation is required to draw definitive conclusions regarding performance, and to determine the possible cause and potential solutions to any problems.

Closing Comments

When an investor wishes to consider a business as an investment they will initially examine the company accounts with a view to carrying out some ratio analysis. This is done to assess the profitability, liquidity, gearing and, in particular, the potential return on investment. In addition, information on the present markets they serve, their market share, the overall size of the business and future plans for expansion (or rationalisation), will all help towards the decision about whether or not to invest.

2.4

SELECTING FINANCIAL STRATEGIES

Raising Finance

Objectives

By the end of this topic you should be able to:

1. Briefly explain the importance of raising finance in relation to the achievement of other functional and corporate objectives.
2. State what is meant by short, medium and long-term finance.
3. Describe at least 10 ways in which a business might raise finance, including their relative advantages and disadvantages.
4. Describe at least 7 factors to take into account when making decisions over methods of raising finance.
5. Select and justify the most appropriate way of raising finance in a given situation.

Key Terms

Personal sources of finance might include savings held in banks or building societies, loans from friends and family, or, even, funds from redundancy payments.

Trade credit is an interest free period in which to pay for goods / services received from suppliers. The typical credit period is between 30 to 70 days.

Overdrafts are arrangements between a firm and its bank or building society to withdraw more money from its bank account than that which is deposited in it, to an agreed limit. Interest is charged on any amounts overdrawn.

Leasing is where a business rents a fixed asset rather than purchasing it outright and where the ownership of the asset remains with the finance company.

Hire purchase is where an asset is purchased by putting down a deposit and paying the remainder in instalments over an agreed period of time. The asset is owned once the final instalment has been made.

Sale of assets is the selling of fixed assets owned by the business that are no longer used, or are not considered to be making enough contribution to the business's profits.

Retained profit is profit re-invested after all expenses, tax and any dividends to shareholders have been paid.

Loan capital is where a business is advanced a set figure and repays the amount over an agreed period of time, at an agreed rate of interest.

Mortgages are loans used to purchase land and buildings and are usually secured on such property.

Debentures are a type of loan where the money to be raised is divided into smaller units (debentures) and members of the public are invited to lend money to the business for a fixed period of time (usually long-term) at a fixed rate of interest. They are bought and sold on the Stock Exchange.

Share capital is finance raised by selling shares in the business - to family and friends in the case of private limited companies, or members of the general public in the case of public limited companies.

Venture capital is finance supplied by merchant banks and specialised commercial banks or venture capital companies, who usually expect to take a minority shareholding in the business for a set period of time.

Government grants are financial assistance from the European Union, and UK government agencies, available for specific geographical areas, purposes, industries and projects.

Introduction

How Raising Finance Interrelates with Other Functions

Raising finance is essential to achieve the objectives of other functional areas and, for example, to achieve corporate objectives relating to growth and expansion. In such a scenario additional finance may, for instance, be required to pay for:

- a major marketing campaign to increase brand awareness, sales and market share.
- new product development to appeal to a broader customer base.
- new plant, machinery and equipment to enable the production of greater volumes.
- the training and development of staff to use the new machinery and cope with greater sales volumes.
- the additional materials, labour, etc required to produce greater volumes.

This section of our Elementary Explanations re-caps on the methods of finance covered in Unit 1 of our Elementary Explanations, which are not just relevant to a business start-up but to a growing business. It also considers other long-term methods of finance including debentures and retained profit, and short-term methods such as trade credit which is also important in securing the working capital requirements of a growing business.

The Difference Between Short, Medium and Long-term Methods

As our elementary explanations for Unit 1 highlighted, there is much controversy over what time period constitutes short, medium or long-term. The most frequently quoted is:

- **short** is up to one year.
- **medium** is one to five years.
- **long-term** is more than five years.

Short-term methods are usually used to fund **working capital** requirements ie to pay for running expenses as they fall due and also to fund investment in short-lived machines and vehicles. These include trade credit and overdrafts.

Medium-term finance is generally used to fund the **purchase of assets with a medium term life**, eg plant and machinery. This includes leasing and medium-term loans.

Long-term finance is generally used to fund the purchase of **long-life assets**, such as buildings and acquisitions. This includes long-term loans and share capital.

Elementary Explanations for AQA GCE Business – A2 U3: Strategies for Success

Method	Description	Advantages	Disadvantages
Personal sources	May include savings, loan from friends and family, redundancy payment.	• No interest payments (unlike loans).	• Owner carries the financial risk.
Trade Credit	Securing an interest free period in which to pay for goods / services received. The typical credit period is between 30 to 70 days.	• Interest free (unlike overdrafts).	• Possible loss of discount for prompt payment.
Overdrafts	Arrangements between firm and bank/building society to withdraw more money from account than that deposited in it, to an agreed limit.	• Simple and quick to arrange • Flexible and convenient • Relatively cheap in short-term - interest only charged on outstanding bank balance at end of each day.	• Expensive if used regularly for large amounts as interest usually charged 2-4% over base rate. • Repayable on demand ie they can be recalled at any time without notice.
Leasing and Hire purchase	**Leasing:** business rents a fixed asset rather than purchasing it outright, ownership remains with the finance company. **Hire purchase:** firm purchases asset by putting down deposit and paying remainder in instalments over agreed period of time. Asset owned once final instalment made.	• Use of asset without capital outlay. • Flexibility in changing equipment. • Often updated with little extra cost. • Service / maintenance often included. • Payments can be offset against tax. • Additional advantage of hire purchase: Balance sheet position improved once final instalment made.	• More expensive in long run than purchasing the asset outright.
Sale of assets	Sale of fixed assets owned by the business no longer used, or not making enough contribution.	• No interest payments (unlike loans). • No dilution of ownership and control (unlike shares).	• Need to ensure sale will not restrict future flexibility. *NB Some business sell assets and lease them back providing injection of cash and continued use of asset.*
Retained Profit	Profits reinvested (after all expenses, tax and any dividends to shareholders have been paid).	• Available immediately – no need to publicise assets or shares for sale, apply for and negotiate loans. • No interest payments (unlike loans). • No dilution of ownership and control.	• May not be popular with shareholders who would rather receive greater dividends. • Sole reliance on profits could mean expansion is slow and limited.
Bank loan	Business is advanced a set figure and repays the amount over an agreed period of time, at an agreed rate of interest.	• Relatively simple and quick to arrange, providing satisfactory financial history and collateral (if required), plus sound plans.	• Interest payments – increases costs, gearing and affects cash flow. • Collateral on which to secure the loan is often required.

© APT Initiatives Limited, 2009

Mortgage	Loans to purchase land and buildings, usually secured on such property, paid back over agreed period eg 5 to 20 years.	• As with loans.	• As with loans, plus… • Cost of professional valuation of property. • Arrangement fee (eg 1.25% of amount borrowed).
Debentures	Type of loan where money to be raised is divided into smaller units and public is invited to lend money for a fixed period (usually long-term) at a fixed rate of interest. Bought/sold on Stock Exchange	• No dilution of ownership or control (unlike shares).	• Debenture holders have priority over all shareholders and, unlike dividends on shares… • The interest must be paid even if the firm is not making a profit.
Share capital	Finance raised by selling shares in the business - to family and friends in the case of Ltd's, or members of the general public in the case of plc's. The success in raising finance in this way would depend upon whether the company is perceived by existing and / or potential investors to be soundly managed, have a good history of dividends and sound proposals for investment.	• No interest payments (unlike loans). • Dividend payments to ordinary shareholders are not fixed.	• Can be a slow process. • Dilutes ownership and control – ordinary shareholders entitled to vote; share in profits. If converting from ltd to plc… • Process of share issue particularly slow and expensive, not worthwhile unless large sums involved – cost of underwriting, fees to solicitors / advisers, printing, advertising. • Threat of take-over. • Greater disclosure requirements.
Venture capital	Finance supplied by merchant / specialised commercial banks or venture capital companies, who usually expect a minority shareholding for set period of time. Venture capitalists invest in new, expanding, and start up businesses with substantial growth potential. The word venture implies risk.	• No interest payments (unlike loans). • Can provide large sums – often around £2 million plus. • Most offer expert management support. • May find it easier to secure further funding from other sources in the future, as attracting interest from a venture capitalist implies the business has significant potential.	• Can be complex, time consuming process – requires in-depth business plan, financial forecasts. • Legal and accounting fees at the negotiation stage, whether or not firm succeeds in securing funds. • Dilution of ownership, control & profits - most VC's expect minority shareholding between 15-40% over 3-7 years and may also appoint a non-executive director to take part in major business decisions. • Many VC's want a relatively quick return - few invest for longer than 7 yrs (more often 5).
Government grants	A range of financial assistance from the European Union, and UK government agencies, available for specific geographical areas, purposes, industries and projects.	• Usually lower interest rate than bank loans.	• Applying can prove costly – preparing accounts and / or cash flows certified by an independent accountant. • Conditions often apply. • Non-financial costs eg grants may be publicised.

Factors Affecting Choice over Methods of Raising Finance

General

This final sub-section briefly explains the various factors which influence the type of finance used / will affect the appropriateness of a particular method of finance in a given situation.

The Purpose

The purpose for which the finance is required will have a significant influence on the method used. For example, the purchase of stocks of raw materials may be best financed by short term methods, such as trade credit or an overdraft. This is because stocks can usually be quickly changed into cash in order to pay suppliers, or pay off the overdraft which is repayable on demand, and which can prove costly if used for fixed assets, as these take time to generate sufficient funds to settle the debt.

Business Objectives

If the owner's objectives are simply to survive then owner's savings or reinvested profits are likely to be used. There is no need to make use of alternative methods which only serve to make the business accountable to an outside body or increases costs. If expansion is the objective, retained profits or owner's savings may be insufficient to fund such an objective, and shares, venture capital, or mortgage loans may enable expansion to take place at a much quicker rate.

Personal Preferences of the Owners / Key Decision Makers

The personal preferences of owners, in particular, their attitude towards sharing ownership and control can have a significant impact on the method chosen to raise finance. If, for example, the owner of a new business start-up wants to retain full ownership and control, then share capital or venture capital is not likely to be found acceptable.

Legal Structure

Unlike sole traders or partnerships, limited companies can obviously sell shares to raise finance. Because companies can raise a substantial amount of finance in this way, they are usually larger, and have more assets to offer as security.

Financial Position

A sound credit history, healthy profitability and liquidity position, and the need for security, may be required in order to secure a loan and interest potential investors. Banks and building societies, will be particularly interested in liquidity, ie whether the business is able to meet debts as they fall due. They are also likely to examine key financial ratios such as:

- interest cover, to assess the business's ability to pay its interest payments out of operating or net profit.
- gearing, which measures the proportion of capital employed provided by loans.

The business may use these ratios to assess the risk involved. The higher the gearing, the higher the risk, as the business is committed to paying interest on loans before it can reinvest profits and / or pay dividends to shareholders.

On the other hand, shareholders and venture capitalists will be more interested in profitability.

Age

The more established a business is, the more likely it will be able to secure finance. New businesses have no credit or financial history and are considered more of a risk. They will need to do much to convince the financier or investor that their business will be success, including in depth market research, detailed sales forecasts and cost calculations.

Size

Small and medium-sized businesses are often considered to be high risk. They tend not to have sufficient assets on which to secure finance or make sufficient profits to attract investors. In addition, as a business grows it becomes more difficult to control and co-ordinate, and many sole traders or partnerships often resort to selling shares and forming limited companies, as a means of minimising the risks involved, because of the protection of personal assets this type of business provides.

Reputation

A firm's standing in the market place will clearly have a direct affect on the interest it receives from investors. The more widely known and established, the more likely it will attract investors / secure loans. (NB this is closely linked to age and size).

Government Policy – Tax, Tax Benefits and Grants

The government is responsible for setting taxes and deciding upon the level, and type of financial assistance available to businesses. Reductions in corporation tax may enable a business solely to rely on retained profits.

Tax benefits on leasing and hire purchase agreements may encourage a business to use such a method.

Finally, if government grants or loans are available they may be used by a business if it qualifies for such funds, due to their cheapness in comparison with other methods of raising finance.

Interest Rates

A steep rise in interest rates may force a business to choose methods of finance other than loans or leasing agreements as these prove too costly.

Closing Comments

There are clearly a wide range of factors that need to be taken into account when making a decision over the best method to use to raise finance. Out of all the methods a decision to sell shares should not be taken lightly as it brings significant long-term disadvantages especially when it involves changing legal status to a plc. These include divorce of ownership and control, threat of takeover and greater disclosure of information. The disclosure requirements, together with the work involved in keeping shareholders satisfied, has actually led some company founders to buy back shares and convert back to private company status – for example - Andrew Lloyd Weber's Really Useful Theatre Company.

© APT Initiatives Limited, 2009

Implementing Profit Centres

Objectives

By the end of this topic you should be able to:

1. Define the terms profit centre, full costing, absorption costing and marginal or contribution costing.
2. Outline how profit centres can aid decision making, motivation and control.
3. Outline how profit centres are established and how costs can be allocated.
4. Outline at least 3 potential difficulties or disadvantages associated with implementing profit centres.

Key Terms

A **profit centre** is a unit within the business that generates both revenue and incurs costs and has its own income statement (or profit and loss account).

Full costing is where **all** the indirect costs incurred by a business are **totalled** and then divided and allocated to the different cost centres according to one criterion eg according to output by volume or value.

Absorption costing is where **each** overhead is absorbed **separately** by the profit centre, for example, rent and rates could be allocated according to floor space taken up by the centre.

Marginal or contribution costing is where direct costs only are allocated to the profit centre. Indirect costs are only included when preparing the whole firm's profit and loss account.

What is a Profit Centre?

It is a common mistake to think that a profit centre refers to those parts of the business which are profitable. Instead it refers to a unit within the business for which data on both revenue and costs are recorded. The unit can be a division, branch, department, product range, single product or, even, a group of machinery, location, or person. They are generally responsible for earning revenues <u>and</u> controlling costs.

Role, Purpose and Benefits

Overview

Whatever the nature of a business, if it is multi-faceted with differing sources of revenue and costs it is important, from an overall management perspective, to know how each section of the business is performing. Splitting the business into profit centres is the equivalent of treating each 'centre' as though it was a separate business. This approach should significantly assist in improving strategic decision making regarding present / future investment and development, and help in the effective control and motivation of staff of each aspect at a tactical / operational level and, ultimately, help to maximise the business's overall performance. This is explained in further detail below.

Monitoring and Control

The implementation of profit centres enables individual financial performance to be monitored, and timely, corrective action to be taken as required. It also permits a meaningful comparison between the goods / services provided by a profit centre, and other organisations dedicated specifically to providing similar goods / services.

Motivation and Performance

This aspect of accounting is often known as responsibility accounting because it is all about identifying responsibility and ensuring that underperforming units are not hidden amongst the more profitable. The aim is to ensure "there is no hiding place" for weak products and units. Consequently, the use of profit centres should help motivation and performance, as each individual becomes more fully aware of how they can have an effect on costs and profit - this is likely to help motivate them to fulfil their responsibilities.

It may also be easier to generate team spirit amongst smaller units, rather than the whole business, which can be good for morale, motivation and overall performance.

Costs and profit linked to targets can also form the basis of financial incentives for staff.

Decision Making

Knowledge of how individual parts of the business are performing in terms of profit, as well as comparative information on competitors and external factors affecting the business, helps to ensure appropriate, well-informed decisions are made that make the most effective use of resources in order to maximise the business's potential.

Because power and responsibility regarding costs and profit is delegated, decision-making should also be speeded up. Day to day decisions are also likely to be more thought through, and of better quality, as managers are more accountable for their actions.

Establishing Profit Centres – the General Approach

In order to create a profit centre, the following is a broad summary of the approach necessary:

1. Break down the products / services the business provides into those which satisfy different markets or market segments.

2. Record the revenue received for each product / service profit centre.

3. Allocate the direct costs involved in providing service / products to each profit centre.

4. Summarise the 'common' fixed costs of the business and allocate these costs into the profit centres on a rational basis eg accommodation costs (rent, rates, insurance, heating, lighting etc) would logically be apportioned on a square footage basis.

This approach would provide an accurate and meaningful picture of the return on investment or the percentage profit or turnover for each profit centre, thereby significantly aiding business development decisions, and the optimisation and utilisation of resources.

More detail is provided below on how costs can be allocated on a logical basis.

Methods of Allocating Costs

General

In order to allocate costs to the various profit centres, costs need to be divided into direct - those which can be directly related to a particular product or process - and indirect (the reverse of the above). Whilst direct costs, by their very nature, can easily be allocated to a cost centre, the question arises as to how indirect costs should be allocated.

There are three main ways for allocating indirect costs / overheads to a cost / profit centre. These are summarised below.

Full Costing

This is where **all the indirect costs** incurred by a business are totalled and then divided and allocated to the different profit centres according to one criterion eg according to output by volume or value.

Refer to the following example.

A firm sells 3 products: product A, product B and product C.
Sales for each product represent 30%, 45% and 25% of total sales, respectively.

Using full costing, 30% of the total indirect costs would, therefore, be allocated to A, 45% to B and 25% to C.

Advantages	Disadvantages
● Simple to use. ● Inexpensive. ● If used to price products – ensures all sales revenue covers costs and any cost increases are passed on to the customer.	● Inaccurate – can be misleading and lead to poor quality decision making.

Absorption Costing

This is where **each overhead is absorbed separately** by the profit centre according to a logical criterion – for example:

- **Rent & rates** – floor space taken up by the centre.
- **Heating & lighting** – as above; machine hours used.
- **Administration** – number of employees working in the centre; direct labour hours or costs.
- **Depreciation** – value of machinery; machine hours used.
- **Insurance** – value of machinery / premises.
- **Storage costs** – storage space used; material costs.

Advantages	Disadvantages
● Fair – takes into account the different rates of usage. ● More accurate – ought to ensure more accurate pricing policies.	● Not all costs can be divided accurately: some workers may be multi-skilled – therefore, used by more than one centre; some floor area may be common to profit centres. ● More expensive to carry out – requires careful measurement.

Marginal or Contribution Costing

This is where direct costs only are allocated to the profit centre. Indirect costs / overheads are only included when preparing the whole firm's profit and loss account.

Advantages	Disadvantages
• Simple to understand. • Allows a direct comparison. • Focuses attention on products only making a small contribution.	• Misleading – cost centre may generate a high proportion of overheads yet be seen as making a positive contribution to profit. • If used to set prices, need to be careful to cover total fixed costs.

Potential Difficulties and Disadvantages of Implementing Profit Centres

There are several potential disadvantages associated with the establishment of profit centres. These are outlined below:

- **Co-ordination** – harder as the firm is divided into more units.

- **Increased pressure** on junior managers.

- **Interdepartmental conflict and competition** as centres begin to view their activities apart from the activities of other centres, and eventually lose sight of the overall business goal(s). Staff may begin to concentrate far too much on generating revenues and / or controlling costs rather than providing the sensitive service required to satisfy client needs.

- **Actual profit may bear no resemblance to the performance** of the profit centre – much is dependent upon demand. Consequently, incentive schemes based on these may act as a de-motivator in these circumstances.

- **Not all revenues or costs can be directly associated** with a particular part of the business.

Closing Comments

This section has highlighted how profit centres can significantly improve strategic decision making and aid control, motivation and performance at tactical and operational levels and, ultimately, the business's overall performance. It has also highlighted how separating the business into a number of profit centres, where each area has successfully been given the authority to run itself as a business within a business, with its own profit and loss account, can create conflict. Each profit centre may begin to view their activities apart from the activities of other centres and eventually lose sight of the overall business goals. Regular communication between such centres is, therefore, important to ensure such conflict does not arise.

Cost Minimisation

Objectives

By the end of this topic you should be able to:

1. Define the term cost minimisation.
2. Outline various ways in which a business might seek to reduce material costs, labour costs, rent and leasing payments, business rates, water rates / bills, energy costs, telephone bills, advertising and promotional expenditure, printing, postage and stationery costs, travel expenses, expenditure on maintenance and repairs, legal and professional fees, bank charges and interest payments.

Key Terms

Cost minimisation involves identifying all the costs involved in producing a business's product or service and investigating whether any of these costs can be reduced without affecting sales or the quality of the product or service provided.

Cost Minimisation as a Means to Achieve Financial & Corporate Objectives

Cost minimisation is a strategy that involves identifying a business's costs and examining whether or not any of these costs can be reduced without affecting sales or the quality of the product or service provided by the business. Remember (from Unit 1) a business costs consist of the following:

- raw materials, including any materials used in packaging.
- wages and salaries and employer's national insurance contributions.
- rent / leasing or hire purchase payments on any buildings, machinery, equipment or vehicles rented, or leased, as opposed to purchasing outright.
- government taxes – VAT on sales, business rates.
- water rates.
- energy eg gas, electricity, oil bills.
- telephone.
- advertising and promotion.
- printing, postage and stationery.
- travel expenses eg petrol, diesel, accommodation, train and air fares.
- repairs and maintenance.
- legal and professional fees including accountancy and insurance.
- bank charges and interest on any loans taken out.

Cost minimisation can help to achieve a business's overall aim of maximising profit and return on investment, as well as market share. It can help to achieve the latter by enabling the business to be more competitive on price.

Cost minimisation is an important strategy for public sector organisations as it can free financial resources for other uses and / or help to lower taxes.

The remainder of this section will examine how a business might seek to reduce specific costs.

Ways of Minimising Costs

Material Costs

Material costs may be reduced through some or all of the following:

- Regularly checking and comparing prices between different suppliers for individual items and re-negotiating prices where appropriate.
- Securing alternative, cheaper (reliable) supplier(s) – though not at the expense of quality. Material costs might, for example, be cut by making use of overseas suppliers in countries where labour costs are cheaper.
- Buying in bulk to secure discounts wherever possible – where the additional stockholding costs (see below) do not outweigh the discount secured. It may be possible, for example, to partner up with another business in order to make such purchases.
- Ensuring that early settlement discounts are taken through effective cash management. Most suppliers will give 2½% to 5% discount for seven day or monthly settlement. 2½% per month = 30% per annum return on capital.
- Reducing the level of stock held and, thus, the costs of holding stock – without risk of stock-out ie a situation where customer orders cannot be met - resulting in lost sales. Costs of holding stocks include the costs of storage and finance, the risk of theft, damage, deterioration or obsolescence, as well as the opportunity cost, for example, the interest that could be earned on money if it was not tied up in stock. Keeping stock levels to a minimum is particularly important for businesses such as supermarkets and / or restaurants, due to the perishable nature of the stock involved. Over-ordering / stockpiling of ingredients and / or poor stock rotation would lead to ingredients going past their shelf-life and unnecessary wastage, resulting in increased costs and lower profits. Such a strategy will, however, only lead to a reduction in costs if the reduction in stockholding costs does not outweigh any increased ordering and handling costs arising from more frequent deliveries and / or loss in discounts previously received on bulk purchases.
- Finding or developing new lower cost materials if possible eg Goodyear Tyre and Rubber Co. increased its use of synthetic rubber to counteract the rising cost of natural rubber.
- Improving the ability and / or motivation of staff to eliminate any unnecessary wastage of materials arising from poor quality or careless work eg through improved induction and training programmes and / or better supervision, and / or staff incentives – as appropriate.
- Keeping equipment well maintained to ensure efficient operation ie less wastage of materials (and energy).
- The introduction of TQM or elements of TQM such as kaizen groups or quality circles to continually seek out ways to reduce losses arising from wasteful practices.

Wages and Salaries

Wages and salaries may be reduced by:

- Reviewing staffing requirements and cutting staff hours eg by introducing shorter working weeks where possible and / or staffing levels – though not at the expense of the level of service as this may affect customer satisfaction and sales. Cutting staffing levels may also increase costs in the short term if redundancy payments are required.

- Making use of flexible working practices eg through the use of a core / periphery workforce and ensuring the right balance between full-time and part-time and temporary staff to ensure staff are not being paid when they are not fully employed. This is particularly important for businesses with seasonal sales.

- Keeping overtime pay to a minimum, for example, by taking on temporary staff to secure any additional hours required. Overtime can be an expensive way of securing the additional hours required at time and a half, for example, in the longer term.

- Investment in training - trained staff are likely to be more productive, ie quicker at their job and make less mistakes, resulting in less waste and fewer accidents. As a consequence, less supervision may be needed, thus cutting labour costs. Employees may also be more satisfied and motivated - thus minimising labour turnover and associated costs ie recruitment, selection, training, for several reasons. They may feel more confident and secure in what they are doing - helping to satisfy safety needs. They may feel management value them as they are willing to invest time and money in them - helping to satisfy esteem and ego needs. They might be able to undertake more interesting / challenging work that enables them to use more of their abilities, thus helping to satisfy self-actualisation needs.

- Outsourcing non-core / critical activities eg such as warehousing and distribution to another business that can perform these tasks more cheaply, without a drop in quality or reliability. This may be – for example – as a result of the other business being located in an area where labour (and, possibly, other production) costs are cheaper and / or specialising in these tasks and / or being able to benefit from greater economies of scale. The decision to outsource does, however, need to be carefully considered due to the loss of control and the negative effect on the workforce currently employed in these activities. It may mean redundancies which involve a cost and may have a damaging effect on the morale of the employees who remain – at least in the short-term.

- Investment in automation ie replacing skilled labour with machinery. Machines can be quicker and more reliable than humans, thus producing more in the same amount of time, and reducing not only labour input costs but also the cost of materials and supplies. This obviously incurs an initial capital outlay and may also involve redundancy payments in the short-term.

Rent on Premises, Leasing of Vehicles or machinery

Rental and / or leasing payments may be minimised by:

- Renegotiating cheaper payments with the landlord or leasing companies – this may be secured by agreeing a longer lease.

- Reducing the floor space required and, thus, rental payments, by reviewing and re-designing current production / office layouts to make more efficient use of space.

- Making use of homeworking / teleworking if possible, for example, allowing each office employee to work from home 1 day a week which could reduce floor space requirements by 20%.

- Subletting any space that can be freed up – if the lease permits this.

- Off-shoring some or relocating all of the business to a location where the rent is cheaper – though not at the expense of a fall in passing trade (where applicable) and / or proportionately higher distribution costs. Many UK business have, in fact, relocated to Eastern Europe and / or Asia where wage rates and other production costs, besides cheaper property prices, are much lower. NB The strategy of relocation and off-shoring is considered in detail under 'Operational Strategies' below.

Business Rates

Business rates may be reduced by moving to a:

- smaller premises.
- different geographical area where rates are lower.

Water Rates / Bills

Water bills may be reduced by:

- Ensuring pipes are well insulated against frost.
- Keeping water-using equipment well maintained.
- Encouraging staff to check and report leaks and ensuring leaks are repaired quickly.
- Investigating and taking up opportunities for re-using process water.
- Using alternative sources ie rainwater and / or grey water ie domestic wastewater that has not been contaminated by human excrement eg water from baths, sinks, washing machines, dish-washers, etc wherever possible.
- Investing in water-minimising controls where possible eg push taps, flow regulator / restrictors, spray nozzles on hoses, low-flush toilets and sensor-activated urinal flushing.
- Investing in more water efficient equipment when equipment comes to the end of its useful life or the lease of equipment expires. Such equipment may be more expensive in the short-term, but will be cost-effective in terms of savings on the water bill in the long-term.

The environment agency provides detailed advice on how businesses can conserve water:
http://www.environment-agency.gov.uk/business/topics/water/32070.aspx

The envirowise website also contains a wealth of information on how to reduce water costs:
http://www.envirowise.gov.uk/uk/Topics-and-Issues/Water.html

Energy eg Gas, Electricity, Oil Bills

Energy bills may be reduced by:

- Getting better deals from alternative suppliers by shopping around. This can be done quickly and easily via websites such as uSwitch.com that enables homeowners and businesses to instantly compare price from every energy supplier: http://uswitch.com/gas-electricity/ppc/energy1-b/?gclid=CNmXua3GzZsCFV8...
- Carrying out operations at night (wherever possible) to take advantage of off-peak tariffs.
- Turning off lights and equipment when not in use.
- Closing doors and windows and sealing any cracks as soon as they appear.
- Reducing the level of thermostat by 1 or 2 degrees and insulating rooms, hot water storage tank and pipes wherever possible.
- Fitting all lights with energy saving bulbs. This may incur a fairly substantial initial cost but could result in substantial savings in energy bills and overall financial benefit in the long-run. They last 6 to 10 times longer and save energy.

- Making bulk purchases of fuel (where possible) before the winter season begins – securing discounts for bulk and / or off season purchases
- Installing programmable thermostats.
- Keeping all machinery / equipment (including air conditioning) well maintained.
- Investing in more energy efficient equipment / machinery when equipment comes to the end of its useful life, or the lease expires. Such equipment / machinery may be more expensive but, again, could lead to substantial savings in the long-term.
- Invest in alternative sources of energy (eg sun, wind, water) for power eg by using solar panels, wind turbines, hydropower. The price of solar panels has fallen significantly in recent years to the point where the cost of investing in them can be recouped within around 6 years and the savings after this point are likely to be substantial.

Telephone

Telephone bills may be reduced by:

- Getting better rates and tariffs for landlines and / or mobiles by shopping around for the best deals.
- Making phone calls through the internet using Voice over IP (VoIP) technology, especially when travelling abroad - where the alternative of using hotel landlines and / or mobile phones can cost substantially more.

Advertising and Promotion

Advertising and promotion expenditure may be reduced by:

- Shopping around to get the best rates for TV and print media.
- Sending promotional literature via email and or with despatches of orders.

Printing, Postage and Stationery

Printing, postage and stationery may be reduced by:

- Corresponding with customers via email – sending order confirmation, delivery notes and invoices via email instead of through the post.
- Corresponding with suppliers via email and sending payment electronically through BACS transfers.

Travel Expenses

Travel expenses may be reduced by:

- Using price comparison websites to find the cheapest chain of fuel stations and ensure staff only fill up at these stations.
- Keeping vehicles well maintained.
- Planning meetings and car journeys to avoid staff travelling in the rush hour and, thus, the time staff spend idling in traffic which wastes fuel.

- Investing in satellite navigation systems to minimise the chance of staff getting lost and wasting fuel as a result.
- Booking airline and train tickets in advance to obtain the cheapest ticket prices.
- Negotiating better deals for car rental and hotels.
- Using video or teleconferencing or internet based (VoiP) technologies instead of travelling to carry out meetings face to face wherever possible.
- Reducing the number of vehicles the company requires to lease or buy, insure and pay road tax, etc by using a pool system as opposed to assigning individual cars to individual employees.
- Investing in smaller, more fuel efficient models when vehicles need replacing, or the lease expires.

Repairs and Maintenance

Repairs and maintenance expenditure can be reduced by:

- Investing in planned, preventative maintenance

Legal and Professional Fees

Legal and professional fees may be reduced by:

- Shopping around to get the best rates for insurance, accountancy, auditing (where applicable) and solicitor's fees.

Bank Charges and Interest on any Loans

Bank charges and interest on any loans may be reduced by:

- Shopping around to get the cheapest form of credit available.

Other Ways to Cut Costs

Many seasonal businesses reduce trading hours or, even, close completely during the quieter months of the year in order to cut costs. This is popular in the seaside hotel trade. The rationale for this strategy is that expected sales revenue during this period is less than the variable costs involved in remaining open. If remaining open results in a negative contribution, it is financially worthwhile to close even though there are fixed costs to cover and equipment is unused. But most businesses continue to trade during the lean season because either:

- sales revenue exceeds variable costs and a positive contribution (albeit small) is made from remaining open; or
- in the case of a new and growing venture, the owners are prepared to accept the loss in order to build up trade.

Businesses might, however, consider reduced opening hours (eg in retailing) or a reduction in service (eg in travel and transport). Reduced opening / reduced service will impact upon sales revenue and cash flow but, again, it is a question of comparing the downward impact on sales revenue with the downward impact on variable costs. This tactic would require more flexible working contracts and might initially result in existing staff leaving in order to find full-time jobs (throughout the year) elsewhere.

Closing Comments

The starting point in any cost minimisation programme is to monitor every expense. It is only once a clear understanding has been gained of exactly where money is going, that ways to reduce costs become clear.

Many cost cutting strategies impact upon other functional areas within the business. For example, using alternative, substitute, cheaper materials may require the re-setting of machinery and the re-training of production and, even, sales and marketing staff. Any reduction in labour hours or staffing levels will require the human resources department to draw up and implement a revised workforce plan. A reduction in advertising expenditure could lead to a fall in sales and may require operations to cut back on planned production volumes. Clearly, the impact of cost cutting strategies on other functional areas need to be carefully considered and the finance department will need to liaise closely with any departments affected when implementing such measures.

Allocating Capital Expenditure

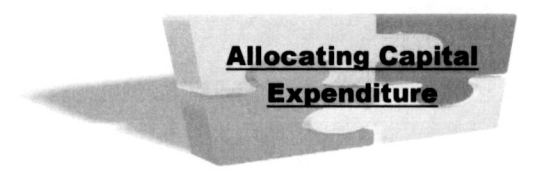

Objectives

By the end of this topic you should be able to:

1. Define and explain the difference between capital expenditure and revenue expenditure.
2. Outline how capital expenditure is treated and allocated in the final accounts of a business.

Key Terms

Capital expenditure is spending on the acquisition, modification or improvement of a physical asset that is likely to last more than a year such as land, buildings, machinery and vehicles.

Revenue expenditure is spending on items used up on the day to day running and management of the business, for example, payment for materials, labour, energy, maintenance and repairs.

The Difference Between Capital Expenditure and Revenue Expenditure

Capital expenditure occurs when money is spent on acquiring, modifying or improving assets that are likely to last more than a year, such as land, buildings, plant, fixtures and fittings, machinery, equipment and vehicles. It includes the installation and legal costs associated with the acquisition, modification or improvement of the asset.

This contrasts with revenue expenditure which occurs when money is spent on day to day running and management of the business, for example, in payment for goods and services which have either already been used or will be shortly. This might include buying advertising space in a newspaper or, perhaps, paying salesmen. It would also include the purchase of stock that has been (or will be shortly) converted into finished goods and sold to customers, as well as the labour used to convert it into a finished product.

The table below provides more detailed examples of capital as well as revenue expenditure in relation to three major fixed assets – buildings, vehicles and machinery.

	Capital Expenditure	Revenue Expenditure
Buildings	<ul><li>The cost of the building.</li><li>The cost of any extension, modification or improvements (materials, labour used).</li><li>Legal fees eg to obtain planning for change of use.</li><li>Architect fees to draw up plans for extension and / or modifications.</li><li>Utility installation costs.</li></ul>	<ul><li>Maintenance.</li><li>Repairs.</li></ul>
Vehicles	<ul><li>The cost of the vehicle.</li><li>The cost of any alterations made to the vehicle to fix any problems that existed prior to purchase (if second hand) or to improve its performance.</li></ul>	<ul><li>Road Tax.</li><li>MOT.</li><li>Insurance.</li><li>Fuel.</li><li>Servicing and repairs.</li></ul>

© APT Initiatives Limited, 2009

Machinery	• The cost of the machinery. • The cost of any alterations made to the machinery to fix any problems that existed prior to purchase (if second hand) or to improve its performance. • Installation cost. • Training cost. • The cost of modifications / upgrades.	• Insurance. • Maintenance / Servicing. • Repairs.

The two types of expenditure are treated differently in a company's final accounts and it is important to distinguish between the two types of expenditure in order to give an accurate reflection of the financial situation of the business.

Allocating Capital Expenditure

In terms of accounting if an expense is a capital expenditure, then:

- The **total** expense is recorded as a **cash outflow** on the **cash flow statement**.
- The **total** expense is itemised on the **balance sheet** under **non-current (fixed) assets**.
- The **total** expense is **not** shown on the income statement (profit and loss account).
- The expense is capitalised and the business **spreads the total cost of the expenditure over the useful life of the asset** ie the asset is **depreciated**.

It is important to appreciate that **the** depreciation of capital items affects both the value of the figures on the balance sheet <u>and</u> the income statement (profit and loss account). If, for example, machinery costs £1 million and is expected to last for 10 years (with no residual value), then, depending on its depreciation policy, the business might decide to make an annual allowance of £100,000 per year. At the end of the first year, the net book value (the value of the asset after the depreciation charge) will be £900,000 and this figure (of £900,000 as opposed to one million) should be recorded on the balance sheet (next to the relevant non-current asset) and so has a direct effect on the net worth of the business. Counter to that, the reduction in value of £100,000 is recorded as a cost against revenue on the income statement (profit and loss account) and so has a direct effect on profit. Refer to the table below

	Cost = £1 million	
End of Year	Net Book value (on Balance Sheet)	Depreciation (Income statement Charge)
1	£900,000	£100,000
2	£800,000	£100,000
3	£700,000	£100,000
4	£600,000	£100,000
5	£500,000	£100,000
6	£400,000	£100,000
7	£300,000	£100,000
8	£200,000	£100,000
9	£100,000	£100,000
10	0	£100,000

Closing Comments

This section of the Elementary Explanations has highlighted the importance of distinguishing between capital and revenue expenditure. The key differentiator is that if the expenditure simply maintains the asset in its current condition, then it is an item of revenue expenditure as opposed to capital expenditure. In which case, the total cost should be deducted fully in the year it occurred and recorded on the income statement as a cost against revenue.

2.5

MAKING INVESTMENT DECISIONS

> # Why Businesses Invest – Helping to Reach Functional Objectives

Objectives

By the end of this topic you should be able to:

1. Define the term investment.
2. State at least four types of investment made by businesses.
3. Give at least 4 examples of how different types of investment may help a business to achieve specific functional objectives.

Key Terms

Investment concerns spending money now in the hope of reaping greater reward (in relation to the original investment) in the future.

Types of Investment

Businesses make investment decisions on a daily basis. Throughout a business's existence, such decisions may concern some or all of the following:

- Investment in capital goods such as land, buildings, vehicles and machinery.
- The purchase of another business, eg competitor or supplier. This may involve all of the above as well as brand names, trademarks and patents.
- Investment in research and development.
- Investment in promotional campaigns.
- Investment in projects involving both research and development, and promotional expenditure, eg the launch of a new product.
- Investment in training.

Why Businesses Invest

To Reap Greater Reward in the Future

Businesses invest in the hope that they will receive greater reward (than the original cost of the investment) at some point in the future.

To Fulfil Functional Objectives

The decision to invest is often based upon the need to fulfil specific functional objectives, for example:

- Investment in capital goods and / or purchase of a competitor business might be essential in order to fulfil an objective relating to growth in sales or market share.
- Investment in new machinery might be essential to fulfil operational targets relating to production volumes, product or service quality, production costs and / or minimising waste and achieving environmental targets.
- The purchase of a supplier's business might be a way of achieving financial objectives relating to cost minimisation and shareholder returns.
- Investment in research and development might be essential to achieve operational targets relating to new product development.
- Investment in promotional campaigns might be essential to achieve targets relating to sales, market standing (image) and market share, or to financial targets relating to cash flow / liquidity by encouraging sales of slow selling lines.
- Investment in training may be considered essential in order to make full use of the workforce's potential and / or to meet targets relating to health and safety.

Closing Comments

There are also many different types of investment decisions, for example:

- Is a particular project worthwhile? Do the benefits outweigh the costs?
- Should we undertake the investment now or wait until later?
- Should we lease / rent or buy premises / plant / vehicles / machinery?
- Should we do the work for a particular project ourselves or outsource?

In most cases a business will start with quanititative appraisal which concerns looking at the investment from a financial perspective.

Conducting Quantitative Investment Appraisal

Objectives

By the end of this topic you should be able to:

1. Define the terms investment appraisal and quantitative measures of investment appraisal including payback, average rate of return and net present value.
2. Select appropriate methods of investment appraisal in a given situation and calculate and interpret findings.

Key Terms

Investment appraisal considers the benefits of an investment decision in relation to the anticipated costs. Benefits might include increased revenues and / or reduced costs. Costs might include the initial capital outlay and running costs.

Payback is the amount of time it takes for an investment to recover or pay back the initial cost of the investment (capital outlay).

Average rate of return measures the (average) net return each year (profit or savings) generated from the investment as a percentage of the initial capital cost of the investment.

Net present value calculates and then totals the present values of all the expected future cash flows of an investment (using discounting factors based on a pre-determined interest rate to arrive at the 'present values'), and subtracts these from the original cost of the investment.

Forecasting Cash Flows

The first stage in making investment decisions using quantitative techniques, involves forecasting the cash flows in and out of the business in order to determine the likely return / profit of the investment.

Investments typically involve a large initial outflow of cash, which give rise to a series of inflows of cash. Cash outflows are the costs associated with the investment (eg initial capital outlay and running costs). Cash inflows are the expected returns, which may include increased revenues and / or reduced costs as a result of savings made, for example, by the introduction of machinery in place of labour). Cash outflows are then deducted from the cash inflows to show the net cash flows over the estimated life of the investment. Refer to the example provided below.

Year	Cash Inflows (£)	Cash Outflows (£)	Net Cash Flow (£)	Cumulative Cash Flow
0	0	200,000	(200,000)	(200,000)
1	90,000	75,000	15,000	(175,000)
2	120,000	90,000	30,000	(145,000)
3	200,000	120,000	80,000	(65,000)
4	250,000	160,000	90,000	25,000
5	250,000	160,000	90,000	**115,000**

The time at which the investment is made is usually labelled Year 0.
Minus figures are shown in brackets.

Payback

Calculation including Example

Payback calculates the amount of time it takes for an investment to recover or pay back the initial capital outlay. It is calculated by dividing the initial capital cost of the investment by the annual net cash flow ie revenue less expenses or net savings made.

Let us work through a simple example where the original cost and total cash flows over a 5 year period are anticipated to be the same for three separate projects, but the anticipated net cash flows vary each year, as follows:

	Project A (£)	Project B (£)	Project C (£)
Initial Investment	100,000	100,000	100,000
*Cash Flow			
End of Year 1	30,000	10,000	60,000
End of Year 2	30,000	15,000	40,000
End of Year 3	30,000	25,000	25,000
End of Year 4	30,000	40,000	15,000
End of Year 5	30,000	60,000	10,000
Total Cash Flow	150,000	150,000	150,000

*Cash flow is the revenue minus operating costs or the net savings made by the project. It does not include the initial investment cost.

Payback for the three projects can be calculated as follows:

Project C:
After 1 year £60,000 has been paid back. After 2 years a total of £100,000 has been paid back (£60,000+£40,000). Therefore, payback is exactly **2 years**.

Project B:
After year 4 a total of £90,000 has been paid back (£10 + 15 + 25 + 40). Another £10,000 is, therefore, still required from year 5 to cover the original investment. To calculate the exact month in which payback occurs, the amount outstanding, ie £10,000 is divided into the total cash flow expected for year 5 (ie £10,000 / £60,000). This figure is then multiplied by 12, as there are 12 months in a year (or 365 if the number of days were required). Payback is, therefore, **4 years and 2 months** (rounded up). NB This calculation obviously assumes cash flows are constant throughout the year.

Project A:
After Year 3 a total of £90,000 has been paid back. Another £10,000 is, thus, required from Year 4 to cover the original investment. Payback for Project A is, therefore, **3 years and 4 months** (rounded up). (10 / 30 x 12 = 4 months in Year 4).

Interpretation

When using this method to choose between projects, **all other things remaining equal**, the project with the shortest payback will be chosen, the implication being that the project is less of a risk. In the example provided above **Project C** had the shortest payback and so carried the least risk. The risk is lower because it is safer to be exposed to any investment risk for the least possible time.

Average Rate of Return (ARR)

Calculation including Example

Average rate of return measures the (average) net return each year (profit or savings) as a percentage of the initial capital cost of the investment. The formula for calculating the average rate of return is as follows:

$$ARR\% = \frac{\text{Average net return (profit or savings) per annum}}{\text{Initial capital outlay (cost)}} \times 100$$

There are, however, several steps involved as follows:

1: Calculate **total net cash flow** over the life of the project.
2: Calculate the **net return** over the life of the project: Total net cash flow – capital outlay.
3: Calculate the **average annual net return:** Net return / number of years.
4: Calculate the **ARR%**: Average annual net return / initial capital outlay x 100.

Let us work through the following example:

- Capital outlay of a project is £45,000.
- Project has a 4-year life.
- Net cash flow (revenue – costs or net savings) end of year 1 is £10,000.
- Net cash flow end of year 2 is £15,000.
- Net cash flow end of year 3 is £20,000.
- Net cash flow end of year 4 is £20,000.

If we apply the above figures to the steps for calculating ARR outlined above, then:

1: **Total Net Cash Flow** over the life of the project = £65,000.
2: **Net Return** over the life of the project = £20,000.
3: **Average Annual Net Return** = £5,000.
4: **ARR%** = 11.11%.

Interpretation

The ARR% for the above project is just over 11%. This means that for every £1 invested, the project generates an average of just over 11 pence each year.

Net Present Value

Calculation including Example

Net present value is a 'discounted cash flow' method of investment appraisal. Such methods take into account the time value of money, ie the fact that future money is not worth as much as present money – a factor that neither payback nor ARR take into account. For instance, £100 now is worth more than £100 received in 2 years time. This is because money held now could be invested in a bank and earn interest during the course of the two years. For example, assuming interest is 10%, by the end of year 2, £100 invested in the bank would be worth £121. This can be calculated as follows:

Value of original £100 invested in bank by end of Year 1:
£100 + (10% of £100) = £100 + £10 = **£110.**

Value by end of year 2:
£110 + (10% of £110) = £110 + £11 = **£121**.

This process is called compounding and can be expressed in the form of an equation: $q(1 + r)^n$

q = the amount invested.
r = the rate of interest (as a decimal).
n = the number of years the capital is invested

Discounted cash flow methods calculate the present value of money receivable some time in the future, eg what £100 receivable in 2 years time is actually worth today. This requires the reverse of the compounding process above (explained in the calculation provided below).

Net present value calculates and then totals the present values of all the expected future cash flows of an investment. It does this by multiplying the expected future cash flows by discounting factors (based on a pre-determined interest rate) to arrive at the 'present values', and subtracting these from the original cost of the investment.

For example, let us assume that a firm is considering an investment (Project Z) with the following cash flows:

Year 0   (£50,000)
Year 1   £20,000
Year 2   £30,000
Year 3   £15,000.

By the end of the first year, the project is forecast to earn £20,000. To consider the alternative, the firm asks how much it must invest in the bank <u>now</u>, to get £20,000 out in a year. Assuming a 5% interest rate, this can be calculated as follows:

£q x 1.05 = £20,000
£q   = £20,000 / 1.05
£q   = **£19,048** (rounded up)

The second year sees the project earning £30,000. The firm, therefore, asks how much it must invest in the bank <u>now</u> to get £30,000 in two years time, assuming a 5% interest rate. This is calculated as follows:

£q x 1.05^2 = £30,000; thus £q x 1.1025 = £30,000; £q = £30,000 / 1.1025; £q = **£27,211**.

This means that the firm must invest £27,211 <u>now</u> if it wishes to receive £30,000 in two years time, at compound interest, with a constant rate of 5%.

The third year sees the project earning £15,000. To calculate how much the business must invest in the bank <u>now</u> to get £15,000 out in three year's time, the following formula is used:

£q x 1.05^3 = £15,000; thus £q x 1.157625 = £15,000; £q = £15,000 / 1.157625 = **£12,958**.

NB The factors – 1 / 1.05, 1 / 1.05^2 and so on, are provided for students in the actual examinations.

By adding all these 'discounted cash flows' for the three years, the total is **£59,217**. This figure must be compared with the original investment in Project Z, ie £50,000. Comparison shows that project Z has a return that is <u>more</u> than 5%, ie a return greater than the alternative of putting the money in the bank.

© APT Initiatives Limited, 2009

Using the figures provided in the discounted cash flow example above, net present value is simply arrived at by deducting the cost of the original investment from the total discounted cash flows (£59,217 - £50,000). In this example **Net Present Value** is, therefore, **£9,217**.

Interpretation

In general, if the NPV is positive – as in the example we have provided above - then the investment will be accepted. If negative, then the investment will be rejected.

Closing Comments

All quantitative methods involve estimating cash inflows and cash outflows, which can not only be time consuming, but imprecise, due to the conditions of market and cost uncertainty (which are considered further in the following section). It can be argued that the most accurate appraisal methods are the discounted cash flow techniques such as net present value, as these take into account the time value of money. However, accuracy is more dependent on the accuracy of the data used in the forecasts.

When trying to maximise the accuracy of forecasts, a business should carefully select and scrutinise the source and quality of data used in their generation. The more reliable the source and the better the quality of the data provided by the source, the greater the certainty over the accuracy of the figures.

Finally, in conclusion to this section, it should be pointed out that each method of investment appraisal discussed above should not be viewed as an alternative to another - in practice businesses usually use more than one method. They may also take into account qualitative factors and these are considered in a subsequent section below.

Investment Criteria

Objectives

By the end of this topic you should be able to:

1. Define the term investment criteria.
2. Evaluate investments against specific criteria in a given situation.

Key Terms

Investment criteria are pre-determined conditions laid down by key decision makers within the business that potential investments must meet - for example - a certain percentage return, within a certain timeframe.

Introduction

For each investment appraisal technique reviewed, firms will often set minimum criteria that the investment must achieve before they can be considered for further investigation and, ultimately, accepted. For the majority of firms the investment decisions will be based on financial criteria. Non-financial criteria may, however, also be important and these may stem from within or outside the business.

Financial Criteria

General

The majority of points raised in this sub-section essentially summarise what has already been outlined in the previous section on conducting investment appraisal using quantitative techniques.

Maximum Capital Outlay

A business may specify a maximum capital outlay beyond which all investments must be rejected.

Minimum Payback Period

A business may specify a minimum payback period in terms of years and / or months ie minimum point of time by which the investment must have paid for itself financially. Therefore, if an investment's payback period is anticipated to be within this cut off point it will be considered acceptable and, at the very least, worthy of further evaluation. If it falls beyond this point it will instantly be rejected.

If two possible investments are being considered and only one can be chosen due to financial constraints, then the project with the shortest payback will be selected.

Minimum ARR% or ARR% Higher than the Rate of Interest

A business may specify a minimum ARR% ie net return on investment that must be achieved. The investment will be considered acceptable or worthy of further consideration if the forecast ARR percentage meets or exceeds this percentage.

Alternatively, the business may specify that the investment must generate a return higher than the current / forecast rate of interest.

In the case of alternative investments, then the investment with the highest ARR% will be chosen.

Positive NPV

A business may specify that the project should only be accepted if the NPV is positive and rejected if the NPV is negative.

In the case of alternative investments then the one with the largest positive NPV should be selected.

Non-financial Criteria

Non-financial criteria may include reference to the fact that the investment must:

- Comply with legislation.
- Match industry standards and codes of practice.
- Improve its reputation and / or relations with its staff, customers, suppliers, the local community, or other stakeholder group.
- Strengthen and / or protect the business against anticipated future threats.

NB Non-financial criteria are covered in more detail under 'qualitative influences on investment decisions' below.

Closing Comments

It should be appreciated that all investment decisions should be based upon a comparison of the costs and benefits – which may or may not be financial. In terms of investment criteria, all investments where the cost is greater than the benefit should obviously be rejected. Only those investments where the cost (financial or other) is less than, or equal to, the benefit (financial or other) should be considered.

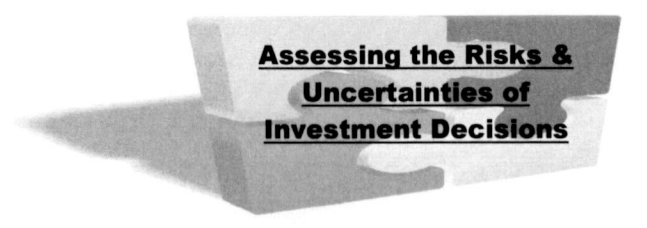

Assessing the Risks & Uncertainties of Investment Decisions

Objectives

By the end of this topic you should be able to:

1. Define the terms risk and uncertainty in the context of investment decisions.
2. Briefly explain why investment decisions involve risks and uncertainties.
3. Explain how sensitivity analysis, decision trees and higher discount rates can help assess the risks and uncertainties of investment decisions.

Key Terms

Risks associated with investment decisions concern the chance that the hoped for or expected outcome is not achieved. It exists where the exact outcome of a particular action or event (in this case investment decision) is unknown, but the possible outcomes and their individual likelihood of occurrence <u>are</u> known.

Uncertainty over investment decisions exists where the likelihood of occurrence of certain events are unknown.

Sensitivity analysis involves identifying critical assumptions upon which forecasted expected outcomes are based and then testing how much the expected outcome may alter if any of these assumptions vary.

Decision trees set out diagrammatically the alternatives relating to a possible problem / issue and all the possible outcomes that stem from these alternatives, together with the likelihood of the different outcomes occurring, and the associated financial consequences.

Risk and Uncertainty Associated with Investment Decisions

When making decisions about investment a business will have to accept a certain degree of risk, ie the chance that their expected or 'hoped for' outcome is not achieved. This is because whilst expenditure is incurred today, the benefit expected to be enjoyed from the investment occurs sometime in the future, yet the future is uncertain.

Forecasting cash flows can be very difficult to do accurately and all projects involve an element of uncertainty ie where the likelihood of occurrence of certain events are unknown. This is because there are numerous factors outside a business's control and, although a decision to invest today may be appropriate (given the current market conditions and economic climate), market and economic conditions may change and have a negative (or positive) effect on a project that requires considerable investment. For example, with regard to the market, consumers can be fickle and the introduction of a new competitor may prevent a business achieving its original sales revenue target, thus making its sales forecasts inaccurate, and ultimately preventing a business recouping the cost of its original investment. Likewise any change in interest rates could also affect both a business's forecast for sales (cash inflows) as well as its costs (cash outflows), if it has funded the investment on borrowed capital. The more unstable the business environment, the greater the uncertainty over the cash flow figures.

Assessing Risk and Uncertainty

Appraising the risks involved with a particular investment decision is not an easy task. It involves management finding answers to the following questions:

1. What is the expected return to be generated by the investment?
2. What sort of spread of possible outcomes might result?
3. Are any of the possible outcomes likely to threaten our very survival?
4. Can the risk associated with a particular investment be reduced?
5. What is the relationship between the reward and level of risk involved?

Businesses can take a number of actions to help manage risk and uncertainty in their investment appraisal. These are considered in turn below.

Managing Risk and Uncertainty

Sensitivity Analysis

Sensitivity analysis involves identifying critical assumptions upon which forecasted expected outcomes are based and then testing how much the expected outcome may alter if any of these assumptions vary.

When a business predicts costs and revenues, there will be certain variables for which assumptions must be made, eg suppliers hold their prices constant, or perhaps increase them by 2% per annum. There are assumptions about consumer patterns of demand, about competition and about prices. To allow for the possibility that the prediction of cash flow may be incorrect (and this is very likely, given the nature of prediction), variables are changed to produce a range of possible outcomes. This, in effect, is showing 'sensitivity' to the nature of the forecasts.

To fully assess the risk involved, firms will then look at the worst answer and assess the likelihood that the variable will change by such an amount.

Decision Trees

Decision trees set out diagrammatically the alternatives relating to a possible problem / issue and all the possible outcomes that stem from these alternatives, together with the likelihood of the different outcomes occurring, and the associated financial consequences. They are based on probability theory, ie the likelihood of an event happening. This is usually expressed as a decimal on a scale of zero to one; 0 meaning definitely will not, 1 meaning definitely will.

Decision trees are used when there are a number of possible actions, with a number of possible outcomes, and qualitative factors are not considered significant. For example, they may be used to make decisions between:

- options for improving existing products or services.
- options for improving existing technological processes.
- potential products and services.
- different markets.
- different locations.

To show how decision trees are constructed the following scenario will be used. A business has £600,000 (£0.6m) available to invest in new product development and cannot decide between two potential products. The initial stages involved in constructing the diagram, would be as follows:

Working from left to right:

1. Draw a square – this represents the decision.
2. Set out the alternative course of action / different options to choose from, ie Product X and Product Y. These are represented by a straight line stemming from the decision box, with the option written above the line.
3. Show the initial costs of decision – usually written below the line representing the option.

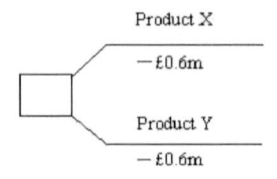

```
            Product X
       ┌────────────────
       │   − £0.6m
   ┌───┤
   │   │
   └───┤   Product Y
       └────────────────
           − £0.6m
```

4. Draw circles to represent possible outcomes – at the end of each option.
5. Identify the possible outcomes of each decision. In the above example, the firm believes that success or failure are the only possible outcomes. These are represented by straight lines stemming from the circle, with the outcome written above the line.
6. Determine the probability of each outcome eg from past data / market research. These are usually written to the side of, or underneath, the possible outcome.

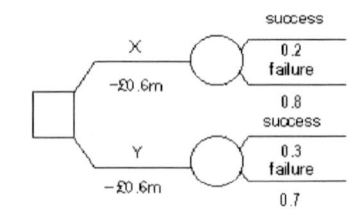

```
                        X              success
                  ┌───────────○        0.2
              ┌───┤  −£0.6m   │        failure
              │   │           │        0.8
              │   │                    success
              │   │      Y            0.3
              └───┤───────────○        failure
                     −£0.6m            0.7
```

7. Estimate the financial outcome, eg via market research and past data relating to the success / failure of previous products, and discussions with production engineers and cost accountants. (Written at the end of the line representing the possible outcome).

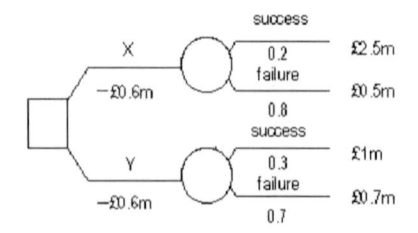

```
                        X              success
                  ┌───────────○        0.2      £2.5m
              ┌───┤  −£0.6m   │        failure
              │   │           │        0.8      £0.5m
              │   │                    success
              │   │      Y            0.3       £1m
              └───┤───────────○        failure
                     −£0.6m            0.7      £0.7m
```

Calculating the optimum decision involves the following: *Working from right to left:*

8. Calculate the expected values of each option (ie the weighted average of the possible options) at each probability point. For example: the expected value if Product X is a success is £0.5m (£2.5m x 0.2), and if it is a failure is £0.4m (£0.5 x 0.8).

© APT Initiatives Limited, 2009

9. Total the expected values at each probability point, and write the total expected value (EV) in the circle. For Product X this is £0.9m.

10. Deduct the expected value from the initial cost of the investment. For Product X this would be £0.3 (£0.9 - £0.6m). This figure is usually written to the left of the beginning of the line representing each option.

11. Put a line through all options other than the most profitable. If the Expected value for Product Y is calculated as with Product X above, then this would be £0.19m (£0.79m - £0.6m). Consequently, Product X is the most profitable option.

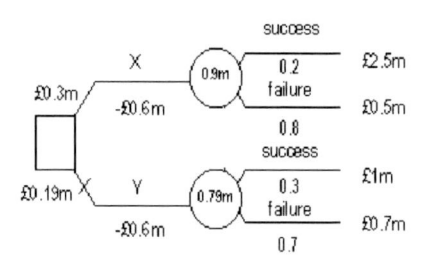

```
                              success
              X          ┌─── 0.2      £2.5m
         ┌─( 0.9m )──────┤    failure
  £0.3m  │    -£0.6m     └─── 0.8      £0.5m

                              success
              Y          ┌─── 0.3      £1m
  £0.19m ┤─( 0.79m )─────┤    failure
              -£0.6m     └─── 0.7      £0.7m
```

Though the expected value of choosing Product X is higher than Y, it is important to consider the risks involved. With Product X there is the risk that only £0.5m will be made which would result in a loss of £0.1m. With Product Y, success is more likely and, more significantly, failure will not actually result in a loss. A risk adverse organisation may, therefore, choose Y, because although there is a lower expected value, there is no possibility of losing money, based on the firm's estimates.

Setting Higher Targets Relating to Payback and ARR or Higher Discount Rates

To allow for greater risk, the firm may set more demanding targets such as a shorter payback period, higher ARR% and / or higher discount rates, thereby implying the opportunity cost is greater, given the higher risk.

Closing Comments

Business involves decision making against a background of uncertainty and, often, the potentially most profitable course of action is the one that carries the greatest risk.

Evaluating Quantitative & Qualitative Influences on Investment Decisions

Objectives

By the end of this topic you should be able to:

1. Define and explain the difference between quantitative and qualitative influences on investment decisions.
2. Outline the pros and cons associated with using quantitative techniques of investment appraisal ie payback, accounting rate of return and net present value.
3. Describe at least 3 qualitative influences on investment decisions.
4. Take into account quantitative and qualitative factors when evaluating investments.

Key Terms

Quantitative influences are factors that can easily be measured eg the size, weight and amount of something. In the context of a potential investment this might, for example, concern the forecast net financial return and the length of time it takes to pay back the initial cost of the investment.

Qualitative influences are factors that cannot easily be measured eg thoughts, feelings and outcomes in terms of human relations, accomplishments and skills. In the context of a potential investment this might, for example, concern the potential impact on staff morale.

Introduction

When making decisions about a particular investment, a business will consider the benefits of an investment decision in relation to the anticipated costs and, in doing this will take account of both quantitative and qualitative factors. Quantitative factors are factors that can be easily measured, eg the size, weight and amount of something. Qualitative factors are factors that cannot be easily measured, eg thoughts and feelings and outcomes in terms of human relationships, accomplishments and skills. For example, a decision whether or not to invest in new machinery, may involve consideration of the following quantitative and qualitative factors:

Quantitative Factors	
Costs	**Benefits**
• Initial capital and installation costs. • Training costs. • Cost of any redundancies. • Running and maintenance costs. • Cost of any financing – interest	• Reduction in running (including staffing) and maintenance costs. • Reduction in costs associated with reworking /disposals due to improved quality. • Increased profits as a result of the above.

Qualitative Factors	
Costs	**Benefits**
• Poor staff relations and • Fall in reputation as an employer as a result of redundancies.	• Improved morale and • fewer accidents (which could be quantified) due to better safety of use.

© APT Initiatives Limited, 2009

Evaluation of Quantitative Methods of Investment Appraisal

Evaluation of Quantitative Methods in General

Quantitative methods of investment appraisal and techniques for dealing with risk and uncertainty such as sensitivity analysis and decisions trees can be a highly valuable aid to decision making. They force managers to investigate cash flows and consider possible options, outcomes and consequences. They do, however, have their limitations which mainly concern the fact that cash flows can be difficult to estimate and so such techniques are only as accurate as the estimates upon which they are based.

Therefore, as stated at the end of a previous section, the more reliable the source and the better the quality of the data provided by the source, the greater the certainty over the accuracy of the forecast figures.

Wherever possible, information should be obtained from an independent body in order to eliminate bias, as this may result in inaccurate forecasts. For example, a business considering investment in new machinery in order to increase productivity and profits, should gather data on the performance of the machinery, not just from the machine supplier but also:

- independent experts; and / or
- other users of the machinery.

This is particularly advisable if the supplier is relatively new / unknown within the industry.

Furthermore, any data used to forecast cash flows should not only come from a reliable source, but be detailed and thorough, based (wherever possible) on in-depth testing and market research, using a sample size large enough to produce statistically reliable results.

The pros and cons of individual quantitative investment appraisal techniques are outlined below before turning to qualitative influences on investment decisions.

Evaluation of Payback

The advantages / uses and disadvantages / limitations of using payback as a method of appraisal in comparison to other investment appraisal methods are summarised in the table below.

Pros	Cons
• Simple to understand. • Easy to calculate. • Useful initial screening method. • Emphasis on early return - forecasts more likely to be accurate. • Useful measurement of risk – the sooner the payback, the less the risk. • Useful if liquidity is more important than profitability. • Useful where product has short life span, eg fashion industry, new technology – important to cover cost before the need to invest again arises.	• Ignores timing of payments. • Ignores cash earned after pay back and, thus, the overall profitability of the project – criteria used is speed of repayment. • Discriminates against projects which involve long pay back period (short-term view). • Ignores inflation and opportunity cost – future money is not worth as much as present money (unlike NPV). • No attempt to consider the simple alternative of putting the cash in a bank.

Evaluation of ARR

The advantages / uses and disadvantages / limitations of using the accounting rate of return are summarised in the table below.

Pros	Cons
• Simple to understand. • Relatively easy to calculate. • Uses yield in all years. • Useful where a quick estimate of overall profitability is required. • Allows comparison to be made with the simple alternative of putting the cash in a bank.	• Timing of return ignored. • Calculates average profits – profits may fluctuate significantly during the life of the project. • Ignores inflation and the opportunity cost – future money is not worth as much as present money (unlike NPV).

Evaluation of Net Present Value

The advantages / uses and disadvantages / limitations of using net present value are summarised in the table below.

Pros	Cons
• Takes into account amount and timing of all cash flows. • Takes into account time value of money / opportunity cost of putting money in bank. • Discounted factor can be adjusted for risk.	• More complex and time consuming to calculate – requires not just estimating cash flows, but also discount rates. • Assumes opportunity cost stays the same throughout the project.

Qualitative Influences / Factors

Business Objectives

If profit maximisation is the business's objective, then it is most likely to choose an investment with the largest return.

If survival is the objective and the business is worried about liquidity, then it is likely to choose an investment which offers the quickest payback.

If improving market image / standing is the business's objective then it might invest in a project which helps to raise its quality image, eg new machinery to improve product quality, even if it increases costs / offers no return (in the short-term).

Corporate Image

Many businesses now take into account ethical considerations and may undertake investment where the costs outweigh the benefits. For example, a business may invest in new machinery to cut down on harmful emissions, in order to promote a 'green' image.

A business may also refuse to invest in a project that could increase revenues and / or reduce costs / and increase profits, if it means making lots of redundancies, in order to protect its 'caring' image as an employer.

Employee-Employer Relations

Investment can have a significant impact on an organisation's human resources. For example:

- Purchase of an existing business may involve redundancies, restructuring and / or retraining.
- Investment in new technologies may involve redundancies and / or retraining.
- Launch of a new product may involve retraining.

As a result of such changes a business may encounter hostility from the workforce which could affect the speed with which the cost of the investment is recouped. When considering the potential resistance to changes, a business may decide not to go ahead due to the potential damage it may do to human relations.

Attitude Towards Risk

Key decision makers within an organisation will have different attitudes towards risk. Some may be averse to risk, and thus, refuse to consider investments where, though the potential rewards are high, the risk is also high.

Closing Comments

It is highly likely that a question on investment appraisal in the examination will provide scope for you to evaluate the investment using both quantitative and qualitative information. The quantitative information is likely to be made obvious in the case study. The qualitative factors affecting the investment decision may not be so obvious and may require more thought on your part. Remember, answers that secure the top marks – for analysis and evaluation are those that provide two sides to an argument and a logical and balanced conclusion. Thus, in the context of investment appraisal, the best answer will be the one that takes both quantitative and qualitative factors into account.

3

MARKETING STRATEGIES

3.1

UNDERSTANDING MARKETING OBJECTIVES

Marketing Objectives

Objectives

By the end of this topic you should be able to:

1. Define the term marketing objectives.
2. State at least 3 examples of marketing objectives.

Key Terms

Marketing objectives are goals or targets that must be achieved by the marketing function (department) within a business to ensure the business's corporate objectives are achieved.

Overview

One of the very first sections in these Elementary Explanations explained how functional objectives help to achieve a business's overall corporate objectives. Marketing objectives are the goals or targets that must be achieved by the marketing function (department) within a business to achieve the business's corporate objectives. They provide a focus for decision making and for setting and agreeing marketing strategies and plans. They can also aid the motivation and control of staff involved in the marketing function. The former because they provide a common goal for individuals within the marketing department to focus on achieving. The latter because they provide a means of measuring performance.

Common marketing objectives concern:

- Product or brand awareness / recognition.
- Sales, Customer base.
- Repeat business or brand / customer loyalty.
- Market standing / position (image).
- Market share or leadership.

Common Marketing Objectives

Product or Brand Awareness / Recognition

Raising or increasing awareness of a product or brand may be a key objective of a business that:

- is just starting out.
- is launching a new product or brand.
- wants to sell more of an existing product or brand to the same market (market penetration).
- wants to break into a new market with an existing product or brand (market development).

In general, raising or increasing awareness will involve investment in some form of promotion. NB Market penetration and market development is discussed later in this section on marketing.

Customer Base, Sales

Establishing or increasing a business's customer base and, especially, achieving a certain level of sales (in terms of value or volume) are, perhaps, the most common marketing objectives. It is likely to not just involve a promotional campaign to raise awareness of a business's product or service, but some sort of incentive to encourage customers to purchase the product or service for the first time.

Repeat Business or Brand / Customer Loyalty

Generating a certain level of repeat business and / or brand / customer loyalty are important objectives for businesses that provide products or services that need to be replaced or renewed in the immediate, short or medium term. This includes a wide range of businesses of which supermarkets, insurance brokers and car manufacturers, are just a few examples.

Generating repeat business / customer loyalty might involve:

- investment in enhancing or maximising product / service quality
- the use of special offers and promotions including bonuses for repeat purchases.
- regular communication with customers to remind them of the business's presence and inform them about new products or special offers.

Market Standing / Position (Image)

Targets relating to market standing or position are concerned with creating an image (distinct from competitors) in the mind of the business's target market, or trying to change customers' perceptions of the business and / or its products / services.

Objectives relating to market standing, position or image are likely to become important when a business:

- faces significant competition and it is vital to make its products / services stand out and be perceived to be better than rivals' products / services.
- wants to target a new market segment.
- wants to encourage more customers within a chosen target market to purchase its product / service for the first time.

Achieving targets relating to market standing / position involves researching the perceptions of customers and investment in promotion to change (or reinforce) perceptions.

Market Share

Market share is the sales, in terms of value or volume, achieved by one particular business (or one particular product or service provided by a business), in relation to the market as a whole. It is calculated using the following formula:

$$\frac{\text{ABC's product or service sales value or volume}}{\text{Total sales value or volume of whole market}} \times 100$$

It can be calculated yearly, quarterly, monthly or weekly and is a common objective for firms operating in highly competitive markets. Ways in which it might be increased include:

- improving quality / benefits and making customers aware of this through promotion.
- reducing selling price to lower than that of competitors.
- offering special offers.
- more effective promotion in general.

Marketing Objectives and the Link with Overall Business Objectives

It is important to re-emphasise that marketing objectives should be based on and support the overall business / corporate objective. For example:

If a business is new or introducing a new product, then the corporate and marketing objectives might be as follows:

Corporate Objective	Marketing Objective(s)
Survival, Breakeven.	• Gain recognition. • Establish a customer base.

If a business is established, then the corporate and marketing objectives might be as follows:

Corporate Objective	Marketing Objective(s)
Sales growth. Expansion	• Establish and extend brand loyalty. • Increase market share. • Develop new products for a different customer base.

SMART Marketing Objectives

It is also important to emphasise that, like all objectives, marketing objectives should not be vague but S.M.A.R.T, ie **S**pecific, **M**easurable, **A**greed by the key individuals concerned, **R**ealistic / achievable (given the strengths and weaknesses of the business, and opportunities and threats facing the business), and **T**imescaled. For example:

- *To increase awareness of product X amongst the target market by 25% within the year.*
- *To increase sales of product Y by 10% within the next 6 months.*
- *To increase repeat purchases from 40% to 55% by the end of the year.*
- *To increase share of the market for product Z, by 10%, within the next year.*

Closing Comments

It should be remembered that marketing is not just relevant to commercial profit making organisations, but public sector and non-profit making organisations. Some examples of non-profit making marketing objectives and ways in which they might be achieved are provided below.

Objective	Strategies / Tactics for their Achievement
• To reduce demand for a particular product / activity considered to be harmful to health by X% by X date.	• All year round TV adverts highlighting the dangers of smoking and where to obtain free information and advice.
• To reduce the occurrence of accidents relating to a particular activity by X% by X date.	• Late October / Early November TV adverts highlighting the dangers of fireworks. • Christmas adverts highlighting the dangers of drinking and driving. • Quarterly TV adverts highlighting the importance of wearing seatbelts in cars.

Assessing Internal and External Influences on Marketing Objectives

Objectives

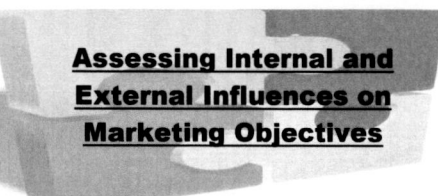

By the end of this topic you should be able to:

1. Outline at least 3 internal influences on marketing objectives.
2. Outline at least 4 external influences on marketing objectives.

Key Terms

Internal influences on marketing objectives are factors stemming from inside the business that can affect decisions over, or success in achieving, marketing objectives – for example – the business's corporate objectives; availability of finance; size, quality and motivation of the workforce; productive capacity and methods.

External influences on marketing objectives are factors stemming from outside the business that can affect decisions over, or success in achieving, marketing objectives – for example – changes in political, legal, economic, social, market and technological factors, competitor activities, the cost of inputs and the quality and reliability of suppliers.

Overview

When making key business decisions, whether these relate to marketing or other functional areas, a business must take into account both the internal and external factors affecting its operations. Such factors may help or hinder the business in achieving its objectives.

Internal influences on marketing objectives are factors coming from inside the business that can affect decisions over, or success in achieving, marketing objectives. External influences on marketing objectives are factors stemming from outside the business that can affect decisions over, or success in achieving, marketing objectives. They may provide new opportunities, or may threaten a business's ability to achieve objectives in the short, medium, or long term.

At every stage of the marketing process, the business should take into account these factors. This is essential to ensure that the marketing objectives and strategy decided upon are achievable / realistic, and that any judgements or modifications made at the review stage, are fair and appropriate.

Internal Influences on Marketing Objectives

Corporate Objectives

Previous sections highlighted how objectives are set for the whole business and that these provide the boundaries for setting functional objectives. Thus, corporate objectives will not just influence financial objectives but also a business's marketing objectives. These must be consistent with and support the achievement of overall corporate objectives.

Amount of Finance Available

The amount of finance a business has available will influence the amount that can be spent on marketing activities and this will influence the business's marketing objectives and plans for their achievement. A healthy financial situation in terms of the level of profit being generated and / or gearing ratio can, for example, enable a business to invest more in marketing and so set more ambitious marketing objectives.

Size and Quality of Human Resources

The size, ability and motivation of the workforce will influence a business's marketing objectives. For example:

- Objectives that concern increasing sales volumes can only be achieved if any additional staff required are available to produce and / or sell greater volumes to customers.
- The more multi-skilled the workforce, the more able it is to develop new products to meet new or changing customer needs and, thus, objectives relating to customer base, sales and market share.

Operational Issues – Production Capacity and Methods

The productive capacity of a business will, obviously, constrain how much can be produced or (in terms of service industries) how many customers can be served at any given time, and this will, obviously, limit a firm's marketing objectives relating to growth in sales volumes – at least in the short-term.

The production methods used eg job, batch or flow may also influence a business's marketing objectives. For example job production provides considerable flexibility in meeting unique customer needs and adapting to changing customer needs. In contrast flow production provides less scope for meeting unique customer needs and so might restrict objectives relating to, for example, extending the customer base.

If products are unable to be consistently produced in line with customer requirements, in the right quantities, at the right time, then this will undoubtedly affect the achievement of marketing objectives.

External Influences on Marketing Objectives

Political and Legal Factors

This concerns the government and the extent to which it intervenes in markets, regulating business activity. Different political parties have different viewpoints on what is and is not good for business. Policies on privatisation and the EU have provided numerous opportunities for business but have also led to increased competition, making it more difficult for a business to achieve its objectives, eg in terms of sales and market share.

The government is also responsible for setting legislation which often acts as a constraint, influencing decisions relating to marketing and employment, in particular. Being a member state of the European Union has brought increased legislation with certain sectors being particularly affected.

The government also influences business activity through its policies on taxation which can have a direct affect on the disposable income of consumers and, thus, demand for a business's product or service and the achievement of its marketing objectives.

Economic Factors

Economic factors concern the level of interest rates, exchange rates, inflation and employment. Changes in these may affect a business's cost structure and / or the amount of disposable income a consumer might have to spend on goods and services. In a recession, for example, where unemployment is high, firms providing luxury goods tend to be particularly affected. They may have to revise their objectives relating to growth in sales and may be forced to downsize or de-layer, in order to cut costs and avoid closure.

Social, Ethical and Market Factors

This concerns changes in demography and changes in the values, attitudes, needs and expectations of customers, employees, and society as a whole.

Changes in the size and structure of the population may lead to changes in demand for a business's product or service. For example, an ageing population is leading to increased demand for certain types of holidays, medicines and household equipment, thus enabling businesses operating within these markets to set objectives relating to growth in customer numbers and sales. People are also far more health conscious leading to new products and markets, and more ambitious growth objectives for businesses operating within these markets. People are also becoming increasingly concerned about the environment and this could impact on the demand for, and thus, marketing objectives of, businesses providing services in the travel industry.

Technological Change

This concerns the methods and machinery used to produce products as well as the actual product itself.

Advances in technology have led to completely new markets eg digital cameras and television, and once popular products becoming obsolete. Technological advances also enable businesses to invest in new cost saving machinery and equipment which may help to achieve objectives relating to sales growth and market share.

Competitor Activities

Businesses are affected by the success or failure of competitors as this may result in increased or decreased demand for their products or services. New competition or more aggressive marketing tactics from competitors may, for example, make it difficult for a business to achieve its objectives relating to sales growth and / or market share.

Cost of Materials, Quality and Reliability of Suppliers

Increases in the cost of materials (or other inputs), as well as the quality and reliability of its suppliers will affect the ability of the business to meet and / or exceed customer expectations and objectives relating to sales growth and / or customer loyalty, for example.

Closing Comments

Although marketing objectives will be influenced by a business's corporate objectives it should be appreciated that the marketing department is likely to have considerable influence on decisions concerning overall business objectives. This is because a business's corporate objectives should be based upon a detailed knowledge and understanding of the marketplace (as well as a business's internal capabilities), and one of the key functions of marketing is to research and keep up to date with changes in the marketplace and factors in the external business environment affecting the demand for its products or services.

3.2

ANALYSING MARKETS & MARKETING

Reasons For, and the Value of, Market Analysis

Objectives

By the end of this topic you should be able to:

1. Define the term market analysis.
2. State at least 3 reasons for undertaking market analysis.
3. Explain the value of market analysis.

Key Terms

Market analysis is a process that attempts to identify and measure market characteristics through a range of market research techniques in order to inform decision making and planning. It may, for example, include identifying and measuring market size, segments, growth, share, level and intensity of competition, and distribution channels.

Overview

Market analysis is a process that attempts to identify and measure market characteristics. Remember (from Unit 1):

- A **market** is a place where buyers (or demanders) and sellers (or suppliers) get together to exchange products and services (for money). It consists of customers and consumers, competitors and distributors.

Remember also that:

- Consumers are individuals or businesses that actually **use** a business's product or service but **do not necessarily pay** for this use.
- Customers are the individuals of businesses that **purchase** a business's product or service for themselves or on behalf of other individuals or businesses ie consumers.

Market analysis may, for example, attempt to identify and / or measure the following:

- current market size in terms of customer numbers, sales value and volume.
- market segments, consumer requirements and profiles.
- market trends.
- projected market growth.
- level and intensity of competition including market shares of competing businesses.
- distribution channels.
- skills and capital requirements.
- cost structure.
- potential profitability.
- social, legal, political, economic and technological factors affecting the market.

Such data is obtained through a range of market research techniques. Remember also (from Unit 1):

- **Market** research consists of desk (secondary) research and field (primary) research methods.
- **Field** research is used to gather primary data ie data which does not already exist 'first hand' data). The most common methods used to gather primary data include face-to-face, telephone or postal surveys, and direct observation.
- **Desk** research is used to gather secondary data ie data which already exists ('second hand' data). Much secondary data can be obtained free from libraries or from the Internet, in the form of government reports, national and local newspapers, trade publications, international / national reference books / directories and Annual Company Reports. Secondary data will also include past records generated from within the business itself - for example - on market share, profit and contribution.
- The exact method used by a business to gather the data it requires will depend upon the research objectives, as well as the amount of time and finance available. With regard to these factors, primary data is usually more up-to-date and tends to be much more specific to a business's needs. It is, however, generally more time consuming and costly to obtain.

Reasons for Market Analysis

As stated in our Elementary Explanations for Unit 1 there are four main reasons to carry out market research and analysis:

- **Descriptive** – to identify what's happening now, eg is the market increasing or decreasing? Who are our customers? Are our sales increasing or decreasing?
- **Predictive** – to identify what is likely to happen in the future eg to help forecast sales levels.
- **Explanatory** – to establish why something is happening, eg why has there been a drop in sales?
- **Exploratory** – to investigate new possibilities / strategies, eg through product trials and test marketing.

Overall, analysis of a market can help to identify, test and measure business opportunities and the business's potential within a market. It generates vital information to aid decision making and planning. Knowledge of the market and, in particular, how customers are reacting or might react to new products / services, or changes to other elements of the marketing mix (eg price changes, new promotional campaigns or distribution channels, etc) can help a business to ensure it has the right resources (eg stock, workforce, equipment, etc) to meet customer requirements and expectations.

The Value of Market Analysis

Carrying out market research and analysis can be time consuming and costly, and many entrepreneurs would argue that 'gut feeling' or 'hunches' alone are all that is required to build a successful business. Basing marketing decisions on hunches can save costs in the short-run, for example the costs involved in researching the market and test marketing prototypes. The time it takes to implement new strategies is also minimised, which may help a business to gain a competitive edge.

Launching new strategies on hunches alone, however, without any researching or testing, runs a greater risk of failure. Market research and analysis is more likely to detect potential problems / weaknesses with particular decisions / strategies, thus saving costs not only in terms of the initial investment, but also the effect that failed strategies may have on the long-term reputation of the business. Market research and analysis is also becoming more and more important to the achievement of business objectives, because of:

- the rapid pace of change (mainly relating to technological change resulting in shorter product life cycles).
- increased competition (as a result of government policies such as privatisation, deregulation).
- more sophisticated and demanding customers (as a result of improvements in education).

Closing Comments

Whether a business undertakes market research and analysis before making a particular decision, or bases a decision on gut feeling, will largely depend on the following:

- the **resources** (eg finance, human resources) available to the business.
- the **risk** involved.
- the **attitude** of the key decision makers **towards risk**.

If, for example, the business has limited financial resources, then a decision may be taken on a hunch. If, on the other hand, a particular strategy requires significant capital investment, and thus, the cost of failure is particularly high, it may be wise to invest in extensive market analysis. Whether it does this or not will finally depend upon the degree of risk the key decision makers are willing to take.

Methods of Analysing Trends

Objectives

By the end of this topic you should be able to:

1. Define the terms sales forecasting, sales forecast, trend, moving averages, extrapolation, correlation and test markets.
2. Select, apply and interpret appropriate methods for measuring and forecasting sales in a given scenario.
3. Explain how correlation can be used in analysing markets.

Key Terms

Sales forecasting concerns attempts to predict the future behaviour of sales.

A **sales forecast** is a prediction of the sales (in terms of volume or value) that will be achieved in a given period of time.

A **trend** is the general pattern or underlying movement of the data being examined.

Moving averages (or rolling averages) are a collection of averages calculated for a group of data shown over a certain number of (usually) equal time periods.

Extrapolation involves the use of past data to establish trends (ie the general direction in which the data is moving), which are then projected forward into the future.

Correlation refers to the relationship between two variables eg the weather and sales of ice creams.

Test marketing involves the launch of a product on a limited scale in a representative part of the market to assess consumer reaction and forecast future sales.

Test markets are segments within a market (eg a geographical area or demographic group) considered to be representative of the market as a whole. They are chosen to trial a new product or service in order to assess the likelihood of its success within the whole market, and identify potential problems / weaknesses and allow them to be rectified prior to a full launch.

Introduction to Methods of Measuring and Forecasting Sales

Role and Value

Sales forecasting concerns attempts to predict the future behaviour of sales. Measuring and forecasting sales can help a business to plan the use of resources and ensure the smooth running of the business. This is because if a business is able to predict its level of sales volume accurately, then many other important variables might be forecasted. For example, if a business estimates it might sell 10,000 units in one month, then it can plan for material purchases, labour requirements, production scheduling, distribution and cash flow, to name but a few.

It might also help to plan for price changes, especially if the forecasted volume does not allow a business to achieve its objectives.

A longer term forecast might help a firm to establish whether it can achieve possible sales targets given its current capacity, and help with decisions over capital investment.

Sales forecasting, therefore, plays a significant role in marketing, production, financial and human resources planning.

Overview of Methods

Sales forecasting techniques can be categorised as quantitative or qualitative:

- **Quantitative** techniques are based on an analysis of numerical data.
- **Qualitative** techniques are based on opinions and experience and are generally used when numerical data is scarce or the market changes quickly (which makes quantitative techniques less reliable).

Businesses often use both techniques to develop sales forecasts. The techniques specifically required by the AQA Unit 3 specification are, however, quantitative and these establishing and extrapolating trends through moving averages, and the use of correlation and test markets

Establishing and Extrapolating Trends through the Use of Moving Averages (Time Series Analysis)

The Value of Establishing the Trend

Although a business might not be able to predict the precise values in the future (by definition of the word 'forecast'), it might simply refer to the trend in order to view the general pattern and underlying movement of the data. If a particular market is seen to be growing or falling (in terms of the general movement), then this might well influence the business's strategy. For example, it might need to consider increasing or reducing capacity, moving into a different market, or placing greater emphasis on marketing to encourage greater sales.

Establishing the Trend

Establishing the trend involves calculating 'moving averages'. The essence of this technique is to smooth out fluctuations in a series of data so that the underlying trend can be identified. For example:

- a business selling garden furniture is likely to experience more sales in the Spring and Summer than in the Autumn and Winter.
- a business selling a product that is sensitive to the trade cycle, such as a new car dealer, will sell many more cars during a period of economic growth than during a recession.

By manipulating the data and taking averages, it is possible to forecast sales more easily.

Calculating the trend / moving average involves the following steps:

1. Selecting a number of time periods for calculating the average. NB This should be done on a rational basis, eg if the data consists of the quarters of a year then four quarters should be used to calculate the average. Alternatively, if the data consists of years and there is an obvious peak every third year, then three years should be used.

2. Totalling the first available set of values up to the number of the time periods selected and calculating the average, eg Quarter 1 + 2 + 3 + 4 divided by 4.
3. Repeating the process for the set of data, eg Yr 1 Qtr 2 + 3 + 4 + Yr 2 Qtr 1, and so on.

A numerical example will help you to understand the process. In the figures provided in the table below sales appear to rise and fall every five years. Consequently averages have been calculated using five sets of data.

Time (year)	Point in Cycle of data	Data Sales (units)	5 point moving average (Trend)*	Variation (Data – trend)
1	1	350		
2	2	370		
3	3	395	370	25
4	4	375	377	-2
5	5	360	383	-23
6	1	385	386	-1
7	2	400	390	10
8	3	410	396	14
9	4	395	400	-5
10	5	390	402	-12
11	1	405		
12	2	410		
13	3	?		

* The trend is inserted in the middle of the points of data for which the average is calculated, eg the first average is for yr 1 to yr 5, and is inserted opposite year 3 (because it is an average for all five points).

By turning the data into averages and plotting the averages, it is possible to identify the general movement of the data (ie the trend). Refer to the diagram below:

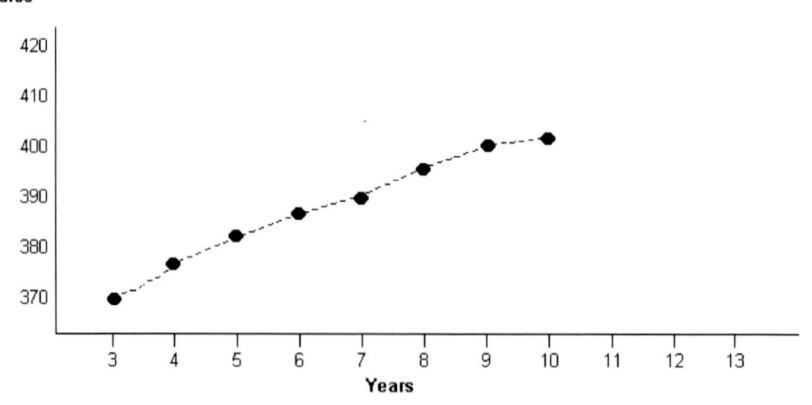

The trend is clearly upward, although there appears to be a flattening off of the data.

A Note of Caution: By definition of this being a moving average (ie a trend) a business should not regard this flattening off as a one-off, because the trend seen is the result of a calculation of many points of data (5 time periods in fact). The business must, therefore, look very carefully at the reasons why this might have happened.

© APT Initiatives Limited, 2009

Extrapolating Trends to Forecast Sales

Extrapolation involves the use of past data to establish trends (ie the general direction in which the data is moving), which are then projected forward into the future. By calculating the moving averages and using this to plot the trend it becomes possible to forecast the trend because it is easy to forecast the path of a relatively straight-line (ie relative to the fluctuating pattern of the actual data). This is done by continuing the line into the future. Refer to the diagram below. The forecasted trend for year 13 is **407**.

It is possible to draw optimistic and pessimistic predictions.

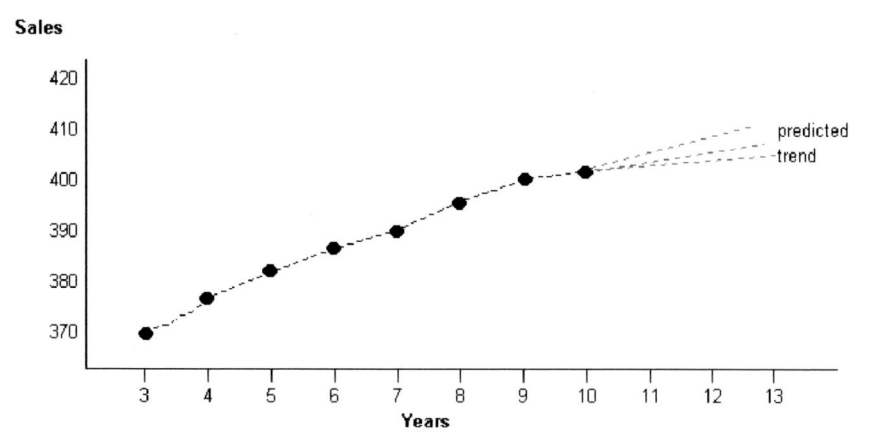

There are limitations with this technique, namely that it assumes that the trend will continue. Thus, the accuracy of the technique depends upon trading conditions remaining stable. Consequently, it is only really useful to predict sales in the short-term as so many variables can have an impact on sales in the longer term. (These are considered later in the section on 'Difficulties in Analysing Marketing Data' below). A firm must remember that the further into the future it tries to predict, the less accurate the prediction will become.

Forecasting Taking into Account Average Cyclical Variation

The calculation of the trend then allows **variations** to be calculated between the actual and trend figures for different points in the cycle. Taking into account these variations can help to increase the accuracy of forecasts. For example, during periods 3 and 8, the variation was positive, meaning that sales were well above the average. In this example, it would be sensible to expect the sales for year 13 to be similarly above average (because there seems to be a five year cycle).

Once the trend has been forecasted, the variation at the particular point in the cycle (known as the cyclical variation) must be used to establish how much the forecasted sales are likely to differ from the forecasted trend. This is done by using all the cyclical variations for the period the business is trying to predict. Year 13 (in the example above) is point 3 in the cycle. Year 3 and 8 are also the same point and, therefore, taking an average of these two, **(the average cyclical variation)**, will produce a figure that can then be added to the trend to find the final prediction. Refer to the figures below.

Average cyclical variation = 25 + 14 = 39 / 2 = 19.5.
Forecasted Sales = 407 (trend forecast) + 19.5 = **426.5.**

Centring

The example above has five points per cycle, but when there is an even set of data, eg quarters in a year, a further calculation is made, to allow points to be plotted against a specific time period and to calculate the cyclical (or seasonal - as in the example provided below) variation.

Time	Qtr	Data	4 point total	8 point total	8 point moving av. (Trend)	seasonal variation	Qtr
Yr 1	1	280					
	2	322					
	3	378			322	56	3
	4	292	1272		330	-38	4
Yr 2	1	312	1304	2576	336	-24	1
	2	354	1336	2640	342	12	2
	3	394	1352	2688	348	46	3
	4	324	1384	2736	347	-23	4
Yr 3	1	328	1400	2784	345	-17	1
	2	330	1376	2776	346	-16	2
	3	402	1384	2760			
	4	324	1384	2768			

In the table above, instead of calculating the average immediately, the data for quarter 1 to 4 are added, then the data for quarters 2 to 4 of year 1 plus quarter 1 for year 2 are added. These two totals are added together and inserted in the 8 point moving total columns (because eight points of data have been used). Then the average of the eight points is calculated, and inserted at the third point in the data. This process is known as **centring**.

Once the trend has been calculated, then the seasonal (or cyclical) variation follows in exactly the same way as the example already considered. The prediction of the final result is also carried out in exactly the same way. Note that, in this case, the trend flattens. This will obviously affect the final prediction.

You might wish to go through the process. If so, your forecasted sales figure for quarter 1 of year 4 ought to be **between 323 and 327.**

Overall Benefits and Limitations of Using Moving Averages and Extrapolation to Measure and Forecast Sales

Calculating moving averages is useful in exemplifying what is currently happening. In addition, making predictions about sales through extrapolation, allows a business to plan. There are, however, a few limitations associated with using such techniques to measure and forecast sales.

1. Firstly, the calculation of moving averages only describes what is happening, it does not explain *why*.

2. Secondly, and more significantly, predictions using extrapolation are based on the assumption that history repeats itself, yet factors affecting markets may change such as, interest rates and new competition, as well as unpredictable events such as war and changes in the weather.

Consequently, it should only be used as a technique to predict sales where trading conditions are stable, and therefore, accuracy is more likely in the short-term.

How Correlation can be Used in Analysing Markets

Introduction

Correlation refers to the strength of the relationship between two variables, for example the relationship between:

- weather and items of food or clothing – for example – in winter, sales of umbrellas are likely to increase and sales of ice creams are likely to decrease.
- expenditure on promotion and sales – for example – an increase in advertising expenditure is likely to result in an increase in sales.
- pay rates and productivity – for example – a rise in pay rates may result in an increase in labour productivity.
- complimentary goods / services – for example – the greater the demand for razors, the greater the demand for shaving foam.
- Substitute goods / services – for example – the greater the demand for houses, the lower the demand for rented accommodation.

Establishing a relationship between different variables might assist a business with the prediction of sales and, in particular, in making decisions about marketing strategy and the various elements of the marketing mix, as well as decisions relating to other functional areas (eg HR and levels of pay).

Graphical Use of Correlation – Scatter Graphs

By plotting the sales of one variable against another, it will be possible to ascertain how closely related the two products are. Such a diagram is referred to as a **scatter graph**, because it appears as a collection of points 'scattered' on a graph.

By plotting correlation in the form of a graph, a business may be able to anticipate future sales or orders of a particular product or service by extrapolating the line of best fit between the two variables.

When producing the graph, the independent variable (the assumed causal factor) is plotted on the X / horizontal axis (using the examples provided above this would be changes in the weather, promotional expenditure, rates of pay, demand for razors, demand for houses). The dependent variable is plotted on the Y / vertical axis. A line of best fit is then drawn between the plotted points.

The degree to which it is possible to draw a straight line through the points, demonstrates the extent of the correlation or the 'closeness' of the relationship between the two variables.

An example of a scatter graph is provided on the following page. This shows the relationship between sales of computer parts (casing for the hard drive, screens, speakers, etc) and sales of computers, ie complimentary products.

Two variables that are closely related and move upwards in the same direction (as in the above scatter graph), are said to have a high **positive correlation**.

Alternatively, some products have a **negative correlation**, ie when the sales of one product rises, the sales of another might fall. This might occur if the products are substitutes. For example, an estate agent will earn revenue from houses that it rents out to tenants, as well as commission from selling houses. Such is the state of the market that when house sales are rising, the market for renting is less profitable, and vice versa.

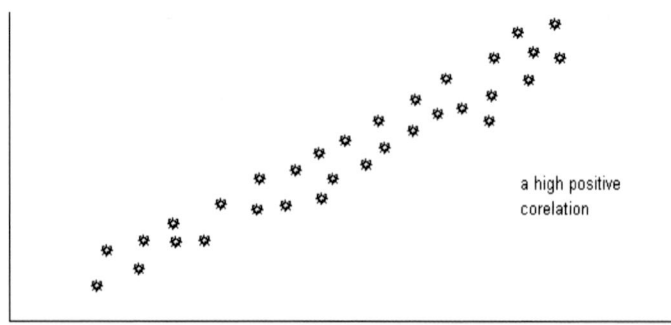

Sales of Computers

[Scatter diagram showing a high positive correlation between Sales of computer parts (x-axis) and Sales of Computers (y-axis)]

a high positive corelation

Sales of computer parts

By establishing the relationship between the revenue from one source and the revenue from another, this might allow the business to change its strategy, or perhaps adjust its rental prices. Refer to the diagram below.

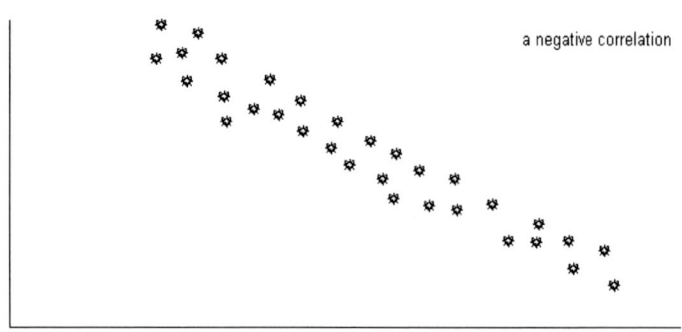

Revenue from renting property

[Scatter diagram showing a negative correlation between Revenue from selling property (x-axis) and Revenue from renting property (y-axis)]

a negative correlation

Revenue from selling property

Variables that have little connection are said to have a **weak or low correlation**. Variables that do not seem to bear any relationship are said to have a **zero correlation**.

Lines of Best Fit

Once correlation (positive or negative) has been established, a line of best fit needs to be imposed on to a scatter diagram before it can be used to make predictions.

Firstly, the mean for each variable's data needs to be calculated and this pair of values needs to be plotted on the scatter diagram.

A straight line is then drawn through this plot so that all the other plots are on, or close to, the line and there is roughly the same number of plots above and below the line.

Note that the closer to the line all the plots are, the higher / stronger the correlation.

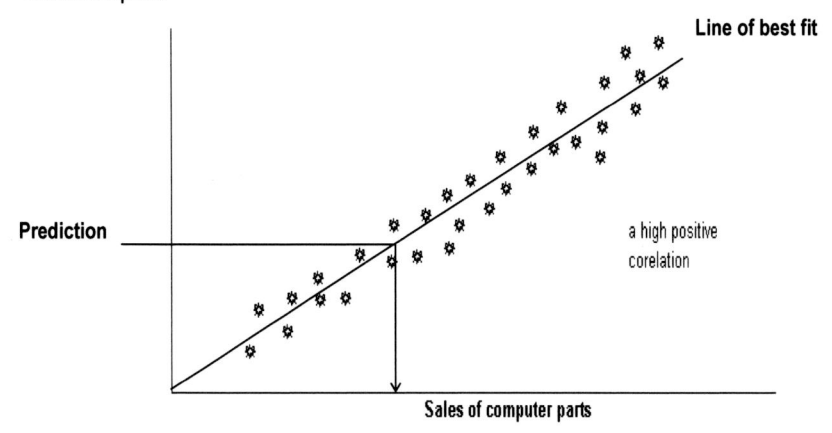

Sales of Computers

Scatter graph showing: Line of best fit, a high positive corelation, with Prediction line drawn from y-axis to x-axis (Sales of computer parts)

Limitations

There are limitations associated with the use of correlation and scatter graphs to analyse relationships and aid decision-making. Namely, that there are many factors that can affect a particular variable. For example, increased investment in advertising may show a positive correlation with sales of a particular product. However, sales may not have increased as a result of advertising expenditure, but as a direct result of say:

- a fall in interest.
- a fall in taxation rates.
- the closure of a major competitor.

Consequently, decisions based on judgements about the relationships between two particular variables should not be made until **all** these **other factors / possible relationships have been taken into account.** This will provide the business with a more accurate assessment of whether it can achieve its objectives, or whether such objectives need to be adjusted.

Test Marketing

The Process of Test Marketing and Review

This involves the launch of a product on a limited scale in a representative part of the market to assess consumer reaction and forecast future sales. Following the test market a business is likely to ask itself the following questions before investing in a full launch:

1. Is it likely to meet a defined **customer need**?
2. To what **segment(s)** can it be sold?
3. What **position** is it likely to occupy in the market place?
4. Does this fit in with the overall **objectives** of the firm?
5. Will it improve or diminish the firm's **image / reputation**?
6. What are the marketing, financial, operational, HR **implications**?

7. Does the firm have the necessary **resources** eg management & staff with the time, skills, experience? appropriate technology and operational systems? adequate finance?
8. If not, can they be **obtained**? at what **cost**?
9. Are the **contribution** possibilities worthwhile?
10. What will be the effect on the firm's **overall financial position**?
11. Are there any **legal aspects** to consider?
12. When is the best **time** to launch? Can the firm **keep to schedule**?

If the majority of the answers to the above questions are in favour (or all if the business is risk-adverse), then the business will launch the product into the market place.

Benefits and Limitations

Test marketing can be particularly effective in determining whether a new product is likely to achieve the desired results. Although it incurs costs and, arguably, may not reflect the whole market, in general it can save huge costs in the long run by helping to improve the product before a national launch, to ensure people buy it.

Closing Comments

This section briefly explained that sales forecasting techniques can be categorised as quantitative or qualitative. **Quantitative** techniques are based on an analysis of numerical data, whereas **qualitative** techniques are based on opinions and experience and are generally used when numerical data is scarce or the market changes quickly (which makes quantitative techniques less reliable). They were developed in the 1960's by American Scientists. The above section has – as required by the AQA specification – focused on quantitative techniques. As pointed out, however, businesses often use **both** techniques to develop sales forecasts. Some examples, therefore, of qualitative techniques are provided below:

- **Personal insight** – based on the experience of a particular individual - inexpensive but accuracy can be low.

- **Historical analysis** – where the performance of one product provides a base for predicting trends in a similar product.

- **Market surveys** – accuracy is dependent upon the sample being representative, the quality of questions asked and reliability of replies, the quality of analysis and conclusions drawn.

- **Panel consensus** – experts discuss and arrive at consensus – accuracy is higher than personal insight, but may still be low.

- **Delphi Technique** – where a panel of experts respond to questions, independently (unlike panel consensus), and each of their responses are presented anonymously to other members of the panel, until they reach a consensus. This avoids experts being influenced by other individuals on the panel (possibly who shout the loudest or have the highest status). Therefore, accuracy is higher than with panel consensus.

The Use of Information Technology in Analysing Markets

Objectives

By the end of this topic you should be able to:

1. Define the term information technology.
2. Explain at least 3 ways in which information technology might be used to analyse markets.

Key Terms

Information technology can be defined as 'the acquisition, processing, storage and dissemination of vocal, pictorial, textual and numerical information by a micro-electronics-based combination of computing and telecommunications' (Department of Employment Information Technology). In simple terms it concerns the application of technology to information.

Introduction

Since the late nineteenth and early twentieth century, with the advent of the telegraph, telephone, typewriter, radio and television, technology has been used to send and receive information. Since the 1950's and the development of the microprocessor, rapid advances have been made that have enabled the sending and receiving of text, speech, numerical information, pictures and diagrams at great speed (almost instantly), within and between businesses and / or countries, to several people at the same time. This has become known as the information technology revolution.

The main information technologies used by businesses today to communicate information, are listed below:

- Telephone and intercom, Mobile phone
- Bleeper, Radio pager
- Telex, Fax
- Prestel / Viewdata / Teletext
- Computer, Laptop computer
- Electronic mail
- Internet, Intranet
- Teleconferencing
- Video-conferencing

The AQA specification specifically requires knowledge of the use of information technology in analysing markets. It should be appreciated, however, that the use of information technology is not just limited to aspects of marketing but all the other functional areas of business.

The Use of Information Technology in Analysing Markets

Data Collection

The first stage of market analysis involves data collection. With regard to this, the sending and receiving of text, speech, numerical information, pictures and diagrams at great speed (almost instantly), within and between businesses and / or countries, to several people at the same time through - for example - mobile phone or Internet technology, has greatly increased the efficiency with which the data collection stage can be carried out.

Data Analysis

Data analysis can be carried out far more quickly and cost effectively on computers using spreadsheet and database software.

Spreadsheets involve data being entered, stored, and presented in a grid on a computer. The grid is made up of a number of cells. Each blank cell is able to carry information which falls into one of three categories:

- Numerical data – numbers entered by user
- Text – spreadsheet headings
- Formulae – instructions given by user which tell the computer to manipulate the numerical data.

Spreadsheets enable calculations to be made and figures to be manipulated quickly and easily and, in the case of marketing, to produce sales forecasts.

Databases are simply electronic filing systems. A file is a collection of common data. It consists of related records. Information on each record is listed under headings known as fields eg name, address, age, and occupation. Databases enable information to be stored on the computer thus reducing the stationery and storage costs involved in holding large manual files. More significantly with regard to analysing market data, they have a file searching, sorting and calculating facility which enables specific information to be quickly and easily retrieved, and data to be almost instantly reorganised for specific purposes, eg re-arranging customers in ascending order of sales.

The use of databases is commonplace in the marketing departments of most large companies. They can be used to store information about customers' purchasing habits and to produce letterheads and mailing lists far more rapidly than manual methods. For example, when a customer purchases products using a loyalty or reward card, or when an Internet purchase is made, the business can build a picture of their purchasing habits, in terms of expenditure, volume, nature of goods, etc and store this information in a database. If it is seen that a customer buys nappies over a period of time, then such information can be used to market other baby products to this customer. In addition, they might, one year later, send a mailshot to the customer about toddlers' toys.

Overall the use of computers speeds up data processing and allows the study of more complex inter-relationships of pieces of survey data, than previously practicable. For example, researchers can take 10, 50, or even 100 different variables for describing the demographic characteristics, behaviour, attitudes, motivations, etc of a particular consumer, and instruct the computer to analyse all consumers interviewed into a limited number of groups, in such a way that each group has a common pattern of characteristics which differentiates it from others. This helps to identify market segments and aids the development of marketing strategies to cater for the needs of specific segments.

Data Presentation

Most spreadsheet packages such as Excel also have their own graphical packages which produce diagrams, charts and graphs, etc automatically. Once the relevant data has been typed there are a variety of presentation methods to choose from to suit different needs thus, increasing the accuracy and speed with which diagrams are produced and market data can, ultimately be analysed.

Closing Comments

As stated in the introduction to this section, information technology is having a major impact on all aspects of business, not just marketing. Some examples are provided below:

- **Accounting and finance:** Spreadsheets can specifically be used for costing and to produce budgets and forecasts and end of year accounts. They are particularly useful in budgetary control, which involves comparing budgeted figures with actual figures, and analysis of the variance, ie the difference between the budgeted and actual figures. Databases can also help control the amount owing by customers as well as ensuring prompt payment to suppliers. Using the file searching and sorting facility it is possible to identify late payers and produce reports which list debtors in order of age (aged debtor reports). Information on stock and sales levels can be stored in a database enabling tight stock control and much tighter budgetary control.

- **Production / operations:** IT can be used in the design and production of products, using CAD (Computer Aided Design) and CAM (Computer-Aided Manufacture). Manufacturing Resource Planning (MRP) software also enables management to quickly find out whether an order can be fulfilled (with existing capacity, in the time available). This is because it automatically calculates the labour, materials, machinery and time required to complete a specific design / fulfil a specific order, and compares this to the capacity and time available.

- **Human resources:** Computers have revolutionised payroll. They automatically calculate monthly pay, tax, national insurance and pension contributions, even bonuses linked to attendance, punctuality and productivity figures. ICT has also changed the way people get paid – most people are paid directly into their bank through electronic funds transfer (EFT). The up-take of e-mail and mobile phone technology has also enabled much more flexible working practices. Employees can work from home, or whilst travelling, with direct links to the workplace via a phone line or laptop computer.

Difficulties in Analysing Marketing Data

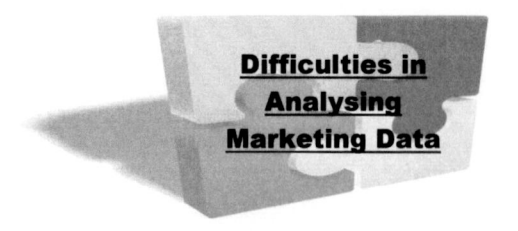

Objectives

By the end of this topic you should be able to:

1. Outline at least 3 difficulties associated with analysing marketing data.

Key Terms

Difficulties in analysing marketing data include the fact that secondary marketing data may not be up-to-date or specific to a business's needs; primary marketing data can be time consuming and costly to obtain and requires the use of skilled personnel; and the fact that numerous external, uncontrollable factors can affect the market for a business's product or service, which can not always be predicted.

Potential Difficulties Involved in Analysing Marketing Data

Limitations of Marketing Data Obtained through Secondary Sources

Marketing data obtained through secondary sources may be relatively easy and cheap to obtain, but it might not be up-to-date and so may not represent what is currently happening in the marketplace.

Secondary marketing data may also not be specific to a business's needs. For instance, a business in the hospitality industry may want to know the leisure pursuits and interests of people aged between 60-65 within a certain region in the UK. Secondary data may, however, only be published detailing the leisure pursuits of people in the whole of the UK with no breakdown between regions. Such data may not, therefore, reflect the leisure interests of people in the particular region in which the business is interested.

Difficulty Securing the Resources Required

Obtaining marketing data first hand ie through primary sources can be time consuming and costly and the business may lack the financial resources and / or skilled personnel required to undertake the research and / or analyse the findings.

If the business lacks the financial resources this may limit the scope of the research and, in terms of field research the size of survey sample, thereby reducing confidence in the results.

A lack of personnel skilled in market research and analysis could also result in the following:

- **Invalid data** being collected ie it does not measure what it is supposed to measure. In the case of field research, this may, for example, happen as a result of poorly worded, ambiguous questions.
- **Inaccurate calculations**.
- **Incorrect interpretation** of the data – with the data not supporting the conclusions drawn.

External Uncontrollable Factors that are Difficult to Predict

Even when the data obtained is up-to-date and specific to the business's needs and has been correctly analysed and interpreted, there is no guarantee that it will represent the near and, in particular, longer term future. This is because numerous factors impact upon the market for a business's product or service over which the business has little or no control, and that cannot always be predicted - for example - changes in competitor activities, or changes in macro-economic factors.

Closing Comments

In light of external, uncontrollable and, largely, unpredictable factors affecting the market for a business's product or service, there is no guarantee that researching and analysing marketing data will prove more useful / effective than decisions based simply on a hunch / gut feeling / instinct. It should be appreciated, however, (as highlighted at the beginning of this section on 'Analysing Markets & Marketing'), that launching new marketing strategies on hunches alone, without any researching or testing, runs a greater risk of failure. Market research and analysis is more likely to detect potential problems / weaknesses with particular decisions / strategies, thus saving costs not only in terms of the initial investment, but also the effect that failed strategies may have on the long-term reputation of a business.

This being said, when hunches are based on years of experience, the strategies implemented may indeed prove successful.

3.3

SELECTING MARKETING STRATEGIES

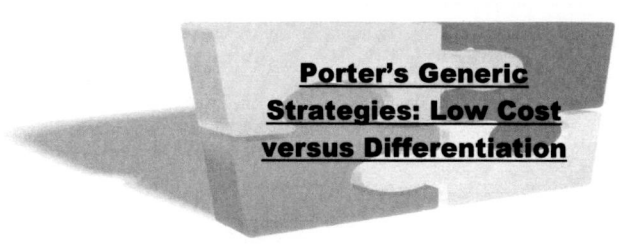

Porter's Generic Strategies: Low Cost versus Differentiation

Objectives

By the end of this topic you should be able to:

1. Define the terms competitive advantage and the strategies cost leadership, differentiation and focus.
2. Outline how cost leadership and differentiation might be achieved and circumstances when each strategy might be appropriate.
3. State at least 2 advantages and 2 disadvantages associated with each strategy.
4. Identify the strategy used by a business in a given scenario and comment on its appropriateness.
5. Select and justify the most appropriate strategy to adopt in a given situation.

Key Terms

Competitive advantage is something that places an organisation above its rivals, for example, the ability to offer lower prices or a faster, more reliable service.

A **cost leadership** strategy involves producing at the lowest possible cost often in order to offer a product or service to customers at the lowest possible price.

A **differentiation** strategy involves making the product or service look distinctively different to those of competitors in the eyes of the customers and in ways valued by customers.

A **unique selling point** or proposition (USP) is a key characteristic of the product or service that differentiates it from similar products or services in the market place.

A **focus** (or **market segmentation**) strategy involves focusing on a small part of the overall market and succeeding through, either, cost leadership or differentiation within that small sector of the overall market.

Introduction

All successful firms have a competitive advantage ie something which makes them stand out from their rivals. If a firm has a competitive advantage that is appreciated by customers and one that is sustainable, (which largely concerns being difficult to imitate), then customers will return time and time again. A business is also likely to be able to secure new business as customers perceive there to be no close alternative / substitute.

The work of Michael Porter identified 3 generic strategies through which competitive advantage can be achieved: cost leadership, differentiation and focus. Each of these strategies are discussed below, together with other strategies a business might implement, depending on the situation it faces in the marketplace.

Low Cost – Cost Leadership

What is It? How can it be Achieved?

Cost leadership involves being the lowest cost producer in order to either:

- offer the **lowest-priced product or service** and, thus, achieve objectives relating to sales and market share, or

- enjoy a **higher than average profitability** and, thus, achieve objectives relating to profit, return on capital employed and / or return to shareholders.

It often involves producing or providing and selling large volumes of a standard 'no frills' product or service and, thus, benefiting from economies of scale ie factors that lead to a reduction in unit cost as a business increases its output / size. But, whatever the nature of the business's operations, emphasis will (fairly obviously) be placed on minimising costs in all areas of the business. This may be achieved, for example, through the use of:

- **new technology** and / or **new methods of production** eg moving to more capital intensive production methods. In this scenario average labour costs per unit might be cut as more capital intensive production processes generally require less labour hours (as machines replace labour and tend to be quicker at carrying out tasks), as well as lower skilled labour resulting in lower wage bills. They should also lead to a reduction in costs arising from poor quality as machines tend to be more reliable, making fewer mistakes than humans.

- **relocating some or all of the business to gain access to lower-cost factors of production** eg cheaper rent on premises, cheaper raw materials and / or cheaper labour.

- **outsourcing non-core / critical activities** eg such as warehousing and distribution to another business that can perform these tasks more cheaply, without a drop in quality or reliability. As the section on cost minimisation above highlighted, this may be as a result of the other business being located in an area where labour (and, possibly, other production) costs are cheaper and / or specialising in these tasks and / or being able to benefit from greater economies of scale.

- **forwards or backwards vertical integration** ie the purchase of suppliers or distributors in order to obtain materials at cost price and / or cut out the middleman.

- **maximising productivity and capital utilisation** in order to ensure the business is not paying for labour and / or machinery that is not being fully utilised, thus minimising wastage of resources and keeping fixed costs per unit to a minimum.

Businesses pursuing a low cost strategy tend to:

- be **streamlined** ie have **few layers in the organisational hierarchy**.

- make managers **fully responsible and accountable** for their sphere of operations, for example, through the use of **cost and profit centres**.

- implement **tight cost control measures and procedures** eg through the use of budgets and close monitoring and supervision of labour and materials.

- use **incentives based on achieving targets relating to costs and cost reduction**.

When is it Appropriate?

A cost leadership strategy is most appropriate when:

- there is significant **price competition** between rivals.
- the business provides a **standard, homogenous product** which is readily available from a variety of other businesses and there is **little scope for differentiation**.
- customers are **price sensitive** or have significant **purchasing power** ie the ability to force a business to reduce its prices.

Potential Advantages and Disadvantages

Overall, a cost leadership strategy can provide a business with a price advantage over rivals and, thus, help to achieve objectives relating to growth in sales volume and market share (assuming competitors are not able to reduce their costs to match the cost leader). Alternatively, it can enable the business to earn above average profit.

Other, less obvious advantages of such a strategy include the fact that it:

- can help deter new entrants to the market(s) served by the business – as it may require significant capital investment to product or provide a product or service at a lower price than the cost leader.
- provides scope to force a new entrant out of the market place through lowering price further.
- helps defend against substitute products ie products or services that partly satisfy the same need as those provided by the business eg tinned salmon vs fresh salmon, driving by car versus taking the train.
- enables a business to cope with pressure to reduce prices from large powerful customers, or the cost incurred in increasing product quality of service levels at the request of powerful customers.
- enables a business to more easily absorb any increases in the cost of inputs and so insulate the business against powerful suppliers.
- enables the business to cope more effectively when demand falls or costs rise as a result of changes in external factors eg recession, changes in interest rates.

There is one main disadvantage associated with such a strategy, namely that:

- there is a danger customers may perceive the product or service to be of lower quality than other providers in the marketplace.

Differentiation

What is it? How can it be Achieved?

Differentiation involves making the product or service look distinctively different to those of competitors in the eyes of the customer and in ways valued by the customer. The aim of differentiation is to either:

- increase profits by charging a higher price (which should more than cover the extra costs incurred in offering a more unique product / service); or
- increase market share by offering a better product/service than rivals, at the same price.

NB Within the public sector, it might be to achieve Centre of Excellence status in order to attract higher funding.

In mass markets, where there are numerous similar products and services competing for market share, businesses attempt to make their product / service stand out from others through developing a unique selling point (USP) ie a key characteristic of the product or service that differentiate it from similar products or services in the market place. A USP, however, may actually relate to the price of a product. Product differentiation, on the other hand, does not directly concern the price of a product / service. It can, however, enable a business to charge a higher price, as customers are willing to pay more for something they see as offering greater added value.

There are two main sources of differentiation:

a) **Actual (physical) advantages** such as:

- improvements in design leading to better performance and / or appearance.
- additional features eg CD player or rear windscreen wipers in cars.
- better quality materials possibly increasing life of the product or taste as in the case of food.
- better packaging.
- easier access – more convenient location.
- faster, more reliable delivery.
- after sales services eg guarantees, warranties.

b) **Perceived (psychological) advantages,** ie the belief that one product is better than another when there are no significant phyisical / tangible differences. This is achieved through branding and advertising. For example, many advertisements, in particular TV, attempt to create an image about the company or product that the customer wishes to be associated with.

Successful product differentiation requires:

- thorough awareness and appreciation of **who the customer or consumer is** and **what they value.**
- in–depth **knowledge of competitor products / services.**
- **innovation** and **flexible organisation.**

With regard to the first bullet point, many businesses may use intermediaries, ie wholesalers, retailers or agents to get their products to the end user. In such cases, is the customer the retailer or member of the general public, or both? These two groups will have different needs and values. Consequently, the business will need to decide which group to base the differentiated strategy upon.

With regard to the second bullet point, developing unique products or services that stand out from competitors requires **customer and competitor research** to identify exactly who the customer is (in terms of soci-economic groups, geographical area, etc) and, in particular, what they value. Customer research (including qualitative research) can be time consuming and costly to obtain. It is also likely to require considerable investment in:

- **research and development.**
- **new technologies** and / or **staff training.**

This is to enable products to perform better eg to be more reliable or longer-lasting than those of the competition, or services to be improved to more closely meet the needs of customers.

Finally, successful product differentiation also requires the development of **a culture where innovation is encouraged not stifled**, and **a flexible organisational structure** which enables management and staff, to make timely responses to changes in competitor activities and customer needs.

When is it Appropriate?

A differentiation strategy is most appropriate when:

- there is significant **competition** between rivals.
- the business does not provide a **standard, homogenous product** readily available from a variety of other businesses and there is **plenty of scope for differentiation**.
- customers are not **price sensitive**.

Potential Advantages and Disadvantages

Differentiation allows a firm to charge a higher price and thus enjoy greater profits and / or attract more customers and so increase sales and market share.

It can help build customer loyalty as customers become attached to the unique attributes offered. Thus it can:

- help keep customers from purchasing the product's of rivals.
- reduce the threat of substitutes.
- deter new entrants into the market.

Because there are few, if any, close substitutes it can also:

- reduce the power that large customers have to push firms down on price.
- enable the business to pass on any increases in the cost of inputs in the form of higher prices to customers, ensuring the profitability of the firm is maintained.

There are some risks and disadvantages associated with a strategy of differentiation. This mainly concerns the fact that seeking out ways to differentiate the product or service that are difficult for competitors to imitate can be difficult to do and, more importantly, costly. Customers are also becoming more and more sophisticated and tastes can easily and frequently change, thus necessitating ongoing investment to identify and develop new ways to make the product / service stand out in ways that customers value.

Focus

What is It?

For businesses that cannot succeed either in terms of cost leadership or differentiation in terms of the whole industry, then one possibility is what Porter called a **focus strategy**. This means focusing on a small part of the overall market and succeeding through, either, cost leadership or differentiation within that small sector of the overall market.

Advantages and Disadvantages

Focusing on a small sector of the overall market can enable a business to gain a better understanding of the needs of the market for a particular product or service, and thus, more efficient allocation of resources and more rapid response to changes.

A **focus differentiation** strategy in particular can enable a business to meet the needs of customers more precisely than competitors, and thus, help secure customer loyalty, gain market leadership in a particular segment and maximise profits. As already stated above, a high degree of customer loyalty helps to:

- discourage other firms from entering the market.
- protect against substitute products.

Large buyers also have less power to negotiate as there are generally very few alternatives for them to choose between.

The main disadvantages associated with a focus strategy are the **lower volumes** and, thus, lower overall potential sales and profits that can be made in comparison to a business that focuses on the whole market.

Because of the lower volume, businesses adopting a focus strategy also have less power with suppliers. However, a firm with a focus-differentiation strategy is better able to pass increases in costs (supplier and other) on to the customer as they are less price-sensitive.

As with any strategy, there is always the risk of other firms imitating the strategy. Market and environmental circumstances are also constantly changing and this can affect the make-up of segments and may necessitate a change in strategy.

Closing Comments

Porter stresses the dangers of not devising a strategy based on one or other of these generic strategies. Firms that seek to be all things to all people risk being "stuck in the middle" and, therefore, failing to develop a competitive advantage. However, more recent research has suggested that firms can employ a hybrid strategy ie low cost and differentiation and that such firms can outperform other firms that adopt a single generic strategy.

Given the dynamic challenging environment in which most businesses operate today, one thing is certain - that flexibility in strategy (and tactics) is clearly required in order to respond appropriately to changing environmental and market conditions.

Suggestions for further research:

Porter, M.E. (1980) Competitive Strategy, Free Press, New York.
Porter, M.E. (1985) Competitive Advantage, Free Press, New York,

For an up-to-date appraisal of Porter's Generic Strategies including their limitations:

Bowman, C. (2008) Generic Strategies: a substitute for thinking?

Ansoff's Matrix Marketing Strategies (& Other Strategies)

Objectives

By the end of this topic you should be able to:

1. Define the terms market penetration, market development, product development and diversification.
2. Briefly explain the risk associated with each strategy.
3. Outline ways in which each strategy might be achieved.

Key Terms

Market penetration involves increasing sales of present products to present markets.

Market development involves increasing sales of present products by selling to new markets.

Product development involves selling new products to present markets.

Diversification involves selling new products to new markets.

Overview

The Ansoff matrix (developed by Igor Ansoff) is a well known model to use when making strategic decisions about marketing, and specifically over strategies for achieving growth in a national and an international context. The model provides four main strategies for a business to choose between which concern products and markets. Refer to the diagram below.

PRODUCTS

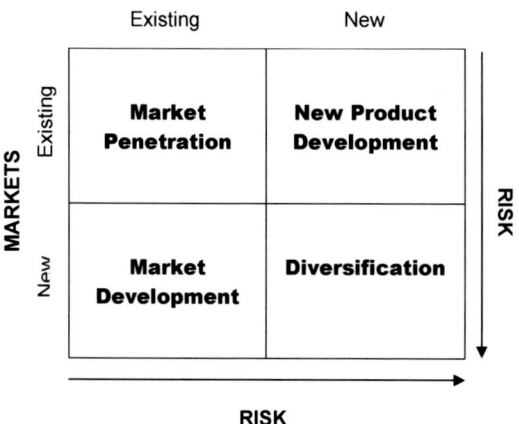

	Existing	New
MARKETS Existing	Market Penetration	New Product Development
MARKETS New	Market Development	Diversification

RISK (increasing along both axes)

© APT Initiatives Limited, 2009

Options can actually be compared in terms of the degree of risk involved. As the diagram above exemplifies, any strategy that involves the business in new markets, or new products, carries risk. A strategy that involves both of these (diversification) carries the greatest risk. This is discussed further below.

Market Penetration

Market penetration involves selling more of the same products to the same type of people / present markets. It is considered the **least risky** of the four strategies as it involves products and markets in which the business has already gained experience. But, it is only possible if either the market is growing, or the firm has sufficient competitive advantage to gain market share from rivals.

It can be achieved by:

a) increasing the frequency or quantity purchased amongst existing users / customers.
b) attracting users of competitors' brands.

It, therefore, requires a sound knowledge of customer purchasing habits and competitor activities and, possibly, market research into the attitudes and opinions of non-users. The latter may reveal that changes are required to various aspects of the marketing mix (excluding the product itself). The emphasis is, however, often on promotion, for example:

- more effective promotion of present product benefits / uses.
- identification and promotion of new product uses.

Alternatively, increasing the average quantity purchased by existing users may simply involve a minor change to the print on packaging. Simply adding the words *'and repeat'* to the directions on the back of a shampoo bottle has, for example, been an effective way of increasing the quantity purchased.

Market Development

Market development concerns increasing sales of present products by selling them to new markets. This strategy assumes that there are new markets which can be exploited profitably. It is **more risky** than market penetration as it involves one unknown and requires more extensive market research.

Market development can be achieved by:

a) targeting new segments of different age groups, social and economic classes, industry or household, in present geographical markets, or
b) targeting new geographical markets, nationally or internationally.

It is often a difficult strategy to adopt when there are strong cultural differences. Like market penetration, the emphasis is often on promotion as market development is usually achieved through careful advertising to effectively position the product in the new market place.

Product Development

Product development involves selling a new product to present markets. New products are always important especially in an industry that is subject to rapid change. But, research and development is a high cost and a risky activity. It should be appreciated, however, that new does not necessarily mean a brand new product, which often involves considerable investment, and thus, risk.

For example, it could simply involve:

- changing the material, ingredients, colour.
- adding a new feature.
- introducing a new size.
- improving the functional performance by making the product longer-lasting.

Diversification

Diversification involves selling new products to new markets. It is considered to be the **most risky** strategy as the firm is dealing with two unknowns, and it usually requires considerable research and significant investment.

Conversely, however, diversification can actually help to **spread risk** – as the business becomes less vulnerable to changes in one particular market. It is often adopted when a business faces saturation, or intense competition, or declining sales in its current market as a result of other factors, eg recession.

There are two main types of diversification:

- **Related.** This involves diversifying into areas which have a link with the organisation's present markets and products. For example, a biscuit manufacturer might diversify into cereals - both products are within the food industry.
- **Unrelated.** This is where a business enters a completely different industry. For example, a biscuit manufacturer diversifying into the financial services sector.

In general, the more unrelated the diversification:

- the higher the cost involved; and
- the greater the risk.

Other Strategies

Withdrawal / Retrenchment

In most case when we talk about strategy we think in terms of expansion. The Ansoff Matrix, for example, is about the direction of growth. If there is a threat to long term survival, expansion might be an appropriate strategy – especially if expansion involves moving into new and more profitable areas. However, a more appropriate, successful strategy might take the form of cutting back the size of the organisation.

At first this might be considered as rather defeatist and it might induce a spiral of decline but, just as a dentist drills out decay to fill a tooth in order to save it, so a business might cut out the deadwood in order to save the rest of the business. Such a strategy only makes sense if you cut out declining activities in which the firm has no competitive advantage, in order to concentrate on core activities in which it has some competitive advantage.

The retrenchment might take the form of:

- deleting certain products or services.
- moving out of certain market segments.
- moving out of certain geographical areas.

Retrenchment often involves **redundancies** as a result of downsizing (reducing the size of the workforce), delayering (removing one or more management or supervisory levels), or closure of some branches / offices. This is especially hard to deal with when companies have enjoyed long periods of growth, and may result in the following:

- A **reduction in the feeling of job security** amongst employees, leading to poor morale and motivation, which may negatively affect productivity.
- **Increased stress and loss of promotion prospects** (as a result of delayering) resulting in higher labour turnover. However, some employees might like the **extra responsibility / empowerment** delayering might bring.
- **Reduction in fixed overheads and increased capacity utilisation** – as a result of branch / office closure.
- A **lack of certainty in its investments.** Shareholders will not wish to invest in a business that grows and cuts back unevenly, and neither, for that matter will banks be willing to lend, unless it is on a relatively short-term basis.

Consolidation

If competition within a particular market is becoming increasingly intense, then consolidation may be more appropriate to help the business survive into the medium-term. This may involve a focus on improving productivity and efficiency in order to enable the business to compete effectively.

As stated above, whilst strategies relating to diversification can spread risk, they can in themselves be risky, as a business has little knowledge or experience in how to meet the needs of this new market segment. Thus, consolidation as opposed to diversification might be more appropriate in the face of intensifying competition.

Do Nothing – Maintain Existing Operations, Product and Markets

There is also the obvious strategy of simply maintaining current operations and doing nothing different. This is not necessarily a negative option. If the environment is static, the company is in reasonable shape in terms of operations, markets and profitability, and the owners are satisfied, then a 'no change' to current strategy may be the optimum decision.

Closing Comments

The right strategy will depend upon the particular situation facing a business, as well as its objectives and resources. For example:

- If there is plenty of opportunity in the current market - a strategy of market penetration would seem logical.
- If there is fierce competition in the current market - this may force the business to consolidate or look for new, less competitive markets.
- If the business has a strong R & D department - then the business may be able to pursue a strategy of product development with confidence.

Building on previous points raised in these Elementary Explanations, the most effective strategy should be the one which takes into account both internal and external factors, ie which build on strengths, explores opportunities and is realistic given the business resources and conditions in the external business environment, as well as agreed / fully supported by the key people involved in implementing the strategy.

Methods, Risks and Benefits in Entering International Markets

Objectives

By the end of this topic you should be able to:

1. Outline at least 4 benefits of entering international markets.
2. Outline at least 6 factors that increase the risk when entering international markets.
3. Outline at least 5 ways of minimising the risk associated with entering international markets.
4. Outline at least 4 methods of entering international markets.
5. Explain the difference between, and outline the relative advantages and disadvantages of, a strategy of standardisation and adaptation in the context of entering international markets.

Key Terms

Benefits of entering international markets include survival from recession in domestic markets, the spreading of risk, economies of scale, enhanced image / status and, ultimately, the achievement of objectives relating to growth in sales and profits.

Risks of entering international markets mainly concern the lack of knowledge and experience and contacts in the market which is aggravated by the differences in social, political, legal and economic factors that exist between the domestic and foreign market, as well as the additional costs involved, and potential problems with coordination and control.

Methods of entering international markets include direct exporting, indirect exporting, licensing, franchising, foreign independent presence and joint ventures.

Direct exporting is where a firm keeps production in the home country but independently researches and selects a foreign wholesaler or retailer to sell its products to a foreign end-customer, or independently researches and sells it products direct to a foreign end-customer.

Indirect exporting is where a firm keeps production in the home country but sells its products to a foreign market through an intermediary in the home country, or a foreign agent.

Licensing is where a business obtains a licence to sell another business's product in exchange for a fee.

Franchising is where a business gives another business the right to produce its product together with its name, logos / brands in exchange for an initial fee and annual royalty payment (usually a percentage of the sales turnover or profit).

Foreign independent presence involves a business actually setting up facilities in the chosen foreign market and operating from there.

Joint venture is where two businesses combine resources. In the case of international marketing it often involves the exporting firm joining with a locally based firm.

Standardisation (or globalisation) is where a business entering a foreign market sells the same product / service abroad as sold in the domestic market and in the same way, ie with the same marketing strategy ie promotion, price, channel of distribution, etc

Adaptation (or localisation) is where a business entering a foreign market adapts the marketing mix to suit local needs.

General Introduction

International opportunities arise from economic growth and rising living standards abroad. This leads to higher demand for goods and services, including higher demand for foreign goods / services. Alternatively, they can fall due to recessions abroad, which reduce demand and export opportunities. The onset of globalisation, with more efficient transport and telecommunications systems than ever before, makes opportunities to market products internationally easier to identify.

There are several potential benefits and reasons for seeking out and taking up international opportunities. There are also many potential problems / barriers, that may need to be overcome and that can increase the risk associated with venturing into international markets. These are considered below, following a discussion of the various ways in which a business can enter a foreign country.

Potential Benefits of Entering International Markets

Survival from Recession or Saturated Markets and the Achievement of Growth and Profit Objectives

If a market, or even an entire economy, is not growing at a rate that allows a firm to achieve its objectives, then instead of spending money attempting to draw more customers to the firm from the domestic market, it might decide to penetrate new markets abroad. Essentially this means researching different countries, to ascertain which is the most likely to purchase its products, at the right prices.

Objectives relating to profit may be achieved if a business is able to sell at a higher price and / or secure lower costs (production, distribution). The latter may be achieved by actually setting up a manufacturing base in a country it has chosen to enter where production costs are lower.

The Spreading of Risk

Although expanding overseas may be risky (explained further below) it can actually help to spread risk as the business is no longer dependent entirely on one country for its revenue and is less vulnerable to changes in the economic climate of one particular country. This is especially important for income elastic products, ie ones that are sensitive to levels of economic activity.

Economies of scale, Increased Competitiveness and Achieving Objectives

Economies of scale are factors that lead to a reduction in unit cost as a business increases its output / size and scale of operations (internal economies) or an entire industry develops (external economies). Internal economies include purchasing, technical, specialisation, financial, marketing and risk bearing economies. Economies of scale are discussed in more detail in the section on Operational Strategies below.

Increasing the size and scope of the markets a business serves is likely to help the firm to achieve greater economies of scale, particularly with regard to purchasing economies and also risk bearing economies as stated above, because it reduces the business's dependence on any one market.

It should be appreciated, however, that a business may seek to achieve economies of scale simply by relocating to similar sized premises abroad (as opposed to actually expanding its existing operations).

For example, it may deliberately re-locate to a different area or locate to another country where the industry in which it operates is more developed / established and, thus, benefit from external economies of scale, as follows:

- **Reduced labour costs** – Local colleges and government training schemes are usually set up to support growing industries. This means that the business does not have to bear the training costs.

- **Cheaper ancillary services** – As an industry expands it attracts smaller firms which try to service its needs, resulting in the establishment of a wide range of support services, eg banking, insurance, waste disposal, maintenance, cleaning. The more firms that set up the more competitive the price, thus resulting in lower costs.

- **Reduced research and development costs** – The bigger the industry in the foreign country, the greater the opportunity for firms to combine resources to fund R & D, thus reducing the costs a firm might incur trying to do this on its own.

Lower costs can improve a business's competitiveness both at home and overseas and achieve objectives relating to sales, market share through lower prices and / or allow the business to enjoy higher margins and, thus, achieve objectives relating to profit and return on investment.

Enhanced Image / Status and the Achievement of Objectives

Foreign countries / cities are also renowned for their reputation for certain products. For example, Paris for perfume, Milan for fashion. The reputation of these locations may provide substantial marketing benefits to a business, for example, increasing customer perceptions of the quality of the product, thereby increasing sales and / or allowing the business to charge a higher price, thereby increasing margins.

Potential Problems, Challenges and Risks Associated with Entering International Markets

Overview

A frequent error made by firms entering overseas markets is the assumption that *"abroad is the same as Britain"*. The fact is that there are particular problems associated with any marketing of goods and services abroad. These problems are over and above the normal problems and risks associated with business in the UK market. These problems exist even when business firms enter the markets of the other 26 members of the EU, or when they enter the US market (eg Marks and Spencer have a history of failure when establishing stores in the USA).

The peculiar problems associated with marketing abroad are considered in turn below.

Lack of Knowledge and Experience

The main risk associated with entering overseas markets is the fact that the business is venturing into an area in which it has **no previous experience**, and so **inappropriate decisions might be made regarding product, price, place, promotion, etc** resulting in poor sales. This is especially the case with entry into foreign markets in light of the considerable differences that may exist between home and foreign markets outlined below. These not only concern differences in the attitudes, needs and preferences of customers, but also the way in which businesses are regulated and are allowed and / or expected to operate.

Social, Cultural, Religious and Language Differences

There may be significant differences between people's tastes, attitudes, beliefs and perceptions in the foreign market compared with the domestic market which has implications for the product / service provided and the way it is promoted. For example:

- Indian food is generally much spicier than English. A business selling food products abroad may, therefore, have to adapt the ingredients used in the manufacture of its products and /or develop new ones in order to accommodate different tastes. If it does not the product may not sell. Adapting existing products and in particular developing new products is likely to require significant investment in market research and new product development, and might require changes to production processes and retraining to ensure the new products can be made to the specifications and standards required.
- The rights of women in certain countries might restrict their buying power, making the launch of new products for women in such countries problematic.
- A business must make sure that the 'message' conveyed in its promotional campaigns does not conflict with attitudes and beliefs held (as well as complies with any legislative differences). If brand values clash with the cultural values of the individual country, then the product will not sell.

More obviously, differences in language can lead to communication problems and will, for example, require changes to packaging to ensure people can read the messages and product information displayed.

Political Differences

Many areas of the world are renowned for being unstable, (eg parts of the Middle East and Northern Ireland), and / or anti-foreign investment. With regard to the latter, countries may seek to allow new, local businesses to grow and take action to restrict foreign businesses from flourishing (protectionism). This might take the form of financial help with grants or subsidies. There might also be limits on the amount that can be imported (known as quotas).

China was very much anti foreign investment pre 1990's. During the 1990s, however, there was an enormous amount of inward investment in China. This was due to the political climate becoming more welcoming to the wealth that market economies create. The attraction of cheap labour, government incentives, political co-operation and a market of well over 1 billion people encouraged many businesses to make large capital investments in China.

Legal Differences

There may be differences, for example, in terms of product labelling, safety, environment and advertising. Therefore, operating across international borders increases the complexity and costs involved in keeping up to date with changes in legislation.

Differences in Business Practices and Customs

Differences in culture and religious beliefs impact on the way people behave and expect others to behave in business situations. A lack of awareness and / or appreciation of these differences could lead to failure to gain key contracts.

Economic Factors

Economic factors include differences in living standards, levels of income, unemployment, taxation and inflation, as well as interest rates and exchange rates.

These might not only affect the spending power of individuals, (and thus, a business's sales), but also a business's costs, and overall profit. Movements in exchange rates, in particular, represent an additional source of risk to firms involved in international marketing. Different currencies result in transaction costs in currency conversion and changes in exchange rates can have a significant impact on a firm's costs, the demand for its products, and its profitability. Therefore, it is worthwhile looking at exchange rates in greater detail.

The exchange rate is simply the price of one currency in relation to another. An increase in value of the pound is called an appreciation. This means that the pound is stronger and that the pound costs more in terms of foreign currency. A decrease in the value of the pound is called depreciation / devaluation. This means that the pound is weaker and that the pound costs less in terms of foreign currency.

The simple rule to remember is as follows:

- A **fall** in the value of our currency against foreign currencies (known as depreciation) makes our **exports** (ie products sold to foreign customers) **cheaper** to customers in those countries where the rate has changed against our currency, but makes **goods imported into our country** (from countries where the rate has changed against our currency), **more expensive** for us.

- A **rise** in the value of the currency (known as appreciation) makes our **exports more expensive** to those customers where the rate has changed against our currency, but makes **goods imported into the country** (from countries where the rate has changed against our currency) **cheaper for us.**

Any change in exchange rate will affect a business entering overseas markets in a number of ways:

1. **Exports:** If a business resorts to exporting goods in traditional ways by physically moving goods across national boundaries, then the price paid by foreigners for these products imported from abroad will be affected by the exchange rate.

2. **Investment in operations in foreign countries:** If a business decides to set up physical facilities in a foreign country to serve customers in that country, then any initial investment it puts in will be affected by the exchange rate.

3. **Remitting profits:** If the business sets up operations abroad but maintains its headquarters in the UK any sending back of profits to the UK will also be affected by movements in the exchange rate.

4. **Imports:** if a business sets up operations in the foreign country but imports raw materials from its domestic market or other countries to the foreign market, then the price it pays for these materials will be affected by exchange rates.

Negotiating a long term contract for either the purchase of raw materials or the sale of finished products (if possible) will provide some insulation against exchange rate movements. Trying to negotiate long-term contract does, however, involve predictions into the future and, therefore, an element of uncertainty and risk.

Alternatively, if the business does decide to set up and manufacture its products in the foreign market where it decides to sell its products, then sourcing supplies of materials in this market will also reduce the impact of exchange rate movements. It might actually result in positive publicity as the business would be seen to be supporting businesses in these countries. It might, however, not be a cost-effective strategy if suppliers offering competitive prices cannot be found in these countries.

With regard to the profits received from sales in other countries, if the pound becomes stronger, then the business will actually receive less money when it converts the profit back into sterling and vice versa. It should be noted, however, that many organisations with overseas operations in a different currency zone maintain separate financial activities. Funds are only transported internationally when conditions are appropriate / advantageous.

NB A single European currency negates problems associated with fluctuating exchange rates for businesses obtaining supplies and selling their products or services solely within the Eurozone.

Absence of, and the Need to Build Trust with, Locally-based Firms

Any venture abroad by a UK company may require assistance from local firms to act as agents or strategic partners. The former, ie agents, act on a commission basis to undertake a specific task. The latter, ie strategic partners would become a partner for mutual benefit. It takes time to build a network of contacts and so the newcomer will face problems at first.

Lack of Customer Awareness of Brand Name

Coca Cola and McDonalds are global brand names known throughout the world. The same cannot be said of many less famous UK firms venturing into new markets. Therefore, one task facing the newcomer will be to build up brand recognition and trust and this will require considerable investment in promotion.

Additional and Increased Costs

Unless the business sets up a manufacturing base near to the geographical markets it chooses to serve, there will be increased transport costs involved in getting products to these new markets.

In addition, in order to communicate with customers, suppliers and employees across international boundaries, new technologies may need to be budgeted for.

Entry into foreign markets is also likely to require considerable market research (see below) at a significant cost.

These additional costs may mean that the venture incurs a negative cash flow for a considerable period of time.

Problems with Coordination and Control

As a business grows it becomes harder to maintain effective coordination and control, particularly when it involves diversification into new geographical markets. (Co-ordination and control concerns ensuring the right people, finance, and physical resources, are in the right place, at the right time, and that everyone is working towards a common goal). This is because the business is not just faced with dealing with more customers, employees, paperwork, levels of hierarchy, locations, etc but different types of customers, employees and administration requirements. The growing complexity of the business makes coordination and control more difficult and can result in diseconomies of scale (discussed further in the section on 'Operational Strategies' below). Diseconomies usually occur when the pace of expansion is too rapid to allow appropriate systems to be developed that would enable effective coordination and control to take place.

Ways of Minimising the Risks

In-depth Research and Analysis

Whether or not a country will be worth entering and, if so, the most appropriate marketing mix, including promotional mix and entry strategy, can only be determined through market research. With regard to this it would be sensible for any company considering entering a foreign market to seek information on:

- market size and trends.
- consumer attitudes and behaviour.
- size and strength of the competition.
- demographic trends.
- socio-cultural and religious features of the country.
- economic trends.
- possible distribution links.
- transportation links and other aspects of the infrastructure eg telecommunications.
- legal and political environment.

Throughout the investigation it should be remembered that *"abroad is different"*. This is not to say that Britain is somehow superior or inferior, but simply that, for instance, people abroad have different needs and tastes, and they operate within a different legal or cultural environment. If businesses neglect these differences, then the strategy is likely to fail. The essential lesson to remember is that we should not assume that what succeeded in Britain is bound to succeed abroad.

The marketing data provides the raw material for decision making. Any deficiency in the data or in its interpretation will lead to wrong decisions being made about the choice of markets to enter, the entry strategy and the marketing mix applied to the products and services sold.

This can incur significant costs and as with any new business venture it should be remembered that there is still no guarantee of success. This is because a business is subject to a range of external uncontrollable factors that cannot be foreseen - even with the best market research - that can impinge upon its success.

Appointing Personnel Experienced in these Markets to Oversee Activities

Given the differences that exist between countries it might be wise to employ local people / companies to advise and guide the business through the language, cultural and legislative differences when undertaking market research and devising the most appropriate mix, including promotional mix to ensure success in these new markets and, even, to run the day to day operations.

Drawing Up a Detailed Business Plan

The actual process of creating a business plan should ensure the venture is properly thought through, and should help to ensure that the right resources are in the right place, at the right time to meet customer expectations. The completed plan should also provide a means of monitoring performance and activities, enabling timely and appropriate action to be taken as required.

Keeping Investment in Fixed Assets to a Minimum

This might be achieved, for example, by renting and leasing as opposed to purchasing land and buildings or vehicles and equipment outright.

Setting Up Any New Business as a Limited Company

This protects the personal assets of the owner(s) / shareholders in the event of failure.

Taking Out Adequate Insurance

Buildings and contents, public liability and professional indemnity Insurance, for example, can be taken out to insure against the risk of things such as fire and theft, personal injury, and errors and omissions (in the case of advisory / consultancy services).

Ensuring Adequate Training and Supervision

This is important to ensure that business activities comply with legislation and, of course, meet customer expectations.

Taking a Stepped / Incremental Approach to Expansion

A business would be wise to consider a stepped / incremental approach to fully test the market and minimise the initial capital investment and risk involved, for example, by initially opening one outlet to serve the new market and only expanding further into the market if this initial venture proved successful.

Methods of Entry into International Markets

General

Simply taking the decision to penetrate a foreign market is only the tip of the iceberg. Even with well-researched evidence that a market exists for a product, there still remains the problem of gaining access to such a market. With regard to this, a firm may decide to keep production within the home country and export goods abroad, or actually allow / move production abroad.

Keeping Production in the Home Country and Exporting

If a firm decides to keep production at home, goods may be transferred abroad to the foreign country either through direct or indirect exporting, as follows:

- **Direct exporting** is where the business independently researches and selects a foreign intermediary ie wholesaler or retailer to sell products to the end-customer on its behalf, or independently researches and establishes a direct link with the foreign end-customer. (The latter has gained in significance with the emergence of e-commerce applications).

    Direct exporting requires significant initial investment (time, effort and money) in researching the foreign market and building relationships and establishing a customer base.

    On the other hand, it develops a better understanding of the market, provides greater control over marketing, and faster feedback from customers which enables more timely response to changing customer needs, especially when it involves a direct link with the end foreign customer. This also secures higher revenues and profits as there are no agents or intermediaries involved.

- **Indirect exporting** is where the business sells its goods to the foreign market through an intermediary in the home country or a foreign agent. It is often used by a business that is new to selling to foreign markets and, thus, lacks the knowledge and experience (in export documentation, shipping, international transactions, etc) required.

Indirect exporting does not require the business to undertake in-depth research and identification of suitable distribution channels in the foreign market, which can be time consuming and costly. The use of a domestic intermediary or foreign agent, however, lowers revenues. It also provides less control over the marketing and merchandising of the business's product, and makes it more difficult to make timely and appropriate responses to customer needs as a direct link with the foreign market is not established.

Production in the Foreign Market

Production in the foreign market may take many forms, including:

- **Licensing.** This is where a foreign business obtains a licence to sell the UK business's product in exchange for a fee.

- **Franchising.** This gives an individual or business the right to produce the UK business's product together with the UK business's name, logos / brands in exchange for an initial fee and annual royalty payment (usually a percentage of the sales turnover or profit). Examples include: Benetton, McDonalds, Burger King, Pizza Hut, KFC, Wimpy, The Body Shop. This is a relatively quick way of gaining access to foreign markets without spending huge amounts of money as the franchisee has to provide the capital to start the business. The franchisee also has a direct financial incentive to be far more motivated than salaried managers, and thus may work harder to make it a success.

- **Foreign independent presence.** Alternatively, the business may decide to set up production facilities abroad and operate from there. Having such a base and a location allows it to be better known. This may enable a business to take advantage of cheaper labour and government incentives. The business is also likely to benefit from lower transport costs, no import / exchange control barriers and greater revenues, as there is no third party involved. It is, however, **riskier** than the entry strategies listed previously, and requires **much greater investment**. It is also far more risky if the business lacks experience and expertise in overseas markets.

- **Joint ventures.** This is where two businesses combine resources, and often involves an exporting firm joining with locally based companies. With joint ventures risks are shared and both companies benefit as they can draw upon each other's strengths. There is, however, greater chance of conflict.

Factors to Consider when Deciding Between Methods of Entry

The exact strategy chosen to gain market access should take into account the following internal and external factors:

Internal Factors	External Factors
● Corporate objectives & strategy	● Size and spread of the market.
● Nature of the product	● Needs / expectations of customers
● Costs and profitability	● Social and economic conditions
● Financial resources	● Competition
● Human Resources - experience and expertise	● Political and legal factors
● Attitude towards and ability to cope with, risk	● Availability and reputation of distributors / distribution outlets.
● Willingness to share control.	

Standardisation or Adaptation / Globalisation or Localisation?

Explanation

Another key strategic decision that has to be made for any firm entering international markets is whether to:

- sell the same product / service abroad as sold in the domestic market and in the same way, ie with the same marketing strategy ie promotion, price, channel of distribution, etc (standardisation or globalisation), or
- adapt the marketing mix to suit local needs (adaptation or localisation).

The first strategy, ie standardisation, is based on the assumption that if the product and the promotional method works in this country then it will succeed abroad. This might be the case when selling to countries which are similar to Britain – such as Germany, Australia, Canada, or the Netherlands. But, business managers should not assume that foreign tastes are the same as ours. Even giant companies such as Marks and Spencer have found that *"abroad is different."* Therefore, the successful formula used in the UK might not work abroad.

The alternative strategy of adaptation is based on the fact that "abroad is different" and, thus, the product offering and / or the marketing mix needs to be adapted not just in terms of the rest of the world as a whole, but for each and every country in which the firm seeks to sell.

Potential Advantages and Disadvantages

Standardisation is obviously less expensive as the company can benefit from economies in terms of product development, purchasing and marketing. However, adaptation may be essential in order to meet the needs and tastes of customers in the chosen markets and, therefore, maximise sales revenues.

To solve the dilemma a business must weigh up the costs involved in adapting the marketing mix (including loss in economies of scale), against the potential benefits in terms of increased sales. If the cost outweighs the benefits, the business should either pursue a strategy of standardisation or not enter the market in question.

Conclusions Regarding the Most Appropriate Strategy

The strategy adopted will vary according to individual circumstances. It will be influenced by many factors, most notably:

- the nature of the product.
- customer expectations.
- the business's objectives.
- the resources available.

Where customer needs and market conditions are fundamentally the same as those in the UK, there is a good case for adopting a standardised or globalised approach.

Where market conditions or tastes and needs are radically different, then there is an argument for adopting a strategy of adaptation – including adapting the product and / or mix for each different market. This will add to costs but it will mean that the product is targeted at a particular market.

Closing Comments

Entry into international markets will incur significant costs, in order to develop and promote products that not only meet customer expectations but comply with legislative and other differences that exist between countries. There are also significant risks associated with expansion overseas. Consequently, it should only be pursued following a detailed survey of each potential country / market to determine whether the risk is worth taking in relation to the potential reward. It should also take place at a pace not too rapid to allow appropriate systems to develop that enable effective coordination and control to take place.

Any company seeking to exploit a market for the first time is likely to require assistance. UK Trade and Investment (UKTI) is a government organisation that can help UK based companies succeed in international markets: www.tradeinvest.gov.uk

Assessing Effectiveness of Marketing Strategies

Objectives

By the end of this topic you should be able to:

1. Explain the need for SMART objectives in order to assess the effectiveness of marketing strategies.
2. Outline the role that market research can play in measuring the effectiveness of marketing strategies.
3. Outline the need to take into account changes in internal and external factors over the period a strategy was implemented when making a judgement over the effectiveness of marketing strategies.

Key Terms

Assessing effectiveness of marketing strategies involves measuring the extent to which a particular strategy has achieved the objective it was implemented to achieve.

Introduction

The very beginning of these Elementary Explanations stated that any strategy should be evaluated in terms of 3 criteria. It is worth reminding ourselves at this point what they are:

1. Is it **suitable** - for achieving the business's objectives and / or addressing specific problems / weaknesses?
2. Is it **acceptable** - to the key stakeholders?
3. Is it **feasible** - in terms of implementation? Eg does the business have the resources eg financial, human, physical? If not, can it obtain the resources required?

The AQA specifications require knowledge and understanding as to how you would assess the effectiveness of marketing strategies. This requires a judgement to be made over the extent to which a particular strategy has achieved what it set out to achieve.

The Need for SMART Objectives

It should be remembered that a marketing strategy is a plan or course of action decided upon in order to achieve marketing objectives. Thus, in order to be able to measure the effectiveness of the marketing strategy, any objectives and targets set (as emphasised previously above), should be:

- Specific.
- Measurable.
- Timescaled.

ie **quantifiable**.

Once quantifiable targets have been established, properly designed monitoring and control systems should highlight any areas where:

- objectives / targets are not being achieved.
- investigation for the non-achievement of objectives / targets should be carried out.
- corrective action is required.

With regard to the above, managers are usually responsible for measuring the effectiveness of staff in relation to targets set within their departments at set intervals. If actual achievement falls below (or above) a certain amount, then the reasons should be investigated.

Market Research

Evaluation of results may also involve further market research consisting of direct feedback from customers, as well as observation of any competitor responses in relation to the marketing strategy.

Findings from the above research should be reviewed regularly (together with sales and financial data) by the key individuals involved, and corrective action taken where required. The latter requires understanding and reacting to both internal <u>and</u> external factors. This may involve minor changes to one aspect of the marketing mix, or a complete change in strategy.

Closing Comments

It is important to remember that the business is affected by a number of internal factors and external uncontrollable factors that can render goals / targets out of date or impossible to achieve. Consequently, any internal and external factors that may have impacted on the achievement of specific targets, should be investigated and taken into account when measuring effectiveness and, in particular, when forming judgements about performance.

3.4

DEVELOPING AND IMPLEMENTING MARKETING PLANS

Components of Marketing Plans

Objectives

By the end of this topic you should be able to:

1. Define marketing plan and marketing tactics.
2. Outline the marketing planning process.
3. Describe common components of a marketing plan including objectives, marketing strategy and tactics, costings / budgets, sales forecasts and timings.

Key Terms

A **marketing plan** is a report outlining a firm's marketing objectives, strategies and tactics, including costings (budget), timings and forecast results.

A **marketing strategy** is a broad plan of action for achieving a firm's marketing objectives.

Marketing tactics are short term measures used to implement strategy.

Overview

Marketing Plans

The marketing plan forms part of a business's overall corporate plan. It concerns the future direction of the business for the next 1 to 5 years (depending on the nature of the business), in terms of the markets it serves / intends to serve, and the products / services it will focus on developing and selling. It is a report that outlines a firm's marketing objectives, strategies and tactics, including costings (budget), timings and forecast results.

The plan should take into account the business's:

- corporate objectives.
- internal capabilities.
- external opportunities and threats.

The Marketing Planning Process

The diagram on the subsequent page outlines the key stages involved in developing and evaluating a marketing plan in relation to the business objectives, ie the process of marketing planning.

The diagram highlights the fact that developing marketing plans requires considerable research and analysis of both internal and external factors affecting the business. These are discussed further in the following section.

© APT Initiatives Limited, 2009

THE MARKETING PLANNING PROCESS

Gather information on present situation – *where are we now?*

Internal – marketing policies, resources, potential
External – uncontrollable factors in the market and economy

↓

Evaluate present situation – Conduct a SWOT Analysis

S&W = Internal eg market share, financial performance, product quality
O&T = External eg market size, competition, economic climate

↓

Make predictive Assumptions

What internal and / or external factors might alter during the period the plan is to be conducted?
Eg the birth rate will decrease by x%, there will be no significant change in legislation,
interest rates will increase by x%, Income tax will increase by x%,
Inflation will remain below x%, the economy will grow by x%.

↓

Set Marketing Objectives – *where do we want to be?*

Eg sales, distribution levels, brand image, market share
Should be SMART, eg *'increase share of market for X by X% by X date'*

↓

Devise the Strategy & Tactics – *how are we going to get there?*

Strategy – decide products and markets; changes to **Marketing Mix**
Tactics – exactly what? by whom? by when?

↓

Implement the Strategy (using the Marketing Mix)

Product, Price, Place, Promotion

↓

Monitor & Review / Measure the Results – *are we succeeding?*

Compare predicted to actual results using budgets, customer feedback
Take corrective action where required

Components of Marketing Plans

Objectives

The first thing the marketing plan should include are realistic marketing objectives based on the business's corporate objectives. The very first section outlined what marketing objectives are and may concern, as well as highlighted the need for SMART objectives. Remember, they are goals or targets that must be achieved by the marketing department / function to achieve the corporate objectives. They may concern, for example, brand awareness, sales and market share, and repeat business.

It is important to emphasise that prior to developing and implementing marketing plans, the business's corporate objectives should be clarified, as any strategy or plans (whether these relate to finance, operations, human resources or marketing) must fit in with the business's overall objective(s).

Marketing Strategies and Tactics

The main bulk of a marketing plan concerns the strategy and tactics. The previous sections have examined marketing strategies in detail. Remember, a marketing strategy is a broad plan of action for achieving a firm's marketing objectives, which should take into account the internal capabilities of the business and its external business environment. Marketing tactics, on the other hand, have not yet been defined. These are short-term measures used to implement strategy, detailing specific actions that need to be taken. Both are expressed in the plan in terms of elements of the marketing mix, as follows:

- **Product / Service** – the key features, quality, branding and packaging required to meet customer needs.

- **Price** – the price required to make an acceptable level of profit, which customers are willing to pay, (taking into account elasticity, costs, competitors).

- **Place** – where the business is to be located, how the product is to be accessed by customers / the distribution channels to be used.

- **Promotion** – the methods to be used to make customers aware of the product and persuade them to buy it (eg advertising, sales promotion, personal selling).

Some organisations may choose to focus on one particular aspect of the Marketing Mix. For example:

- Some of the major supermarket chains – particularly Asda and Tesco – focused on price for a long time. Tesco has, however, re-positioned itself in the marketplace, placing emphasis on product quality through the use of various promotional campaigns.

- With detergents and beers and lagers, the focus is on promotion, with particular emphasis on television advertising.

Even though some businesses place emphasis on one particular aspect of the mix, all aspects will still need to be addressed as all remain important to the customer. Customers need a product / service that:

- meets their needs (product).
- they can afford / provides value for money (price).
- they are fully aware of and informed about (promotion).
- they can access conveniently (place / distribution).

If a business fails to address one particular aspect, they are unlikely to be successful in the long-term. Remember also (from Unit 2) that a business will make strategic decisions about each aspect of the mix, but that the mix needs to be blended effectively to achieve the desired result in terms of sales, market share, profit, etc.

Resources and Costings / Budgets

The plan should detail the resources and costs involved. These costs are expressed in terms of budgets which provide an important means of control. Unit 1 has already required knowledge of budgets in general. Remember, these are agreed plans of action over a given period of time, eg 12 months, expressed in numerical terms. They are not to be confused with forecasts or estimates. Forecasts are predictions of what might happen in the future and whilst budgets may be based on forecasts - for example - of expected demand, budgets are planned targets which staff must strive to achieve.

Marketing budgets include targets for both income and expenditure. They include targets that should be achieved by a certain date, in order to achieve the overall business and marketing objectives, as well as targets for expenditure on all the activities involved in implementing the marketing plan. With regard to the latter funds may be allocated for some or all the following:

- Research and development
- Market research
- Distribution and warehousing
- Above and below the line methods of promotion
- Sales force
- Training and development of marketing staff
- Equipment, fixtures and fittings.

Budgets are generally produced annually, but for control purposes are usually broken down into monthly statements. For example, if the overall marketing objective for the year is to increase sales by 12%, then the marketing budget will show the monthly sales targets required to achieve this objective, as well as monthly targets for expenditure items.

The process of setting the marketing budget should also (as with all budgets) involve **all** those linked with their achievement. This will not only help to ensure that realistic and appropriate targets are set, but help to eliminate potential conflict by making all those concerned aware of the reasons behind the figures. This is also likely to increase the motivation of those involved to achieve the targets set.

Sales Forecasts

The marketing plan should also contain a prediction of the sales (in terms of volume or value) that will be achieved during the time period in which the plan is to be implemented.

Sales forecasts and methods of sales forecasting have been considered in the previous section on 'Analysing Markets and Marketing'. Remember (from this section) that the production of sales forecasts can help a business to plan the use of resources including material purchases, labour requirements, production scheduling, distribution and cash flow. This will be vital to ensure customer needs and expectations are met and, in terms of marketing, that the objectives laid down in the marketing plan are achieved.

Timings – Implementation Schedule

The plan should ideally detail exactly **who** is responsible, for doing **what**, by **when**. This will provide an important control mechanism - enabling progress to be monitored at regular intervals and corrective action to be taken as appropriate.

Closing Comments

Developing a marketing plan uses valuable resources. It is essential, therefore, that mechanisms and systems are set up which enable the plan to be monitored and evaluated, and allow timely, corrective action to be taken, as required.

The best plans will also include contingency plans identifying possible problems and challenges the business may face (eg aggressive competitor reaction) and action to overcome these if they do arise, to help ensure the business achieves the objectives laid down in its plan.

Assessing Internal and External Influences on Marketing Plans

Objectives

By the end of this topic you should be able to:

1. Outline at least 3 internal influences on marketing plans.
2. Outline at least 3 external influences on marketing plans.

Key Terms

Internal influences on marketing plans are factors that stem from inside the business that can affect decisions over or success in achieving marketing plans – for example – the finance available, the skills and abilities of the workforce, capabilities of existing plant and equipment.

External influences on marketing plans are factors that stem from outside the business that can affect decisions over or success in achieving, marketing plans – for example – competitors' activities and social, legal, economic and / or technological factors.

Introduction

For marketing plans to be effective in achieving a business's objectives they, (along with the objectives themselves), must take into account the internal capabilities of the firm and its external business environment. Some of the main internal factors and external factors influencing a business's marketing plan are considered below.

Internal Influences on Marketing Plans

Marketing and Decisions Over Business Objectives

The previous section (Marketing and the Achievement of Business Objectives) emphasised that Marketing objectives, strategy and tactics must be based upon decisions made regarding the overall business (ie corporate) objectives.

The Finance Available

Marketing requires finance to implement marketing plans and fulfil marketing objectives. Developing and launching new products, in particular, can prove costly in terms of market research, promotion and distribution. If finance is not available internally eg through retained profit, the finance department may have to seek external sources, eg through a bank loan. This may add to the cost of producing / providing the product / service, thus necessitating the Marketing department to raise the planned selling price, or accept lower profit margins.

The Marketing department will clearly need to communicate regularly with the Finance department to ensure that sufficient funds are available to implement marketing plans and achieve marketing objectives.

HR Issues: Skills and Ability of the Workforce

Marketing requires people to:

- generate ideas for products / services.
- carry out research.
- form part of a sales team selling and promoting the product, etc.

Producing / providing a new product may require changes to current methods and practices which some employees may not welcome. There are also training implications.

The Marketing department will, therefore, need to work closely with the Human Resources department, to ensure sufficient numbers of people with the appropriate knowledge, skills, <u>and</u> motivation, are obtained to implement the strategy and tactics planned to achieve marketing objectives.

Operational Issues: Capabilities of Existing Plant and Equipment

Marketing objectives and plans for their achievement will also be constrained by the capabilities of existing plant and equipment, not just in terms of capacity to produce greater volumes, but flexibility to produce new products to meet changing customer needs.

External Influences on Marketing Plans

Customer Needs and Wants

Out of all the factors influencing marketing plans, this is the **most** influential factor. For marketing strategies and plans to be effective in achieving a business's objectives they must take into account customer requirements. Remember, the main aim of marketing is to identify, anticipate and satisfy customer requirements. If the plan does not take into account customers needs and expectations, then it does not matter how detailed the plan is, or how efficiently it is implemented, it will not result in business success.

Competitors' Actions, Strengths and Weaknesses

The strategy and tactics laid down in the plan should also take into account the activities of competitors and their strengths and weaknesses. This will be essential to ensure the business designs a marketing mix that helps the business to stand out from competitors.

The business should also be prepared for competitor reaction to any changes in its strategy and tactics. This may affect the achievement of the objectives specified in the plan. Ideally it should anticipate competitor response and plan counter responses to help to ensure the objectives can still be achieved.

Other External Factors

There are a range of other factors over which a business has little or no control, which may impact on customer spending and purchasing habits and the market for a particular product or service. These include changes in social, legislative, economic and technological factors. Some examples are provided below:

- **Legislation:** Changes in legislation can, for example, affect decisions relating to the **product** and **promotion**. For instance, if the marketing plan requires the development of new products, the business will need to take into account product safety legislation and ensure the product complies. Any advertising and promotion specified in the plan must also comply with advertising standards.

- **Social attitudes:** People are becoming increasingly concerned about the impact of a business's activities on the environment. A business would, therefore, be wise to take these concerns into account when making decisions over the **packaging** of its products.

- **Economic:** Changes in interest or taxation rates may affect the amount of disposable income people have available to spend on the business's product or service and the prices they are willing to pay to acquire them, and so may influence a business's **pricing** decisions.

- **Technological:** More and more people can afford the facilities to, and are willing to, shop on-line. This may encourage a business to start selling its product or service on-line.

Closing Comments

At every stage of the marketing process, the business should take into account internal and external factors. This is essential to ensure that marketing objectives and strategy decided upon are achievable / realistic, and that any judgements or modifications made at the review stage are fair and appropriate.

The value of the marketing plan in achieving a business's objectives will very much depend upon the accuracy of the research into internal and external factors, and the assumptions made about changes in these factors during the time period in which the plan is to be implemented. This being said changes in external factors are often difficult to predict. Hence, flexibility needs to be built into the plan to ensure timely response to any changes affecting its implementation, and its appropriateness in achieving objectives.

Issues in Implementing Marketing Plans

Objectives

By the end of this topic you should be able to:

1. Describe at least 5 issues associated with implementing marketing plans.

Key Terms

Issues in implementing marketing plans arise as a result of failing to research and take into account internal and external factors and / or to involve key staff at the marketing planning stage; failure of the marketing department to liaise closely with other functional areas; staff viewing the plan as a rigid document that must be adhered to, resulting in failure to respond appropriately to changes in the internal or external business environment once the plan has been implemented.

Issues In Implementing Marketing Plans

The Need for In-depth Research & Analysis and the Resources & Cost Involved

For marketing strategies and plans to be effective in achieving a business's objectives they, (along with the business objectives themselves), must take into account the internal capabilities of the firm and its external business environment. Carrying out an internal audit of the business and its external business environment and undertaking a SWOT analysis can, however, be time consuming and costly and a business may not have the internal expertise or resources to carry this out. It should, however, recognise its importance and invest enough money to assist the business in making reasonably informed decisions. The following two sub-sections outline the problems arising from inadequate research and analysis at the planning stage.

Lack of Research and / or Consideration of External Factors

If a business fails to fully research and take into account external factors that can affect the business and the demand for its products, then this can lead to a lot of variance eg of sales forecasts and budgets and these documents (as well as the entire plan) can become devalued / lose importance

Lack of Research and / or Consideration of Internal Factors

If a business fails to fully research and take into account its internal capabilities then this can lead to insufficient resources to implement the strategy and tactics laid down in the plan.

Failure to Liaise with Other Functional Areas

Developing and implementing the plan also requires close liaison / communication with the other functional areas of the business. If this does not take place, then it may not be possible to implement the plan due to:

- insufficient cash available to finance the strategy and tactics laid down in the plan.
- insufficient number of people with the appropriate knowledge and skills required to carry out the strategy and tactics laid down in the plan.
- inability to produce products (in line with customer specifications), in the right quantities, at the right time.

Failure to Involve Key Staff at the Planning Stage

The key people involved with the implementation of the plan should be consulted at the planning stage. This does not just include staff working in other departments (mentioned above) who will be affected by the plan, but staff working in the marketing department who are ultimately responsible for its achievement.

The participation of all staff concerned as early as possible, (well before the introduction of the plan) can be greatly beneficial. It allows conflict to arise and be resolved at an early stage, and can significantly improve the original ideas regarding the plan and how it should be implemented, providing first hand information and expertise on the organisation and its work. If this does not take place, then this can lead to a lack of understanding of the requirements of the plan and problems at the implementation stage, including a lack of commitment to carrying it through.

Changes in the Internal and / or External Business Environment

Internal and / or external factors (considered in the previous section) may change affecting the implementation of the plan and its appropriateness in achieving the business's objectives.

Danger of Treating the Plan as a Rigid Document

In light of the above, the plan should not be treated as a rigid document that must be followed, to the extent that initiative is stifled, resulting in slow reaction to changes in the business environment (and internal factors), and missed business opportunities.

Closing Comments

The drawing up of a comprehensive marketing plan is important in maximising the performance and potential of a business. The marketing planning process itself ensures strategies and tactics are properly thought through and thoroughly researched, and that nothing is overlooked that might impinge upon their success.

The completed plan itself helps prioritise and allocate resources and responsibilities to ensure that the right resources are in the right place, at the right time to meet customer requirements and fulfil marketing objectives. It also provides targets which can be used to monitor performance and enable timely action to be taken as necessary. If communicated to employees it can also aid motivation by providing a sense of direction, purpose and urgency.

The construction of the plan does not, however, guarantee success as there are numerous factors outside a business's control that can impinge upon its performance. Plans should, therefore, change as circumstances change to allow the business to react to and stave off threats, and take up opportunities.

4

OPERATIONAL STRATEGIES

4.1

UNDERSTANDING OPERATIONAL OBJECTIVES

Operational Objectives

Objectives

By the end of this topic you should be able to:

1. Define the term operational objectives.
2. State at least 6 examples of operational objectives.

Key Terms

Operational objectives are goals or targets that must be achieved by the operations function within a business in order to achieve the business's corporate objectives.

Overview

Operational objectives are the goals or targets that must be achieved by the operations function in order to achieve the corporate objective(s). They provide a focus for decision making and for setting and agreeing operational strategies and plans. Like all objectives – as long as they are SMART objectives, they can aid motivation and encourage teamwork amongst operational staff, and make it easier to coordinate operations. This is because they provide a common goal for individuals to focus on achieving. They also provide a means of measuring performance and so provide an important means of control.

Types of Operational Objectives

Quality

From AQA AS Unit 2 Business Studies you should already appreciate that quality does not necessarily relate to the most expensive or luxury good. It is all about providing the customer with a product or service that meets their needs / expectations on a consistent basis, however simple or inexpensive the product or service may be.

Targets relating to quality might concern:

- reducing the number of rejects ie faulty products occurring in the production process.
- improving reliability in terms of product / service delivery times.
- reducing the number of customer complaints.
- increasing customer satisfaction levels.

by a certain amount in a given time period.

Achieving targets relating to quality essentially requires:

a) a market orientation to include market research to establish customer requirements.
b) securing good quality supplies, ie raw materials / components.
c) capable processes.
d) effective, committed people.

Targets relating to maintaining or improving quality are important in order to:

- **secure repeat business** – A satisfied customer will be more likely to buy again. If a product/service fails to meet customer's expectations he/she will be less likely to buy again.
- **generate new customers** through word of mouth recommendations – If a product / service meets or exceeds customer expectations then customers are more likely to recommend the business and its product / service to others.
- **minimise costs** ie the costs of re-working, re-testing, re-inspecting poor quality / 'failed' products and / or loss of sales resulting from dissatisfied customers.
- **maintain / improve competitiveness** – If competitors are making quality improvements it is vital to keep up with these activities, else the business risks losing market share.
- **maximise sales and profit** (as a result of 1 to 3 above) and **market share** (point 4 above).

Costs

Operations incurs numerous costs, both fixed and variable eg in terms of materials, machine running costs, labour, maintenance, etc. In fact, the bulk of a business's costs stem from operational activities. Inefficient control of operational costs can, therefore, significantly affect a business's profit. Setting targets relating to production costs – particularly with regard to unit material and direct labour costs are, therefore, very common and are central to the achievement of corporate objectives relating to profit and return on investment.

Volume and Capacity Utilisation

Targets relating to volume or output are also very common and stem directly from corporate and marketing objectives relating to maintaining and / or increasing the customer base, sales (in terms of volume) and market share. They may concern, for example:

- producing a certain number of items in a given time period.
- serving a certain number of customers in a given time period.
- achieving a certain percentage growth within a certain timeframe in either of the above, in order to increase capacity utilisation or achieve marketing and corporate objectives relating to growth in sales.

Capacity is the extent to which a firm's capacity (in terms of labour, machinery, etc) is being used. It is usually expressed as a percentage and is calculated by dividing the actual output into the maximum output possible for a particular period and multiplying by 100. For example, a business capable of producing 5,000 units a month but only producing 4,000 units a month is operating at 80% capacity. It has 20% spare capacity. Maximising capacity is important in order to keep fixed costs per unit down. Achieving targets relating to increased volumes may also allow a business to benefit from economies of scale (discussed in a subsequent section).

Volume targets and capacity utilisation are very much dependent upon the demand for a business's product or service which is, in turn, affected by a range of external factors for example, changes in consumer tastes, interest rates and technology. (These external factors are considered in the following section).

Sourcing Products

One of the very first sections in these Elementary Explanations on 'Functional Objectives' highlighted how objectives relating to the sourcing of products are becoming increasingly important due to the move away from manufacturing towards 'service' industries. They are also becoming more common as a result of media attention over ethical issues. For example, a business may set a target to increase the percentage of products sourced from fair trade countries by X date by X time.

Innovation

Innovation is the successful implementation of new ideas. It is the introduction by business of new products and / or new processes. It should be distinguished from invention which is a purely technical process of perfecting an idea. Innovation is, therefore, concerned with the commercial application of the idea or the invention. SMART objectives relating to innovation may concern undertaking any of the following within a given time period:

- Spending on research and development.
- Developing a new product or process.
- Securing a certain number of patents.
- Launching a certain number of products or brands.

Targets relating to the development of new products and / or processes are particularly common when a business operates in a dynamic marketplace and / or business environment where fast response to competitor activities and / or changing customer needs (and / or legislative requirements) is essential.

Innovation can, however, be costly – not just in terms of research and development costs, but in terms of the promotional expenditure, re-training and / or changes in working practices required to inform customers about the innovation and / or implement new processes successfully.

It should be appreciated that **innovation is not just an operational objective but also an operational strategy.** As suggested, in highly competitive, technological markets, the development of new products or new processes may be essential to set a firm apart from rivals, attract customers and, thus, achieve objectives relating to sales and market share. Innovation is, therefore, considered in more detail in a subsequent section on operational strategies below.

Efficiency (including Time)

Efficiency is concerned with the relationship between inputs used and output achieved. It is all about minimising waste in terms of resources, including time. It involves:

- keeping down the level of waste in production.
- keeping down the time it takes to produce a product / provide a service.
- making full use of resources.
- securing increased output of each unit of input.

It may also involve:

- **Arranging tasks and the workplace in the most efficient, ergonomic way**, so that handling and movement is minimised, visibility and accessibility maximised. This includes providing optimum working conditions which take into account factors such as temperature, humidity, radiation, noise levels and lighting. This should help to ensure effort and cost are minimised, and output is maximised.
- **Investment in automation and new technology.** Machines can be quicker and more reliable than humans, thus producing more in the same amount of time, and reducing not only labour input costs but also the cost of materials and supplies.
- **Investment in planned, preventative maintenance** to prevent machine breakdowns and stoppages in the production process.
- **Running machines for longer** to maximise their output over a given period of time.
- **Improving the ability of the workforce through training.** This increases employees' familiarity with job requirements, enabling them to complete tasks quickly, whilst making fewer mistakes.

- **Increasing labour flexibility** – Consider employing shift work and part-time or temporary staff as opposed to full-time staff, as well as multi-skilled workers. This will enable workers to fill in for absent employees, and ensure maximum use is made of the machinery, equipment, etc available.
- **Improving the motivation of the workforce** – for example – by providing financial incentive schemes linked to productivity, and non-monetary methods of motivation such as, quality circles, increased responsibility, chances of promotion, 'people-centred' management, all of which may encourage employees to work harder.
- **Changing the size and scale of the operation** (capacity) – discussed in the section on economies of scale below.

It can be measured in terms of unit (or average) costs. This is calculated by dividing the total cost (fixed + variable) involved in producing a product (or providing a service) by the number of units produced (or customers served). If one firm produces goods at a lower cost than a rival firm produces goods of the same type and quality, then we say that the first firm is more efficient. This is expressing it in monetary terms but - as suggested above - it can also be measured in terms of time ie the length of time it takes a business to complete a process, produce a product, or provide a service to customers.

The efficiency of a specific input or process can also be measured, eg:

- Labour: the amount produced per employee.
- Capital equipment: the amount produced per machine.
- Production process: the amount of wastage produced.

Targets relating to efficiency may, therefore, concern:

- producing a certain number of products or serving a certain number of customers in a given time period.
- increasing the number of products produced or customers served by a certain percentage.
- reducing the amount of waste generated in the production process.
- reducing the average time taken to produce a product or serve a single customer.
- reducing the percentage of materials wasted in the production process.

Improvements in efficiency lead to a lower average (unit) cost. Hence, targets relating to efficiency can lead to:

- increased profits – and thus greater dividends to shareholders and / or money available for re-investment.
- increased competitiveness – in terms of greater flexibility over price due to lower unit costs, thus helping to achieve objectives relating to sales and market share.
- greater chance of survival in the long term, and thus…
- greater job security for employees.

Improvements in efficiency in terms of time may also result in products being produced and / or customers being served more quickly than competitors and, thus, also help to achieve objectives relating to sales growth and market share.

Environmental Targets

This mainly concerns setting targets relating to process waste and reducing the negative effect a business's activities may have on the environment. Process waste is anything that is a by-product of production and ranges from fumes, industrial effluent, packaging used by suppliers, materials that are treated and then disposed of, eg water used to wash new motor cars.

Process waste can damage the environment, for example, through:

- **Air pollution** – acid rain, CFC's, Carbon dioxide gases causing 'greenhouse effect'.
- **Water pollution** – waste products pumped in to rivers, oil spillages in the sea.

Environmental targets may, therefore, concern reducing any of the following by a certain amount within a certain time period:

- Carbon emissions
- Water pollutants
- Energy usage
- Other waste products occurring in the production process

It may also include achieving targets relating to the **recycling** of process water, packaging and other waste products.

General measures that can be taken to reduce process waste may include:

- Investment in new machinery, equipment and computerised systems that help to reduce, monitor and control process waste.
- Investment in training and supervision – to minimise waste resulting from poor quality work as well as to increase staff awareness, and to help staff adapt to changes to working practices as a result of new machinery / products / processes.
- Planned, preventative maintenance to minimise waste arising as a result of poorly functioning machinery / equipment.
- Investing in new more accurate ordering and stock control systems – to avoid stock deterioration.
- Implementing Just in Time production (discussed later) – to minimise stockholding and the occurrence of stock obsolescence and deterioration.
- Use of alternative materials to increase the longevity of products.
- Use of more 'environmentally friendly packaging'.
- Selling off-cuts for use by other businesses.
- Recycling materials and energy use wherever possible.

All the above have cost implications but these may be balanced by:

- **Better image resulting in greater sales, capital, easier recruitment.** Consumers, investors, employees may be more willing to trade with an environmentally friendly firm.
- **More efficient production.** Less wastage usually means less resource costs, which might ultimately make the business more competitive.

Closing Comments

In general operational objectives are closely related and support each other, for example:

Improvements in efficiency should lead to a reduction in unit costs, and where targets concern reducing the time taken to produce and despatch a product or provide a service to a customer, this increased efficiency results in improved quality of service.

Where improvements in quality concern reducing the number of faulty goods and customer complaints arising from these, this should also reduce unit costs (arising from re-working or re-supplying faulty / damaged goods) and increase efficiency.

Implementing improvements to quality and efficiency, innovating, and achieving environmental targets may require substantial investment. More often than not, however, they only increase costs in the short-term. These costs are generally outweighed by the longer-term benefits in terms of reduced unit costs, increased competitiveness, customer satisfaction, sales and market share.

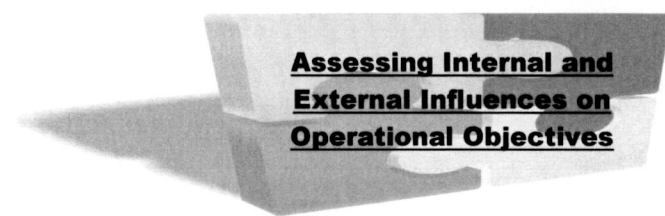

Assessing Internal and External Influences on Operational Objectives

Objectives

By the end of this topic you should be able to:

1. Outline at least 4 internal influences on operational objectives.
2. Outline at least 6 external influences on operational objectives.

Key Terms

Internal influences on operational objectives are factors that come from within the business that can affect decisions over, or success in achieving, operational objectives – for example – the nature of the product, corporate and other functional objectives, the amount of finance available, productive capacity, quality of the workforce and strength of worker representation.

External influences on operational objectives are factors that stem from outside the business that can affect decisions over, or success in achieving, operational objectives – for example – consumer needs and expectations, market and demand factors, competitor activities, social, political, legal, economic and technological factors, as well as the quality, reliability and flexibility of suppliers.

Internal Influences

Nature of the Product

The nature of the product or service determines the resources required (materials, labour in terms of skills, qualifications and experience, etc) to produce or provide it. It also influences the amount that can be produced / provided in any given time period. Thus, the nature of the product will influence objectives relating to costs, volume and efficiency.

Corporate Objectives

Previous sections have highlighted how objectives are set for the whole business and that these provide the boundaries for setting functional objectives. Thus, corporate objectives will clearly influence the functional including operational objectives of the business. These must be consistent with and support the achievement of the business's overall corporate objectives.

Other Functional Objectives

Marketing objectives relating to increasing sales and market share, for example, will directly influence the level of output required by operations staff and, so, targets relating to volume.

Objectives relating to growth through new products either to existing markets or new markets (new product development or diversification in terms of the Ansoff Matrix) will influence operational objectives relating to innovation.

In addition, financial objectives may include achieving certain profit margins which will naturally influence objectives relating to unit costs.

Amount of Finance Available

Achieving operational objectives in the majority of cases, particularly where it involves increasing or improving an element of operations, is likely to incur a financial cost. For example:

- Producing higher volumes is likely to require greater working capital finance.
- Investment in training may be required to improve quality and / or efficiency.
- Cutting costs may be achieved through various means including a move towards a more capital intensive production method involving substantial capital investment.
- Innovation often involves significant investment in research and development.

The amount of finance a business has available or is able and willing to secure through external sources will, obviously, influence the amount that can be spent on operational activities and, thus, the business's operational objectives and plans for their achievement.

Productive Capacity including Size and Quality of the Workforce

The productive capacity of a business will constrain how much can be produced or (in terms of service industries) how many customers can be served at any given time. Hence, it will limit the business's operational objectives, relating to growth in volumes and efficiency in terms of time – at least in the short-term. In the longer-term capacity may be increased, but only if sufficient finance is available to fund this increase and, in terms of labour, any additional staff, with the right skills and experience, can be obtained.

Operational objectives and plans for their achievement will also be constrained by the capabilities of existing plant and equipment and the size and quality of its human resources, not just in terms of capacity to produce greater volumes, but flexibility to produce new products to meet changing customer needs. In terms of innovation, the more multi-skilled the workforce, the more able the business may be to cope with new products and / or processes.

Strength of Worker Representation

Objectives relating to cost minimisation and or increasing efficiency may involve redundancies or significant changes in working practices. These may be opposed and resisted by the workforce and be difficult to achieve, particularly if they have the backing of a strong union.

They might also lead to claims for higher pay, if workers are expected to implement improvements and profits rise as a result, thereby affecting objectives relating to costs.

External Influences

Consumer Needs / Expectations

One of the main functions of operations is to ensure a quality product / service is provided ie one that meets or exceeds customer needs and expectations. Customer needs / expectations, therefore, directly influence objectives relating to quality.

Market and Demand Factors

The size and growth of a market and, ultimately, level of demand for a business's product will, obviously, influence targets relating to production volumes. In a saturated or declining market where competition tends to become more aggressive, emphasis may need to be placed on cost minimisation and improving efficiency in order to maintain competitiveness on price.

Competitor Activities

Businesses are affected by the success or failure of competitors as this may result in increased or decreased demand for their products or services. New competition or more aggressive marketing tactics from competitors may, for example, make it difficult for a business to achieve its objectives relating to output in terms of volume, and may force a business to pursue objectives relating to cutting costs and increasing efficiency in order to secure a competitive advantage through lower prices. Alternatively, they may pursue objectives relating to improving quality in order to maintain sales / market share.

Economic Factors

Economic factors concern the level of interest rates, exchange rates, inflation and employment. Changes in these may affect a business's cost structure and / or the amount of disposable income a consumer might have to spend on goods and services. In a recession, for example, where unemployment is high, firms providing luxury goods tend to be particularly affected. They may have to revise objectives relating to volumes and be forced to cut costs and seek greater efficiencies.

Political and Legal

The government is responsible for setting legislation which often acts as a constraint. New legislation may necessitate costly changes in working practices in order to comply with the legislation - for example - health and safety legislation, which cut into objectives relating to unit costs. Targets relating to the environment are also increasingly common as a result of:

- New legislation introduced relating to the environment and the level of fines imposed on businesses that fail to meet targets on minimising pollution, which are much higher, in real terms, than they ever were.

- Targets set by government for energy use. Large companies gauge themselves against a target set by the government to use less energy than expected, and use this in their marketing to ethical investors. This has led to a move away from coal and oil fired power (fossil fuels) to more modern methods of running a plant such as solar power.

Policies on privatisation and the EU have provided numerous opportunities for business but have also lead to increased competition which, as stated above, forces a business to look at ways to reduce costs and increase efficiency.

The government also influences business activity through its policies on taxation which can have a direct affect on the disposable income of consumers and, thus, demand for a business's product or service and may, therefore, influence objectives relating to output.

Social Influences

Consumers are far more sophisticated and demanding as a result of improvements in education and have, therefore, the power to influence objectives relating to quality.

Changes in the size and structure of the population may also lead to changes in demand for a business's product or service. For example, an ageing population is leading to increased demand for certain types of holidays, medicines and household equipment, thus enabling businesses operating within these markets to set objectives relating to growth in customer numbers and sales which, in turn, influences objectives relating to production volumes. People are also far more health conscious leading to new products and markets influencing objectives relating to innovation.

Targets relating to the environment and the sourcing of products are also increasingly common as a result of:

- The work of pressure groups such as Greenpeace.
- The government actively promoting the need to be conscious about the impact of industrial waste on the environment, and the need to dispose of waste in the correct way.
- An increasingly aggressive media who demand to know what the business plans to do about curbing industrial / process waste and actively seek to expose activities that harm the environment and / or poor working conditions, for example.
- Consumers who (as a result of the above) are far more aware about the effect of greenhouse gases and the wisdom of using recyclable materials, and are increasingly interested in the source of a business's products.

Technological Change

Advances in technology have led to completely new markets eg digital cameras and television, and once popular products becoming obsolete – influencing objectives relating to innovation.

Technological advances also enable businesses to invest in new cost saving machinery and equipment which may help to achieve objectives relating to efficiency and costs.

Cost of Materials, Quality, Reliability and Flexibility of Suppliers

Increases in the cost of materials (or other inputs), as well as the quality, reliability and flexibility of its suppliers will affect the ability of a business to meet and / or exceed customer expectations and can influence objectives relating to quality, volumes, costs, efficiency and innovation.

Closing Comments

It is important to remember that internal and external influences on a business's operational objectives should not only be taken into account when setting objectives – to ensure the objectives set are both realistic and serve to maximise the business's potential, but also when evaluating a business's performance against the objectives set.

4.2

SCALE AND RESOURCE MIX

Choosing the Right Scale of Production: Economies & Diseconomies of Scale

Objectives

By the end of this topic you should be able to:

1. Define the terms scale of production, capacity, economies of scale, diseconomies of scale and unit cost.
2. Outline at least 3 internal economies of scale.
3. Outline at least 2 internal diseconomies of scale.
4. Outline at least 2 other 'costs' associated with increasing the size and scale of operations.
5. Explain, using examples, what is meant by external economies and diseconomies of scale.

Key Terms

Scale of production concerns a business's level of output which depends upon its capacity.

Capacity is the maximum level of output a business can produce within a given period of time using its present resources.

Economies of scale are factors that lead to a reduction in unit costs as a business increases its output / size and scale of operations.

Diseconomies of scale are factors that cause unit costs to rise as a business increases its output / size and scale of operations.

Unit cost / average cost is the total cost (ie fixed and variable) divided by the number of units produced.

External economies and diseconomies of scale arise when an entire industry grows in size.

Scale of Production

Explanation

Scale of production concerns a business's level of output which depends upon its capacity. Capacity can be defined as the maximum level of output a business can produce within a particular period of time eg a week, month, quarter or year, with its present resources, eg capital and labour. Capacity may, for example, be increased by:

- investing in additional capital items eg premises, plant, equipment and vehicles, etc.
- investing in training and staff incentives to increase productivity.
- hiring additional employees.

Importance of Choosing the Right Scale

Choosing the optimum scale of production is a key decision for any business and one that largely depends upon the nature and level of demand for a business's product / service. If capacity is too high in relation to demand then this represents a waste of resources. It means that a business is paying for labour and / or machinery that are not being fully used.
Maximising capacity is vital to any business in order to **minimise wastage of resources / keep fixed costs per unit to a minimum** and, ultimately, **maximise profitability**.

If capacity is too low in relation to demand then in the long-term serious problems can result, each having **a direct effect on costs** and the future reputation of the business. In general, these include:

1. **Long waits for orders to be completed.** If orders have to be met within a guaranteed lead time a business would risk losing customers and / or financial penalties if they failed to complete orders on time.

2. **Less time for routine maintenance.** This could lead to breakdowns and increased downtime which would negatively affect productivity and the likelihood of orders being delivered on time.

3. **Cramped conditions and / or fewer staff breaks.** This makes it more difficult to coordinate and control the business and results in mistakes, and thus, increased returns or complaints and / or staff absence and / or accidents.

4. **Overall drop in morale and motivation increasing labour turnover and associated costs** as a result of the cramped working conditions and / or increased pressure and / or restricted communication with workers. This can, ultimately, result in decreased productivity, increased absenteeism, labour turnover and associated costs.

If demand for a business's product / service is growing, then the decision to increase the size and scale of operations will be influenced by the business's ability to secure the resources (eg finance, labour) it requires.

If the business does increase its scale of operations then it may benefit or suffer from economies or diseconomies of scale.

The Link with Economies and Diseconomies of Scale

As a business grows in scale it may benefit from economies of scale up to a certain level of output. Economies of scale are factors that lead to a reduction in unit cost as a business increases its output / size and scale of operations. (Unit cost / average cost is the total cost ie fixed and variable costs divided by the number of units produced). In other words, doubling the output results in less than double the increase in unit costs. This is mainly because whilst variable costs increase as output increases, fixed costs remain the same (in the short term), and are spread over a greater number of units. Therefore, the average cost per unit is less. In addition, variable costs (and thus the average cost per unit) may actually be lower, due to discounts offered by suppliers on bulk purchases (refer to purchasing economies below).

Beyond a certain point, however, a business will find that its unit costs start increasing as it suffers from diseconomies of scale. These arise from a number of reasons most of which concern the problems of managing large businesses. They are more likely to result when expansion is rapid and appropriate systems are unable to be developed in time to cope with growth.

Economies of Scale

Purchasing

Large businesses are able to buy in bulk, thus reducing unit material (variable) costs. This is because the administration costs involved in handling orders do not rise in direct proportion to the size of the order. In addition, larger orders to suppliers means that they are able to produce in larger quantities, thus benefiting from economies of scale themselves, ie lower unit costs, which enable them to offer their customers more favourable prices on bulk orders.

Technical

As a business grows in size, it can usually afford to install more modern equipment / machinery, which is able to produce items more quickly and more reliably (ie with less error) than manual methods, and therefore, at a lower unit cost (namely labour and material cost).

Greater demand / output also allows a business to set up flow production techniques. These usually require large numbers of unskilled workers (as workers can specialise - see below) and as production is continuous, there are no delays (unlike batch or job), where people are required to move from one process to the next. Consequently, the labour cost per unit is lower. Flow production techniques also often involve the use of specialist equipment which, as stated previously, can increase efficiency and lead to a reduction in costs.

Specialisation

Large businesses are able to split into a number of different departments, with managers specialising in different areas such as marketing, finance, human resources and operations. The workforce can also be divided in such a way that each worker specialises in doing one particular job. In this way people become expert at carrying out one particular task / job as opposed to average at carrying out several. Furthermore, time is not wasted through workers changing from one tool to the next, and little training is required as individual processes are relatively simple. Specialisation, therefore, leads to increased efficiency and a reduction in average cost.

Marketing

There are several economies of scale relating to marketing, as follows:

- Distribution – large businesses may find it more cost effective to acquire their own fleet of vehicles. The cost of distribution will, therefore, be lower as the transport can just be supplied at cost – an external provider of transport would have to add their own margin on top of the cost in order to make a profit.
- Advertising – costs can be spread over a greater output.
- Packaging and market research costs can be shared across increased production levels.
- Personal Selling – the cost of selling 20 products is not double that of selling 10. In addition, the administration costs of selling do not rise in proportion to the size of sale.

Financial

Large businesses are considered more financially secure. They have larger assets to offer as security and are usually more diversified, less vulnerable to competition and, therefore, less risky. Hence banks and financial institutions are more likely to lend them money and offer lower interest rates.

Furthermore, because large businesses are likely to be more widely known they might find it easier to raise funds through shares, as people may be more willing to invest in a company they have actually heard of.

Risk-bearing

Large firms usually produce a range of different products and often operate in several different markets. Diversifying into a number of different activities and markets spreads risk, as it reduces dependence on any one.

Diseconomies of Scale

Communication

Often the larger the firm, the more levels there are through which communication has to flow. This increases bureaucracy, which results in slower decision making, decreased efficiency and increased costs. Individual departments within an organisation may begin to view their activities apart from the activities of other departments and eventually lose sight of the overall goal. It can also lead individual employees to feel isolated and far removed from organisational goals (see below).

Development in information technology eg mobile phones, emails and VoIP (Skype) technology have helped with the communication problems associated with growing businesses, but ensuring effective communication across a range of different units can still be difficult.

Coordination and Control

Co-ordination concerns bringing together the activities of people within the business, ie ensuring the right people, finance, and physical resources, are in the right place, at the right time, and that everyone is working towards a common goal.

As businesses grow, it becomes a major challenge to maintain the tight level of control that is held in small businesses. There are more employees, more paperwork, more levels of hierarchy, more locations, more customers, more markets, and so on. Despite the obvious attraction of growth in terms of revenue and profit, the increase in complexity of a growing business makes coordination and control more difficult. Regular meetings and increased checking procedures may be required to fulfil this function, and this can increase overheads quite significantly in large firms.

Motivation

As suggested above, greater supervision (in order to check and co-ordinate activities) and difficulties with regard to communication, can lead to poor relations between management and workforce, with workers feeling alienated. Ultimately this can lead to low morale and lack of motivation, and result in decreased productivity, increased absenteeism, labour turnover and associated costs.

Technical

This mainly concerns problems relating to mass or flow production techniques, where, if one part of the system breaks down, the whole production process stops.

In addition, an increase in overheads may arise as a result of the need to sustain more complex systems / processes, to aid co-ordination and control.

Other Costs Arising from Growth in Scale

Cost of Financing Growth

On a straight-forward note, an increase in productive capacity is likely to require some form of finance to rent or buy the extra plant and machinery. Such a decision to grow by way of increasing capacity must appear to be justified and well thought through particularly if financed through external sources, otherwise the providers of finance will not wish to take the risk.

With external providers of finance it should also be appreciated that there are financial and non-financial costs depending on the method used, eg interest payments on borrowing, and dilution of ownership and control on the sale of shares.

Strain on Cash Flow

A more complicated issue is that of achieving an increase in output whilst ensuring the cash flow of the business is correctly managed. Many profitable businesses have failed due to their inability to effectively manage cash through periods of growth.

Less Flexibility

One of the great advantages of being a small firm is the flexibility to adapt to changing market conditions and changing customer needs. Corporate America is littered with businesses that grew too large and became extremely complacent about their abilities (as a result of their size). The results of IBM and GM in the early 1990's, with two of the largest corporate losses in history (at that time) is a case in point.

Overworked Employees

Achieving growth in output may involve putting extra pressure on managers and employees. Although this sometimes does prove motivational, there is likely to be a higher rate of absenteeism when there is extra pressure at work.

Closing Comments

All of the above economies of scale occur because of an increase in output (scale) of a particular firm. They can be classed as **internal** economies or diseconomies of scale. When an entire industry grows in size, this can result in **external** economies or diseconomies of scale. Efficiencies may, for example, arise from the following:

- **Infrastructure:** If there is growth of an industry in a particular area eg Silicon Glen in Scotland, then this might mean the local government builds extra roads to facilitate transport to and from the area. This improvement in infrastructure will help to reduce transport costs for all firms in the area, perhaps even those not in that particular industry.

- **Training:** If a firm trains a particular worker and that worker is "poached" by another firm, the second firm gets the qualified worker but with no associated training costs, except the usual induction process.

Diseconomies may occur when demand for resources for firms operating in these growth industries exceeds supply. For example, increased demand for labour, premises and / or supplies might force up the cost of wages, rent and materials / components as firms compete for these resources.

Choosing the Optimal Mix of Resources: Capital & Labour Intensity

Objectives

By the end of this topic you should be able to:

1. Define the terms capital intensity, labour intensity and job, batch, flow and mass production.
2. Outline at least 3 benefits and 3 drawbacks of capital intensive production.
3. Outline at least 1 benefit and 1 drawback of labour intensive production.

Key Terms

Capital or labour intensity refers to the degree to which the production of a product or provision of a service relies more upon the use of capital or labour.

Capital intensive production uses a high proportion of capital resources relative to labour.

Labour intensive production uses a high proportion of labour relative to capital resources.

Job production is where a single item is made or order is processed, from start to finish, usually according to the customer's specifications. It usually involves 'one-off', unique orders which may or may not be repeated.

Batch production is where a large or small quantity (batch) of the same item is produced at the same time. It does not involve the continuous production of items (as with flow production).

Flow production is the continuous production of a large quantity of items.

Mass production is where large volumes of identical products are made to the same standard.

Capital Intensive Strategies

Introduction

A capital intensive production system implies heavy investment in plant, machinery, vehicles and equipment including information technology, which leads to fixed costs being a high proportion of total costs. This is more common to large scale, in particular, mass production and flow production systems.

Flow production is the continuous production of a large quantity of items. It differs from batch and job production (defined later) in that production is **continuous**. It often involves large investment in specialist equipment and machinery and is only appropriate when very large numbers and continuous supply are required.

Mass production is where large volumes of identical products are made to the same standard, thus bringing down the unit cost. As such it can describe both batch and flow methods of production. Unlike low volume batch production, however, it is usually more capital intensive, with specialist equipment being purchased in order to produce a standardised product time after time. Workers are generally not very skilled, often specialising in one particular task, which requires little training.

Benefits

There are often significant costs involved in setting up capital intensive production systems (see drawbacks below). In the medium to longer-term, however, the benefits arising from using a capital intensive process should outweigh the costs as machines tend to be:

- **quicker** than humans at carrying out tasks
- **more reliable** – able to produce consistently, with fewer mistakes than humans.

Therefore, a capital intensive production process might allow a business to:

- minimise production times / complete more orders in a shorter space of time and, thus, more easily keep up to date with increased demand and / or improvements in competitor performance regarding lead times to customers and / or gain a competitive advantage in this respect.
- minimise costs arising from poor quality.
- set more ambitious targets relating to quality, volume and efficiency.

A more capital intensive production process may also enable a business to produce more technically sophisticated products. This would be important in maintaining / gaining a competitive edge, and thus, helping to maintain / increase customer demand for a business's products and, ultimately, sales.

Drawbacks

There are a number of potential drawbacks / problems associated with a move to more capital intensive production methods.

Firstly, there are usually significant set up costs including the initial purchase price of the capital items and, in terms of equipment and machinery, installation and training costs. There are also ongoing costs of maintenance and depreciation. With the exception of any initial training costs, the costs can be minimised through renting and / or leasing rather than purchasing the capital item / asset outright.

Secondly, where it involves a move from labour intensive production, then there are a number of potential problems and difficulties that may be encountered. In addition to the potentially high capital cost, such a move could, for example:

- temporarily **disrupt operations**, resulting in delays to customers while installation and training takes place, unless carefully planned.
- involve **redundancies** – and thus, redundancy payments and cause ill feeling and lower morale amongst remaining employees as these disrupt social relationships, especially if employees have worked together for a long time and there is a strong sense of teamwork.
- lead to some **de-skilling** of the workforce that remains ie less scope for employees to utilise their skills to the full which might even result in lower pay – affecting the achievement of basic and security needs, as well as higher order needs ie esteem and self-actualisation, and thus, potentially lowering motivation and job satisfaction and, ultimately, performance.
- lead to potential **difficulties in learning how to use the new machinery** – causing feelings of anxiety and insecurity – affecting the achievement of safety needs (Maslow).
- encounter **resistance** from the workforce (as a result of points 2-4 above).
- lead to **negative publicity** (due to the above) – affecting sales, at least in the short-term.

In light of the above, the move from a labour intensive production process to a more capital intensive production process requires very careful planning and management in order to minimise the potential disruption to customers and employees.

Labour Intensive Strategies

Introduction

A labour intensive production system is one that uses a high proportion of labour relative to capital, and so, labour costs represent a high proportion of total costs. It is common to businesses that provide individualised / personalised products or services and smaller scale production and to job or batch production systems (see below), as opposed to flow.

Job production is where a single item is made, from start to finish, usually according to the customer's specifications. It usually involves 'one-off', unique orders which may or may not be repeated.

Batch production is where a large or small quantity (batch) of the same item is produced at the same time. It does not involve the continuous production of these items - as with flow production. It is suitable when a limited number of the same product is required at one particular moment in time.

Benefits

Benefits associated with a labour intensive production process mainly concern the fact that there is no up-front capital outlay, lower fixed costs and generally greater flexibility to be gained from employing people over machines. There is also a social benefit – namely the provision of jobs for local people. This can result in positive publicity which may, in turn, help sales – at least in the short-term.

Drawbacks

Labour is a far more complex resource to manage as it involves dealing with human emotions and sensitivities. It may require significant ongoing time and investment in order to attract, motivate and retain staff, especially where competition for labour is high.

The business is also more vulnerable to a range of factors outside its control that affect the availability and cost of labour.

Factors Influencing Choice between Capital and Labour Intensity

There are several factors that will influence the choice between a capital and labour intensive process. The main ones are briefly considered below:

- **Nature of the product** – Some products / services require people to carry them out, for example, hairdressing; the more standardised the business's product / service the greater the relevance and advantages of a capital production process, but this also depends on the level of demand (see below).

- **Customer expectations** – Some processes may be automated but customers prefer personal contact. Many banks and building societies, for example, moved towards the provision of an automated telephone banking service which customers have found frustrating. Some banks have, therefore, reverted back to employing staff to answer customers' telephone enquiries.

- **Level of demand** – The greater the level of demand, the more advantageous the capital intensive production process – due to the high set up costs. As already stated, machinery can produce items or serve customers much more quickly and with less error than humans.

- **The availability of capital and labour** – Machinery or technology may not yet be available to do the job of a human being.

- **The relative cost of capital and labour** – There is a significant difference between countries in the cost of labour. In the developing economies labour is cheap and industries in these countries tend to be labour intensive.

- **Age, size and financial position of the business** – Setting up a capital intensive process can, as stated, be expensive and may not be feasible for a new start-up or small business.

Closing Comments

The move from a labour intensive process to a more capital intensive process can have a significant impact on the staff that remain and negatively affect morale, motivation and performance. In such cases it is vital to ensure the change is managed sensitively and carefully. Making staff aware of the reasons behind the decision and the longer-term benefits would help foster commitment to seeing the change through. Actually consulting staff about the change and how the change should be implemented would also help to minimise potential opposition. It allows conflict to arise and be resolved at an early stage. It also provides first hand information and expertise, which may improve original ideas regarding the changes and how they should be implemented. It is also likely to lead to greater commitment because if the workforce have 'had a say' in the decisions regarding the changes, this can make them feel valued and more willing to see the changes through.

4.3
INNOVATION

Innovation, Research and Development

Objectives

By the end of this topic you should be able to:

1. Define the terms innovation, research and development, and value analysis.
2. Distinguish between innovation, creativity and invention.
3. State the main drivers of innovation.
4. Explain the stages involved in innovation and research and development.
5. Outline the implications of innovation to finance, marketing and human resources.

Key Terms

Innovation is the successful implementation of a new idea eg new product, process, approach, strategy. It should be distinguished from both creativity and invention. Creativity concerns idea generation. Invention is a technical process of perfecting an idea. Innovation requires ideas to be put into action and is concerned with the commercial application of the idea or invention.

Research and development: Research is the study of a particular subject or market in order to further knowledge in this subject or market; development is the application of this knowledge resulting in new products or ways of doing things.

Value analysis is a process which seeks to cut the costs of producing a product without reducing the 'value' of the product from the customer's perspective, and / or increasing the value of a particular product (in the eyes of the customer) without increasing the production costs.

Introduction to Innovation, Research and Development

Types of Innovation

Innovation is the successful implementation of a new idea, for example:

- the successful introduction of a new product to the marketplace.
- the successful application of a new process within a business.
- the successful implementation of a new approach / way of doing things eg a new organisational structure.
- the successful implementation of a new strategy eg successful entry into a new market or, even, creation of a new market.

It is clear from the above that innovation does not just concern new product development. Neither, does it necessarily concern something totally new. It may, for example, involve the modification of an existing product, process or strategy. Innovations can, in fact, be classed according to the extent to which they vary in terms of familiarity to the people involved. For example, they may be regarded as incremental, substantial, radical, or revolutionary.

From a business perspective whatever the type and 'level' of innovation, the innovation should lead to **increased value** either for the customer and / or the business concerned.

Distinguishing between Innovation, Creativity and Invention

Innovation should be distinguished from creativity and invention. The former concerns idea generation. The latter is purely a technical process of perfecting an idea. Innovation requires the idea to be put into action - to be bought to 'life', and is concerned with the commercial application of the idea or the invention.

Drivers of Innovation

Innovation can be driven by:

- changes in demand (demand pull).
- technological breakthroughs (technological push).

Changes in demand may stem from changes in social factors and / or competitor activities, and be evident in declining products / falling sales.

Incremental innovation often takes place in order to extend the life of a product.

More radical innovation is often involved in replacing products that are in decline.

Research and Development

One of the key activities associated with innovation is research and development:

Research can be defined as the study of a particular subject or market in order to further knowledge in this subject or market.

Development is the application of this knowledge resulting in new products or processes.

In detail R and D involves:

- carrying out research into new ideas / areas of interest.
- inventing, designing, testing and developing new ideas to meet customer and / or business needs and complying with legal requirements.
- assisting in the development of prototypes (where applicable) and / or the selection, installation, construction of equipment necessary to implement new products or processes.
- modifying existing products or processes in light of changing business / customer needs and / or competitor activities.
- gaining feedback on new (or modifications of existing) products or processes.

The Stages Involved in Innovation

Identification of New Ideas

The process of Innovation begins with idea generation. New ideas may stem from market research into customers and / or competitor activities, group brainstorming sessions, and / or scientific / laboratory research.

Screening & Selection of New Ideas

A scientific approach is then used to gradually narrow down options and select ideas to go through to the next stage of development. **Value analysis** (see below) is often used to help with the screening and selection of new products, or modifications of existing products.

Detailed Investigation into New Ideas

This stage consists of in-depth research. This may involve consumer research, competitor research, and / or product research ie investigation into materials and methods of production.

Pilot Production / Production of a Prototype

If the above investigation suggests an idea has potential, the business may produce a prototype and / or undergo a pilot stage. In the case of a new product, or a process involving the development of new machinery / equipment, this will enable it to assess whether it can be produced according to the business or customer (whichever is relevant) and legal requirements, and is capable of being produced cost effectively / at a profit.

Testing and Review

This involves the launch of a new product / process on a limited scale to assess consumer / staff reaction and forecast the outcome eg future sales (in the case of a new product) or future savings (in the case of a new process). As previously outlined in the sub-section on test marketing (in the section on 'Methods of Analysing Trends' above), after this initial testing a business is likely to consider the following before investing in a full launch:

1. Is it likely to meet a defined **business / customer need**?
2. In the case of a new product - to what **segment(s)** can it be sold?
3. In the case of a new product - what **position** is it likely to occupy in the market place?
4. Does it fit in with the overall **objectives** of the firm?
5. Will it improve or diminish the firm's **image / reputation**?
6. What are the marketing, financial, operational, HR **implications**?
7. Does the firm have the necessary **resources** eg: Management & staff with the time, skills, experience; appropriate technology or operational systems; adequate finance?
8. If not, can they be **obtained**? at what **cost**?
9. Are the **contribution** possibilities worthwhile?
10. What will the effect be on the firm's **overall financial position**?
11. Are there any **legal aspects** to consider?
12. When is the best **time** to launch? Can the firm **keep to schedule**?

Full Launch

As previously outlined, if the majority of the answers to the above questions are in favour (or all if the business is risk-adverse), then the business will launch the product or implement the new process / approach / strategy on a full scale.

The Use of Value Analysis

Overview

Value analysis is often used to screen out and select products. It is a process which seeks to cut the costs of producing a product without reducing the 'value' of the product from the customer's perspective, and / or increasing the value of a particular product (in the eyes of the customer) without increasing the production costs.

What it Involves

It essentially involves assessing new or existing products against three key criteria, namely:

- **Function** – this concerns what the product is supposed to be able to do, eg the function of a kettle is to boil water.
- **Aesthetics** – this concerns how the product looks, eg in terms of size, shape, and colour – the extent to which it is 'pleasing to the eye'.
- **Cost / economy of manufacture** – this concerns the cost of producing the product ie the direct costs.

Products are subsequently designed to:

- maximise customer value.
- minimise the costs of production.

The relative value placed by customers with regard to these areas will depend upon the nature of the product and customers' individual needs and expectations. For example:

- Machines in a factory need to be more capable of doing the job than aesthetically pleasing;
- In developed economies - the emphasis for clothes may need to be on aesthetics rather than function;
- Cars are often purchased according to their ability to satisfy both criteria equally.

Products are usually assessed by a mixed team of specialists in order to view them from all the required angles. The value analysis team usually includes:

- designers,
- finance staff, and
- sales and marketing staff.

Value analysis requires this team of experts to:

- brainstorm all the essential functions that the product must be able to perform in order to satisfy customer requirements.
- consider the importance of aesthetics in selling the product.
- brainstorm as many ways of achieving these essential function(s) without affecting aspects relating to aesthetics considered important in selling the product.
- cost the alternatives.
- investigate the cheapest alternatives.
- select the best option.

The process usually requires:

- market research to assess the opinions and perceptions of customers.
- the production of prototypes to enable any products or product modifications made as a result of value analysis, to be properly assessed.

The Implications of Innovation for Finance, Marketing and Human Resources

Finance

Innovation can be an expensive and time consuming process and needs to be budgeted for. Payback of innovation is usually a longer period than most capital investment and, therefore, expenditure on innovation must be considered carefully with the finance department. The finance department may also want to carry out some form of investment appraisal before committing funds for the commercial implementation of the new idea.

Marketing

Market research is the process of identifying and investigating the needs of customers and the state of the market. It is tempting to assume that innovation and, in particular, the research and development stage, is solely devoted to the work of scientists in laboratories, probably because the media frequently announces new medical breakthroughs. However, innovation involves a considerable amount of market (as opposed to scientific) research. For example innovation requires:

- Information on customer needs and expectations.
- Reports on new products and processes, which may help, improve current products or production methods in terms of cost and product quality.
- Customer feedback on product tests.
- Customer feedback on any modifications.
- Information on competitor activities.

This market research is essential to enable products to be developed and modified in line with market / customer requirements.

Innovation is also often linked to product life cycles. When a product is nearing maturity R and D is responsible for researching and developing ways to extend the product's life cycle eg by re-launching the same product with one or two design modifications, as well as completely replacing products that are in the decline stage. Close liaison is, therefore, required between the marketing department and R and D function to ensure the timely development and implementation of extension strategies and new / replacement products.

HR

Innovation, whether of products or processes, necessarily results in change which can be unsettling for the workforce. It might involve changes to working practices and / or retraining, especially if the new product or process is technical. Any such changes will, therefore, need to be handled sensitively and carefully.

Closing Comments

Research and development should be fully integrated within the business. Isolating this department will - for example - result in products that either cannot be manufactured at the target cost or, more seriously, products that are not required by customers.

Purpose, Costs, Benefits and Risks of Innovation

Objectives

By the end of this topic you should be able to:

1. Outline at least 7 purposes and associated benefits of innovation.
2. Outline the 2 costs and 2 risks associated with innovation.

Purpose and Benefits of Innovation

The purpose of innovation can be linked to organisational goals often concerning growth, competitiveness and profitability and it can bring numerous benefits in these respects. A wide range of reasons for innovating including potential benefits are outlined below.

- **Improve quality and / or increase added value** - improvements in product / service quality and / or the development of unique product attributes may help improve a business's reputation, attract customers, maximise sales and gain market share, and / or enable higher prices to be charged, thereby maximising profitability.

- **Extend the life of a product** - in order to maintain sales and / or market share.

- **Extend the product range** - in order to expand the customer base and increase sales and / or ensure a balanced product portfolio.

- **Replace declining products** - in order to maintain sales and profits.

- **Respond appropriately to competitor activities** in order to maintain sales / market share.

- **Enter a new market** eg through new products and / or new approaches to marketing - making the business less vulnerable to changes in existing markets and / or allowing a business to more easily achieve objectives relating to growth and profitability - if existing markets are saturated or suffering from increasing competition.

- **Create a new market** - for similar reasons to those cited for entering a new market above.

- **Make use of spare capacity / Increase capacity utilisation** - keeping down fixed costs per unit.

- **Reduce costs (material, labour, energy), increase efficiency and / or productivity** through new types of materials and / or new production processes – providing the business with greater flexibility over price and / or higher profit margins.

- **Reduce the impact of the business's activities on the environment** through new environmentally friendly methods of packaging or more environmentally friendly processes - this may help create a positive image and generate positive publicity which, in turn, can help attract customers, employees and potential investors.

- **Comply with legislation** – new legislation might necessitate changes to products and / or processes – compliance may be essential to avoid financial penalties and negative publicity from non-compliance.

One other benefit arising from a business that manages to innovate successfully is that this can engender a **sense of pride** amongst staff who work there. This can be motivational – helping to satisfy employees' esteem needs. Publicity surrounding the innovation may also **help to attract and recruit high calibre staff** more easily in the future.

Costs and Risks

The Cost of Research and Development and Launch / Implementation

Innovation involves a significant cost in terms of **research and development**. The more novel the product the greater the research and development and market research costs. The more science involved in the R and D process, the more the overall costs involved because research scientists are in short supply so they cost more. Some industries, however, require extensive scientific research and innovation can only be achieved if the business is committed to invest in the appropriate level of scientific technology. For example, in the pharmaceutical industry, companies are unlikely to spend any less than 10% of revenue on R and D and often invest for products between 5 and 10 years into the future.

Technological development has helped to improve and speed up the process of R & D. For example, computer aided design (CAD) enables new products to be viewed on a computer screen in 3D, then quickly and easily modified. This enables firms to invent and modify products much more quickly, thereby reducing lead-time and development costs. The reduction in lead-time enables products to reach the market place much more quickly and ensures a faster response to competitor activities. R and D also allows firms to invent products much more cheaply, as it reduces (and in some cases, eliminates) the need to build expensive prototypes. The reduction in development costs can be passed on to the customer or, alternatively, the business can enjoy higher profits. Overall CAD can help a business be more competitive.

Besides the research and development costs there are the additional costs associated with the launch and implementation of new products and / or processes, for example, training costs and the cost of a promotional campaign to launch a new product. These costs can be substantial.

The High Failure Rate and High Cost of Failure

Only a small number of innovations are successful. The main reasons for this are cited below. Many of these are internal factors that are, largely under the business's control. Some, however, concern external factors that are outside the business's control (such as competition) which are often unforeseen / unexpected:

- Inadequate market research (can lead to other causes below).
- Product defects – poor design, quality control.
- Greater costs than anticipated – rejected or postponed due to inadequate finance / budgetary constraints.
- Poor timing – eg launch of Christmas product in Jan / Feb.
- Inadequate marketing effort to reach target market.
- Inadequate sales force – lack of skills, too few.
- Weaknesses in distribution – eg if they sell to a wholesaler and / or retailer and merchandising is left to them, they may not display the product in a prominent place.
- Staff resistance to change and poor implementation of the changes required.
- Resistance from consumers.
- Competition – close substitutes in the market place.
- Restrictive legislation – eg cloning is illegal in the UK.
- Inadequate technologies – the new product may not be able to be produced cost effectively using current technologies.

Failure is an inevitable part of innovation and can not only lead to loss of the investment, but poor staff morale and increased scepticism and greater resistance to change in the future.

No Guarantee of Success Due to External Factors

As mentioned in the previous sub-section there are numerous external, uncontrollable, largely unforeseeable factors that can affect the success or otherwise of the implementation of a new idea. Even if a business undertakes thorough research and testing, has adequate resources to see the idea through, and is able to implement the necessary changes associated with the idea successfully, the fact is there is still no guarantee of success. A change in market and economic conditions – outside the business's control, might result in failure of the new product. For example:

- Changes in interest rates might affect the demand for a new product and the costs involved in producing it.
- The innovations of rivals might undermine the advantages that the company hopes to gain (discussed further below).

The Ease with which Ideas Can be Copied

One major problem associated with innovation is that ideas can often be easily and quickly copied. It may not take rival companies long to analyse the new improved product (or process) and then produce their own version without the expense of original research and development.

Some innovations may be able to be protected through the use of patents (covered in Unit 1) and / or confidentiality agreements between the business and its employees, suppliers or other stakeholders involved in the research, development and implementation of the idea.

The Impact of Innovations on the Workforce

As suggested in the previous section, some innovations may be unsettling and have a negative impact on employees, especially if new processes replace some of the existing labour force, or new approaches to operations change work groups in other ways.

Closing Comments

Despite the costs and risks involved, innovation is essential in the modern business world. Successful businesses will invest continually in innovation and R and D, as opposed to having one-off programmes of idea / new product development. This is becoming all the more important in light of:

- increased competition.
- rapidly changing technologies.
- higher customer expectations.

For many businesses, when profits fall, it can be tempting to cut costs on those areas where there is no immediate payback. Frequently, R and D is such an area. Most businesses, however, operate within an increasingly competitive marketplace and if they do not engage in innovation they will lose out to rivals who do. In other words, despite the costs and risks, innovation should not be seen as an optional extra but an as an imperative that should be budgeted for.

4.4

LOCATION

Methods of Making Location Decisions

Objectives

By the end of this topic you should be able to:

1. Outline at least 6 quantitative factors affecting location or relocation decisions.
2. Outline how break-even analysis and investment appraisal techniques might be used to help make location decisions.
3. Outline at least 3 qualitative factors affecting location decisions.

Key Terms

Quantitative factors are factors that can be measured in some way. In the context of location decisions they include the nature of the business, the cost and availability of land, premises, finance (to purchase land and premises), access / proximity to supplies, the availability of government incentives, infrastructure, proximity and access to the market, and the state of the local economy.

Qualitative factors are factors that concern people's attitudes, beliefs, feelings, opinions, perceptions, values and prior experience. In the context of location decisions they include tradition, image, labour relations, owner's preference and quality of life.

Investment appraisal - in the context of location decisions - involves comparisons between cash inflows (revenues) and cash outflows (costs) at different locations. It concerns the speed at which the actual investment involved in locating at a particular site is paid back, or the rate of return on the investment.

Break-even analysis - in the context of location decisions - involves examining the behaviour of costs and revenues in relation to the output likely to be achieved at different locations, and predicting what is likely to happen with regard to profit at these different locations.

Introduction

There are a range of aspects to consider in relation to the determination of the best location(s) for a business. Whilst these aspects apply in principle to **all** businesses, the **nature of the business** will determine the importance of each factor. For example, a traditional retail business will need to be located near to its target customer base. In contrast, minimising production costs will be the prime consideration for a manufacturing business.

These factors can generally be broken down into quantitative and qualitative factors. Quantitative and qualitative factors affecting location decisions have already been discussed in detail in our Elementary Explanations relating to Unit 1 (on 'Factors Influencing Start-up Locations'). The main points raised in this former Unit are outlined below. Each of these factors will need to be identified and assessed in terms of their significance for the business in question. The assessment will involve quantification where possible (which may include techniques such as investment appraisal and break-even analysis) and value judgement.

Quantitative Factors

Availability and Cost of Land / Premises

This factor concerns the size / area, contour, suitability of land or premises for further expansion, and likelihood of obtaining planning permission for any required changes.

The price of land / property affects a business's fixed costs. This factor is likely to be relatively more important than other factors for businesses requiring large areas of land or property, eg wholesalers.

If a business has limited funds, renting rather than the outright purchase of property may be the only affordable option. As well as the amount to be paid, consideration needs to be given to the terms of the lease and, in particular, the length of the lease. A short term lease has the advantage that if the location proves unsatisfactory, the business is not committed to make leasing payments far beyond closure. On the other hand, a short term lease has the disadvantage of a possible relocation or increase in the rental in a year or so.

Businesses also require permission from the local planning authority for any new building or any change of use. It is, therefore, important to realise that businesses do not have complete freedom in the choice of location. Not only are they constrained by financial factors, they are also constrained by legal factors.

Availability and Cost of Capital to Purchase the Land / Premises and Fund any Relocation Decisions

A business may have insufficient internal finance to fund a particular location decision and may be forced to borrow in order to raise the capital required. If so, this will increase the fixed costs involved in the location decision. Grants, however, may be available in certain regions to help reduce the fixed costs (discussed later in this section).

Availability and Cost of Labour in terms of Numbers and Levels of Skill

This is often influenced by the availability of social amenities such as housing and medical facilities. As with land and property, the price of labour will vary across regions. This factor affects both fixed (in terms of management salaries) and variable costs.

A business may also take into account the strike record of employees within a particular area, level of absenteeism and labour turnover, and attitude towards work eg flexible working practices. All these have implications for productivity and costs. This factor becomes more important for labour intensive industries, particularly those requiring a highly skilled workforce.

Access / Proximity to Materials / Supplies / Technology

Certain companies still locate close to their principal suppliers. For example, Marmite has a factory close to the brewers in Burton-upon-Trent, who produce all the yeast extract the company uses. This can help to keep transportation (and, therefore, variable) costs down.

This is particularly important for 'bulk-reducing' industries, eg iron and steel, where it is cheaper to transport the finished goods to market rather than transport the raw materials to the manufacturing plant.

This factor is of major importance for most primary industries where firms must locate where the resources can be found.

Government Grants and Tax Breaks

If the government wishes to boost an area of low economic activity, it may provide incentives, such as grants and tax breaks. Such government aid will, obviously, help to reduce costs.

Access and Proximity to Customers (the Market)

Being close to customers is essential for those businesses where customers travel to the premises, and where convenience is an important factor for customers in order to maximise revenues, for example, in the case of supermarkets and hairdressers. The same principle applies to restaurants and hotels. In order to build up a regular customer base and / or generate income from passing trade, premises need to be located in an area that is easily accessible by foot or by car, or public transport. A poor location in this context could clearly result in poor revenues and, ultimately, business failure.

Close proximity to customers is also important for manufacturers in order to gain an edge over the competition in securing key business contracts. Being close to customers means transport costs and lead-times can be reduced, and flexibility of delivery schedules increased.

Other examples relating to proximity to customers include: time share businesses operating solely in holiday destinations, and construction companies having deliberately located in hot climates, to capitalise on the growth in demand for hotels and apartments.

However, not all businesses need to locate close to customers and this is, largely, down to the **development of information technology.** Rapid advances in IT have freed many service businesses from the requirement to be geographically close to customers. Consider the provision of finance services such as insurance. Information and communications technology has meant that a financial service business can base itself anywhere in the country (or even the world), and still offer a good service to customers by electronic links.

Infrastructure

The infrastructure consists of the transport network and utilities which provide a service to the community and to business. So, as well as the road and railway network for example, it includes electricity, gas and water supplies, sewerage, telephone and broadband links.

Traditional theory on location considered access to electricity, telecommunications systems, and a good road network, as essential. These are important in keeping down both fixed costs (in terms of initial utility installation costs) and particularly the variable costs (relating to transport / distribution). But, as the level of infrastructure in the western world has improved, utilities are things that we now take for granted and this factor has become less significant than being close to suppliers or being close to customers.

It is tempting to think that infrastructure is not relevant to **e-commerce** business organisations. However, although an on-line bookseller, for example, does not have to be based in large cities (where rent is high) the product still has to be despatched by 'snail mail', and so it is advantageous to develop a location close to the main transport links. In the 19th century this always meant close to the railways but, today, we find the distribution centres of on-line retailers close to motorway junctions (eg Amazon).

The same principle applies to distribution centres of large 'bricks and mortar' retailers such as Tesco and Sainsbury. There is a great need to be close to the motorway network and many of the largest out of town shopping centres are located close to motorway junctions (eg Lakeside in Essex and Bluewater in Kent).

Location of Competitors

This factor affects revenues. It is tempting to say that any business should locate itself away from rivals as locating near competitors may force businesses to keep prices down if there is very little difference between its product / service. However, locating next to competitors may actually help maximise revenues, as customers are drawn to areas where there is plenty of choice in one central location. There are, in fact, many examples of rival firms clustering together, for example, it is common to see clothes shops, banks, estate agents and solicitors clustering together in the same geographical location.

The State of the Local Economy

The state of the local economy is also an important factor with regard to both costs and revenues. If for example, the local economy is in a recession, labour may be cheap but revenues may be affected due to the high level of unemployment.

Relocation Costs

For an established business that is considering relocating to another area there may be significant costs involved that need to be taken into account. These might include:

- the costs of notifying key stakeholders including customers, suppliers, shareholders, government offices, Companies House.
- the cost of changing business stationery to include the new address and other contact details.
- possible redundancy payments if staff are unable or willing to move and / or the firm is not willing to pay towards staff relocation costs.
- possible lost production time while the move takes place.
- interest payable on any loan used to fund re-location.

Qualitative Factors

Image

Certain locations are renowned for being a source of quality products, for example, Scotland for whisky, London for financial services. Locating in such areas may enable a business to charge higher prices and, therefore, can affect revenues. Although the willingness of a customer to pay a higher price can be measured and so could be quantified, this factor essentially concerns customer's perceptions and so image should be classified as a qualitative factor.

Tradition

Staying in the same place, despite economic attractions elsewhere is an example of industrial inertia. This is often largely due to high investment in fixed assets ie buildings and machinery but, also, the perceived inconvenience of moving.

Labour Relations

A business that values its workforce may refuse to relocate despite cheaper costs and better access to the market at an alternative site, if it means it will lose its current workforce (even if quality labour is available at the alternative site).

Owners' Preference

Despite all the theory involved, there might be a very simple reason, which is not business-based, such as the managing director's husband or wife wanting to play at a particular famous tennis club and this being one of the prime reasons why a business locates in a particular area.

Quality of Life

Linked to the above, a business may locate in an area where there is beautiful scenery, excellent leisure and medical facilities, no congestion, low pollution, low crime rate, etc for the benefit of the owners and employees.

Quantitative Techniques of Analysis

Introduction

For the majority of businesses ie those within the commercial private sector of the economy, in evaluating the options the effect on fixed costs, variable costs, and revenues will require assessment and evaluation.

- **Fixed costs.** These are costs that remain the same (at least in the short term) regardless of the output quantity, eg number of products produced, number of people served, etc. These include, for example, rent (if premises are leased instead of purchased outright), business rates, salaries of managers and financing costs (ie interest payable on loans used to fund a move / relocation).

- **Variable costs.** These are costs that vary according to output quantity, eg number of products produced, number of people served, etc. These include, for example, the costs of materials / components, transporting materials to the firm and goods to the market, the cost of utilities, and direct labour costs.

- **Revenues.** By being based at one particular location, the business might be restricting its access to a particular market. For example, a shop situated on a busy high street is likely to experience higher sales as a result of greater passing trade than one situated in a side street. Lower rent may be possible in a side street but such a shop may have to spend more money on advertising in order to attract customers (although, again, this depends on the nature of product - if the shop is specialised, a high street location may not be needed as there is no competition).

Profitability will generally be the objective of commercial businesses and, therefore, the relationship between costs and revenues is paramount. For example, higher costs may be justified if accompanied by proportionately higher revenues which yield greater profit. Conversely, lower revenues may be justified if accompanied by proportionately lower costs. Either scenario will increase profitability.

For **non-profit making organisations** such as public services the cost element consideration would be the same as for profit making organisations but one would need to assess **level of service** provided as a substitute for revenue. In this case, higher costs may be justified if accompanied with a proportionately higher level of service.

Two of the main techniques for assessing the costs and revenues and potential profitability of location decisions include break-even analysis and investment appraisal. These are considered in turn below.

Breakeven Analysis

Break-even analysis has been discussed in Unit 1 of our Elementary Explanations but not in the context of location decisions. In this context it involves examining the behaviour of costs and revenues in relation to the output likely to be achieved at different locations, and predicting what is likely to happen with regard to profit at these different locations.

If a business is able to break-even more quickly at one location than another location, then clearly there are advantages in this, especially because of lower risk. However, it is important to appreciate that breaking even more quickly might not necessarily mean more profit, because the cost structures might be different (the weighting between fixed and variable costs). Refer to the figures below:

Cost/Revenues/Profit	Site X	Site Y
Fixed costs per annum	£600,000	£860,000
Variable costs per unit	£8	£6
Expected selling price per unit	£14	£14
Breakeven (FC/Contribution)	100,000 units	107,500 units
Expected Demand	190,000 units	180,000 units
Forecast Profit	£540,000 (90,000 x £6)	£580,000 (72,500 x £8)

The above table shows that even though break-even is lower and the potential market is higher at Site X, the profit for Y is greater, given the state of the market.

Another numerical issue to consider is at what point the Site Y becomes more profitable than site X. This level of output must then be considered carefully by the business in terms of the likelihood of reaching it, otherwise, the profitability argument has no weight. Refer to the diagram below.

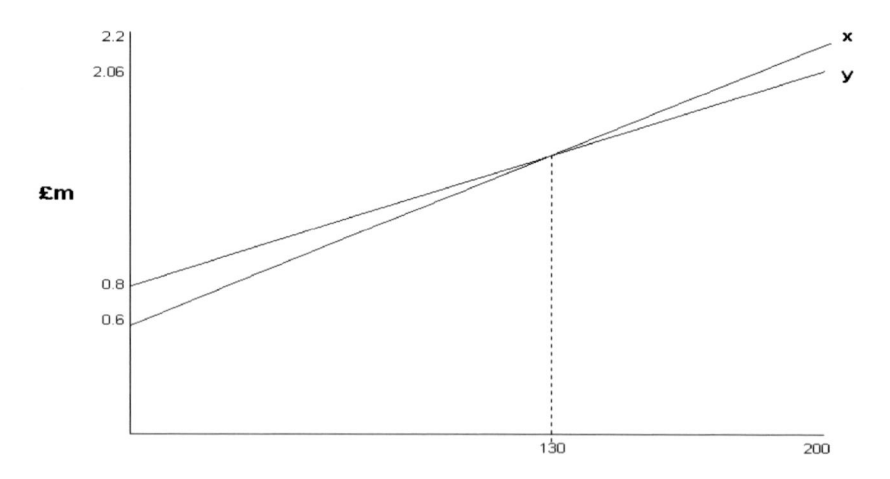

In the above case, the total costs of Site X become greater than Y if output is over 130,000 units. Hence, once this level of output is reached, the business becomes less profitable at Site Y. It must, therefore, assess the likelihood of meeting this level of output <u>consistently</u>.

Investment Appraisal

Investment appraisal has already been considered in depth in a previous section of these Elementary Explanations. In the context of location decisions it involves comparisons between cash inflows (revenues) and cash outflows (costs) at different locations. It concerns the speed at which the actual investment involved in locating at a particular site is paid back or the rate of return on the investment.

If a site has not been purchased, ie if there is no initial investment, then payback and, indeed average rate of return becomes irrelevant. However, discounted cash flow can be used, even though there is no initial investment.

If a business **relocates** - as many businesses seeking growth often do - it will certainly have moving costs and communication costs (in terms of informing its shareholders, suppliers and customers of its new location), as well as possible redundancy payments (if the move is to a location some distance away, or the new location will be more capital intensive). Thus, it is frequently possible to use all three investment appraisal criteria to assess relocation.

Closing Comments

There are other factors not mentioned in this section that a business will consider when choosing between international locations, for example, political stability, exchange rates and ethical issues surrounding the employment of low wage labour. Some of these have already been mentioned in the section under Marketing Strategies concerning entry into international markets. They are, however, also relevant to 'Issues Relating to International Location' - considered in a subsequent section below.

Benefits of Optimal Location

Objectives

By the end of this topic you should be able to:

1. Explain what is meant by the term 'optimal location'.
2. Outline the benefits of the optimal location.

Key Terms

The **optimal location** is one where the benefits of the location (financial or otherwise) outweigh the costs (financial or otherwise).

What is Meant by 'Optimal' Location?

Decisions concerning where to locate are complex. They involve the evaluation of a wide range of financial and non-financial factors.

As the previous section has highlighted - through the use of various examples - not every factor will be relevant to all businesses and some factors will be more important to some than others.

The relevance and importance of each factor will largely depend upon the **nature of the business** and the optimal location will be the location where the **benefits** (financial or otherwise) outweigh the **costs** (financial or otherwise) to the particular business in question.

Benefits of Optimal Location

The benefits of a particular location might be:

- **Lower costs** (fixed and / or variable).
- **Greater revenues** and / or **level of service** eg through greater access to customers and / or improved access to resources enabling the business to respond more quickly to changing customer needs.
- **Greater profits** (as a result of 1 and 2 above) and, thus, greater return on capital employed and greater return to owners / shareholders, and / or **greater funds for re-investment**.

Closing Comments

Ultimately, the optimal location will be the one that helps the business to achieve its prime objective. For businesses in the private profit making sector, this is likely to mean locating in an area that maximises profit. For a non-profit making or public sector business, this is likely to mean locating in an area that minimises costs and / or maximises the service provided to the local community.

The Advantages and Disadvantages of Multi-site Locations

Objectives

By the end of this topic you should be able to:

1. Define the terms site, single-site and multi-site location.
2. Outline at least 6 advantages associated with multi-site locations.
3. Outline at least 3 disadvantages associated with multi-site locations.

Key Terms

A **site** is a physical location of a business.

A **single site** refers to one physical location.

Multi-site refers to the occupation by a business of more than one physical location. This may involve sites in the same or different grounds, town, city, county, country.

Introduction

Multi-site locations occur when a business occupies more than one physical location. This could involve the occupation of an additional site within the same grounds, town, city, county, country as its current site, or an additional site in a different area or country. Businesses that operate sites in more than one country are known as multi-nationals.

Advantages and Disadvantages

Advantages

A multi-site location may:

- **permit specialisation** ie with each site focusing on producing / providing one particular product / service or range of products / services and becoming expert at meeting the needs of customers of that product / service.

- **spread risk** - as the business is less vulnerable to changes affecting one particular site. This is especially the case when it involves sites in different countries, for example, if one country is in recession, and the other in a growth period, occupying a site in the second country will lessen the risk the firm faces, especially if it sells an income elastic product.

- **enable growth** - for example - a retail business may be limited in the number of customers it can serve from one single location, especially given the choice between outlets within driving or, even, walking distance now available. Only by opening another site can it reach a wider customer base.

- **improve the service provided to customers** - if it means the business is located closer to its customers. This is because it should enable the business to better understand and respond more appropriately and quickly to customers' needs / expectations.

- **secure lower costs.** A business with customers that are geographically spread may be able to reduce transport and distribution costs by opening other sites closer to customers. This is particularly relevant to a business serving customers in different countries.
- **avoid some diseconomies of scale** - for example - the optimum size of a factory might be 40 employees with 1 works manager. Increasing the size of the factory on this site might add more to fixed costs and significantly raise the break-even point. In contrast, locating an additional smaller unit elsewhere might be a more economical way of increasing the size and scale of the business.
- **minimise disruption of existing operations.** If a site is running perfectly well, a business might choose to leave this site running and open an additional site elsewhere in order to increase the scale of the business, rather than risk disruption to existing operations.
- **be cheaper than expansion on an existing site.**
- **provide greater flexibility.** For example, in the event that the business had to scale down for any reason, it may be able to close one site and leave the most profitable site running.

Disadvantages

It should be appreciated that many of the above advantages could actually form disadvantages. For example, if it involves specialisation by plant, there may be some **duplication of resources and facilities.** For instance, it is likely to require quality control departments, engineering / maintenance departments and some administrative function to be located at each site, which will **add to costs.** It might also increase the quantity and cost of stockholding. If some stock is common to all sites there might be some duplication of stock.

However, the most common disadvantages associated with multi-site locations generally include the following:

- **More difficult to manage – problems with communication, coordination and control.** It is much more complex to manage a business that is geographically spread out than a business that is based on a single site location. Without effective communication and, potentially, less contact with the original owner / senior managers, individual sites may begin to view their activities apart from the activities of other sites and eventually lose sight of the overall goal.
- **Potential loss in economies of scale.** Suppliers may, for example, not offer discounts on items delivered to two separate sites even if the order relates to the same business, especially if the ordering is not centralised, ie instead of orders for supplies being collated from the two sites and one large order being placed with suppliers, two separate orders are placed at two separate times.

Closing Comments

There may be other advantages and disadvantages than those listed above when it involves sites in different countries. Issues relating to international location are, however, considered in the previous section (as required by the specifications).

Whatever the nature of the business, some of the problems associated with managing two or more business units on different sites, can be minimised by establishing:

- a clear mission, aims and objectives – communicated throughout all levels of the organisation - to ensure everyone works towards a common goal.
- a clear structure with clear lines of accountability, responsibility and reporting procedures.
- regular communication to clarify job requirements, expectations and outcomes.

Issues Relating to International Location

Objectives

By the end of this topic you should be able to:

1. Define the terms off-shoring, protectionism, quotas and tariffs.
2. Outline 2 reasons for international location.
3. Outline at least 6 issues relating to international location.

Key Terms

Off-shoring is the relocation of a business process eg manufacturing, customer service or accounting, from one country to another country.

Protectionism is a policy of protecting domestic producers by imposing barriers such as quotas and tariffs on imports.

Quotas are limits on the amount that can be imported into a country.

Tariffs are fees levied on goods imported into a country.

Reasons for International Location

General

The main reasons for locating operations abroad are to:

- sell to overseas markets.
- secure lower production costs.
- secure lower production costs <u>and</u> sell to markets overseas.

To Sell to Foreign Markets – Global Markets

Selling to foreign markets has already been discussed in the previous section on entering international markets. As this section explained in detail, overseas opportunities arise as a result of economic growth and rising living standards abroad, and selling to foreign markets might be a way of achieving growth and profit objectives as a result of recession or saturation in domestic markets. It can also spread risk and help gain internal and external economies of scale. Certain foreign countries / cities are also renowned for their reputation for certain products eg Paris for perfume, Milan for fashion, and so locating in these areas may provide substantial marketing benefits to a business specialising in these products.

To Secure Lower Costs

Many businesses relocate some or all parts of the business from the home country to another country in order to take advantage of lower costs. Where a business relocates a particular process eg manufacturing, customer service or accounting, from one country to another country, this is called **off-shoring**.

© APT Initiatives Limited, 2009

Many manufacturing firms have, in fact, set up or outsourced production abroad to take advantage of lower production costs – in particular lower labour costs. For example, in 2002 Dyson appliances moved their production operations from their base in Wiltshire to Malaysia. Such a move was expected to reduce production costs by about 30% and was considered essential in order to enable the business to compete effectively with multinational competitors. About 800 key staff including research and development staff, however, remained at Malmesbury where the company had invested a significant £32 million during the previous two years.

Issues Associated with International Location

General

There are other factors to consider in respect of a separate location in another country **in addition to** those previously mentioned. Many of the issues associated with selling to international markets are relevant to the issues a business would face when locating operations overseas. Emphasis in the section on entering international markets was, however, on the difficulties a business might face from a selling perspective. This section is concerned with the **management of operations** as opposed to the marketing of the product or service.

Currency Fluctuations

As highlighted in the previous section on entering international markets, one of the frustrating issues relating to global trade is the need to "deal" with the fluctuation of exchange rates. If a business decides to set up physical facilities in a foreign country, then the key points to remember from an operational perspective are that the exchange rate will affect:

- any initial investment to set up operations in the foreign country.
- any profits sent back to the UK.
- the cost of any materials imported into the foreign country from the business's domestic market, or other countries.

With regard to the cost of imported supplies, negotiating a long term contract for the purchase of these supplies will provide some insulation against exchange rate movements but this involves predictions into the future and, thus, an element of uncertainty and risk. Alternatively, if a business sets up and manufactures its products in a foreign country where it sells its products, sourcing supplies of materials in this country will reduce the impact of exchange rate movements. It might also result in positive publicity as the business would be seen to be supporting businesses in these countries. It might, however, not be cost-effective if suppliers offering competitive prices cannot be found in these countries.

With regard to the profits remitted from operations in other countries, if the pound becomes stronger, then the business will receive less money when it converts the profit back into sterling, and vice versa. As previously pointed out, however, many businesses with operations in different currency zones maintain separate financial activities and will only transport funds across international boundaries when conditions are advantageous.

Barriers to Trade

Some countries are anti-foreign investment and take action to allow new, local businesses to grow by preventing foreign businesses from flourishing. This might take the form of:

- financial help to local businesses (In the form of grants or subsidies).
- limits on the amount that can be imported (known as quotas).
- fees levied on goods imported into the country (known as tariffs).

This is known as protectionism. As the previous section on International markets highlighted, China was very much anti-foreign investment pre 1990's. During the 1990s, however, the political climate became more welcoming to the wealth that market economies create, and the attraction of cheap labour, government incentives, political co-operation and a market of well over 1 billion people encouraged many businesses to make large capital investments in China.

Transport Costs

If a business moves its manufacturing base away from current markets there will be increased transport costs involved in getting the finished product to the end customer. If a business moves its manufacturing base away from current suppliers there will be increased costs involved in getting these supplies to the new base overseas.

Utility Costs

The quality of the water supply, power supply, infrastructure and telecommunications may also be a factor to consider when setting up operations in developing countries.

Legal Differences

There may be significant differences in laws between one country and another. From an operational perspective this might, for example, include differences in employment legislation, or legislation relating to the environment. Such differences will need to be investigated and taken into account in any overseas operations.

Differences in Tax

Taxes can also vary significantly between countries and affect the cost of running overseas operations.

Political Stability

Many areas of the world are renowned for being unstable - for example - the Middle East and the recent conflicts in Iraq and Afghanistan. Setting up operations in such countries subjects the business to increased risk and uncertainty.

Social, Cultural, Religious and Language Differences

Effective communication is essential to a successful business and differences in language can be a significant barrier to effective communication. Culture and religious beliefs also impact on the way people behave and expect others to behave in business situations.

Consequently, a business may prefer to locate operations in countries that speak the same language as well as share similar ideologies to help minimise the possible barriers to communication that may arise within and between businesses.

Ethical Issues

Social and political differences can, in some cases, present ethical dilemmas. For example, locating in countries renowned for the use of child labour, bribery and corruption, the marketing of harmful products, environmental degradation and / or with a poor record on human rights or the treatment of minorities and women, may clash with the ethical principles of the owners, customers and / or other stakeholders concerned. When this receives media attention, it can have a negative impact on sales.

Managerial Control

The further away a firm is from its parent company, the more difficult the coordination and control because of barriers to communication.

Closing Comments

It should be pointed out that for a British company, with the exception of language and currency considerations, locating operations within a member state of the European Union will minimise many of the issues outlined above.

4.5
LEAN PRODUCTION

Introduction to Lean Production

Objectives

By the end of this topic you should be able to:

1. Define the term lean production.
2. State 3 lean production techniques.
3. Outline the benefits generally associated with lean production.
4. Outline the general requirements for lean production to occur.

Key Terms

Lean production involves minimising the use of key business resources (ie materials, labour, capital, factory floor space and time) and eliminating waste without reducing customer value.

What is Lean Production?

Explanation

Lean production is based on a combined focus by management and workers on minimising the use of key business resources, ie materials, labour, capital, factory floor space and time. It is all about **eliminating waste**. Waste is defined as **any activity that adds to cost but not to value**. If it adds to costs but not to value then logically it can and should be eliminated to reduce costs but without reducing customer value.

Waste comes from:

- using more resources than necessary.
- making mistakes (as a result of poor recruitment and / or training).
- overproducing.
- carrying excessive stocks.
- using more space than required.
- spending more money than necessary.
- involving more people than necessary.
- spending excessive time on developing products and services.
- unnecessary movement and transportation.

Lean production was pioneered by the Japanese during the 1960s as a response to the domination of world car markets by American companies. They did so by examining their method of production with a view to making it leaner and fitter. This resulted in massive productivity gains that still allow them to compete with the mass markets of America, without having the obvious benefit (experienced by the Americans) of economies of scale (due to the size of the market).

Summary of Lean Production Techniques

Lean production techniques include:

- cell production.
- just in time production.
- the establishment of kaizen groups.
- time based management techniques and tools such as simultaneous engineering and tools such as critical path analysis.

Each of these techniques is discussed in subsequent sections below. This introductory section provides an initial overview as to the benefits and requirements of lean production, especially in terms of minimising costs and maximising quality.

Benefits and Key Requirements

Summary of Benefits – Minimising Costs and Maximising Quality

In general, lean production techniques can provide **financial** and **marketing advantages** to a business. They help to ensure **costs are low** and **quality high** as they:

- use less time, labour, stock, factory space and capital equipment.
- result in far fewer defects, thus quality and reliability to the customer is improved.

Many lean production (time based management) techniques also aim to reduce the hours required to develop and to produce a new product (through the use of computer aided design and manufacture), providing companies with a further competitive advantage as products are available to customers more quickly.

Summary of the Key Requirements

In general, for lean production to occur, the following are necessary:

- close relations with suppliers based on trust.
- a multi-skilled workforce.
- a committed and motivated workforce.
- a willingness to accept change.
- trust and co-operation rather than conflict.
- management by consent.

Closing Comments

From your research into operational topics required to be studied in the Unit 2 specification you should be aware of the concept of Total Quality Management (TQM). TQM is a proactive, systematic, strategic approach to management that involves all employees and all aspects of the business in meeting or exceeding customer expectations, both externally and internally – with staff being regarded as internal customers. The philosophy is one of improvement and prevention. Lean production is essentially the implementation of a total quality management approach to operations.

The Effective Management of Time

Objectives

By the end of this topic you should be able to:

1. Define the terms time based management, lead time, simultaneous engineering, computer aided design (CAD) and computer aided manufacture (CAM).
2. Outline at least 2 benefits for a business of the effective management of time.
3. Outline how a business might seek to reduce the product development time through simultaneous engineering and computer aided design (CAD).
4. Outline how a business might seek to reduce production lead times, including the use of computer aided manufacture (CAM).

Key Terms

Time-based management involves using time periods and time deadlines as a basis for decision-making. Instead of focusing on the output, the business deliberately targets time issues.

Lead time is the length of time taken between two or more processes.

Simultaneous engineering involves organising the processes / stages involved in product development in such a way as to enable the different stages to be carried out simultaneously, ie at the same time, as opposed to one after the other.

CAD (Computer Aided Design) allows a business to simulate the product on a computer screen and alter the specification, colour, features, in order to change the design, without ever having to build a prototype, thus minimising design costs.

CAM (Computer Aided Manufacture) uses computers to control and adjust the production process. It allows firms to manufacture products in shorter times, with improved quality and reliability, and thus, lower costs.

Overview

What Does it Involve?

The effective management of time involves using time periods and time deadlines as a basis for decision-making. Instead of focusing on the output, the business deliberately targets time issues. It involves minimising lead times ie the length of time taken between two or more processes, for example:

- The length of time it takes for an idea being conceived, invented and developed into a new product / service, up to the point where it is launched into the marketplace (product development lead time).

- The length of time it takes for materials / components starting on a production line to be turned into the finished product (production lead time).
- The length of time it takes from a customer placing an order to the customer receiving the order (customer lead time).
- The length of time it takes from placing an order with a supplier to receiving the goods ordered (supplier lead time).

Potential Benefits

Reducing the time taken to develop an idea, produce a product or serve a customer can cut labour and machine hours used, thereby cutting wage and energy bills. This saving can either increase profits or enable lower and, potentially, more competitive prices to be charged, which can help maximise sales and market share.

Furthermore, if a product can get to the market, or a customer can be served more quickly than competitors, then this can also provide a competitive advantage and so help maximise sales and market share. It also helps to generate sales revenue more quickly and a faster return on investment and, so improves cash flow relating to the investment.

To summarise, the effective management of time can:

- increase productivity.
- reduce costs.
- enhance customer satisfaction.
- increase competitiveness.
- maximise sales and market share.
- maximise profitability.
- improve cash flow.

Time-based Management Techniques

Achieving Shorter Product Development Times – Using Simultaneous Engineering and CAD

Achieving shorter product development times involves the use of simultaneous engineering (otherwise known as concurrent engineering) ie organising the processes / stages involved in product development in such a way as to enable the different stages to be carried out simultaneously, ie at the same time, as opposed to one after the other.

Simultaneous engineering essentially involves / requires the use of:

1. **project teams consisting of experts from different disciplines / functional areas** such as design, research and development, marketing, manufacturing and finance, with a clear understanding of their overall purpose / objective(s).

2. **increased / improved communications between disciplines / functional areas** to ensure the necessary information is made available to those concerned as soon as physically possible. Computer networks are often essential to support data / information transfer between team members.

The use of such a multi-disciplined project team from the start can:

- **generate more ideas** for possible innovations.

- **enable faster feedback and response times** – for example – it cuts down the communication time between an idea being generated, passed on to the relevant specialist to be costed out, and passed on to the market research specialist to assess whether or not it would fulfil a defined customer need at a price they would be willing to pay.

- **provide a much clearer understanding**, by all members of the project team, of any **constraints** facing the new development.

- help to ensure the development of products that are **designed 'right first time'**.

Computers can also help the design process to become shorter. Computer-Aided Design (CAD) allows the business to view a 3-dimensional image of the prototype, without going through the lengthy and expensive process of building models.

Achieving Shorter Production Lead Times – Using CAM

The issue of time-based management can also be extended to the lead-time of production, ie the amount of time taken from when a product begins the manufacturing process to when it completes the process as a finished good.

Achieving shorter production lead times is easier to achieve using flow production, but it can also be achieved using batch production. With batch production, however, the time taken to set up production, change the settings on machines, carry out maintenance, ie the minimisation of **downtime** (or idle time), is a specific focal point for reduction.

Computers can also be used to assist in this process. Computer-Aided Manufacture (CAM) uses computers to control and adjust the production process. It allows firms to manufacture products in shorter times, with improved quality and reliability, and thus, lower costs.

Closing Comments

In a market where consumers' tastes change rapidly, and where there is strong competition, placing emphasis on shorter product development times and quicker lead times would be essential in order to maintain and / or increase competitiveness and, ultimately, maximise sales and market share.

Assessing the Value of Critical Path Analysis

Objectives

By the end of this topic you should be able to:

1. Define the term critical path analysis (CPA).
2. Interpret and complete critical path networks by entering earliest start times and latest finishing times.
3. Explain the significance of critical and non-critical activities.
4. Explain how critical path analysis can help a business to: estimate and minimise the time taken to complete a project; cost projects and make decisions between projects; plan, organise and prioritise resources; motivate staff; and monitor and control activities.
5. Outline at least 2 criticisms of critical path analysis.

Key Terms

Critical path analysis involves displaying all the activities involved in a particular project in diagrammatical form, so as to communicate exactly when the resources are required and for how long. It allows a business to estimate the shortest possible time in which a project can be completed and identifies those activities that must be completed on time in order to avoid delaying the entire project (ie the activities that form part of the critical path).

Critical activities are activities that must be completed on time in order to avoid delaying an entire project.

Non-critical activities are activities that can be delayed up to a certain point without delaying the completion of an entire project.

Overview

Critical Path Analysis (CPA) or network planning or analysis is an important tool in project management. It involves displaying all the activities involved in a particular project in diagrammatical form, so as to communicate exactly when resources are required and for how long. Most, importantly, as the name suggests, it allows a business to identify critical activities ie those that must be completed on time in order to avoid delaying an entire project. This assists management in prioritising resources to ensure a project's timely completion. It is used for complex projects, ie those that require the co-ordination of many tasks. For example:

- construction projects such as the Millennium Dome, bridges, block of flats;
- marketing plans, involving research, advertising and test marketing.

When a business is involved in a project that has a variety of activities, such as building the Millennium Dome, CPA can be used to make the building process more efficient. For example, different materials, various skills of labour and certain capital equipment would have been required for the Dome, but at different times. If they had arrived at the construction site too early, this would have meant money being wasted (by being tied up in non-productive assets). If they arrived late, there would have been wastage in terms of people being paid while waiting for them to arrive. Late arrival of resources may ultimately have resulted in late completion of the project, which could, in turn, lead to financial penalties, poor reputation and loss of future business. Undertaking critical path analysis can help to ensure these things do not occur.

Drawing Simple Networks, Calculating Earliest Start Times, Latest Finishing Time, Total Float and Identifying the Critical Path

Drawing Simple Networks

A project involves activities. Activities can be drawn in a diagram with the following annotation:

Figure 1

A **node** denotes the start and finish of an activity. All networks start and finish on a single node. An **arrow** denotes an activity which has duration, eg waiting for a delivery or actual production. Arrows run from left to right. The length has no significance / bearing on the duration of the activity.

To demonstrate how activities are drawn to represent a project, here is a project with four activities. Notice the activity is normally indicated by a letter, placed above the arrow.

Figure 2

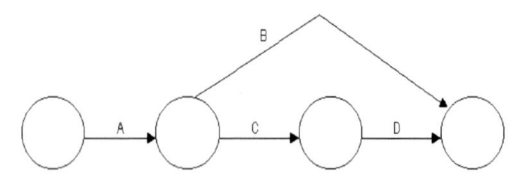

The above network shows that A begins on its own. B and C may begin once A has finished. D may start once C has finished.

Figure 3 below displays a network based on the following information:
A and B begin together, C follows B, D follows A, and E follows C and D.

Figure 3

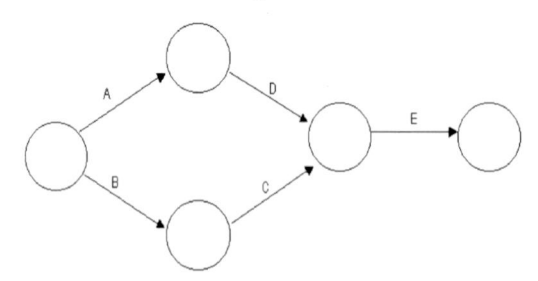

The steps involved in producing a network diagram are as follows:

1. Identify the activities that make up the project.
2. Determine for each activity a) what other activities need to be completed before it can be started; b) what activities depend upon the completion of the activity before they can start.
3. Estimate the duration of each activity.

© APT Initiatives Limited, 2009

This procedure can be demonstrated through the use of an example: A more simple form of project than the ones mentioned in the Introduction above might be one such as a school development plan. This is written by the Head teacher, then passed to three Senior managers, who then consult their departments. After which secretaries type up responses, and then the Head teacher collates these for the final version. Refer to Table 1 below:

Table 1: Activities Involved in the Production of a School Development Plan

Activity	Description	Preceded by	Duration (days)
A	Head teacher does first draft.	-	6
B	Deputy head (curriculum) consults department heads.	A	14
C	Deputy Head (pastoral) consults form tutors.	A	12
D	Bursar consults staff.	A	10
E	Secretary of Deputy head (curriculum) collates responses.	B	4
F	Secretary of Deputy head (pastoral) collates responses.	C	3
G	Secretary of Bursar collates responses.	D	3
H	Head teacher produces final document and despatches to printers.	E,F,G	5

This can be represented in the following diagram:

Figure 4

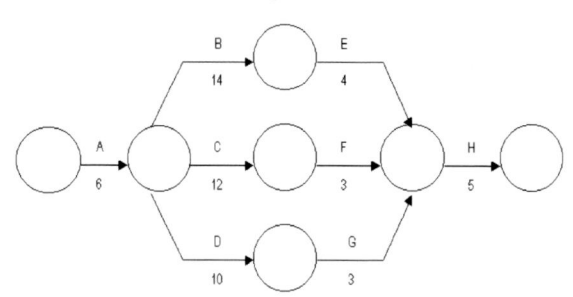

Notice the duration of each activity is inserted underneath each activity arrow.

Calculating Earliest Start Times and Latest Finishing Times

Having drawn the network, it then becomes possible to work out the minimum duration time of this particular project. This is done by calculating the Earliest Start Time and the Latest Finish Time of each activity. The division within each node is done for the purpose of filling in these variables as well as the reference number of each node:

Figure 5

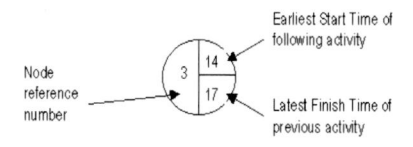

1. Node reference No – **allocated in any logical manner** – usually from left to right.
2. Earliest Start Time **of each activity = the earliest time an activity may begin, which will depend on the duration of previous dependent activities.**
3. **Minimum duration** of the project = the earliest time the project may finish, given the sequence and duration of all the activities.
4. **Latest Finish Time** of each activity = the latest time an activity must finish, so that the entire project can finish within the minimum duration time.

To determine the EST's:

1. Place a zero in the upper right hand segment of node 1.
2. Add the duration time of each activity to the EST of this activity to give the EST of the next activity.

NB If there is more than one activity entering a node, this indicates that both of the activities must be completed before the next activity can begin. Therefore, the *highest* figure is the one that must be taken.

The **minimum length of project** equals the EST in the final node.

Let us apply the above to our previous example - refer to figure 6 on the next page. The EST of A is zero. Thus, the EST of B, C and D is 6 days. These three take different lengths of time, so by adding the duration of each to 6, this gives the EST of the following activities (E, F and G).

Node 6 is of interest: Activity G will finish by 19 (16 + 3, see Node 5), activity F by 21, and E by 24, therefore 24 is inserted. This is because activity H cannot start until all three activities are completed, not when the first one is finished. Hence the minimum duration of this project is 29 days.

For the project to finish within 29 days, it is necessary to establish the latest time each activity could finish, with a view to calculating the delay time allowed on each activity.

To determine the LFT's:

1. Give the last node of the project an LFT equal to its EST.
2. Working backwards from right to left, subtract the length of the activity from the LFT of the node at the point of the arrow, in order to get the LFT at the node of the start of the arrow.

NB Where a node has more than one arrow starting from it, the *lowest* figure is chosen.

Let us apply the above to our example – refer to figure 6: Working backwards the LFT of E, F and G is 24. By subtracting the durations of these three activities from 24, this will provide the LFT of B, D and E respectively. For example, the LFT of C is 21, meaning C might be delayed such that it is not completed until 21 days, yet the project will still be finished by 29 days. Looking at LFT in Node 4, ie 21 + F(3) + H(5) = 29 days.

Node 2 is of interest. Although in Node 5 the LFT of D is 21, and 21 – 10 = 11, this would mean that if 11 was inserted into Node 2 LFT, then the project would be delayed - counting the days from B to E to H would take it to 34 (11 + 14 + 4 + 5), ie well over the minimum duration time of 29.

Figure 6

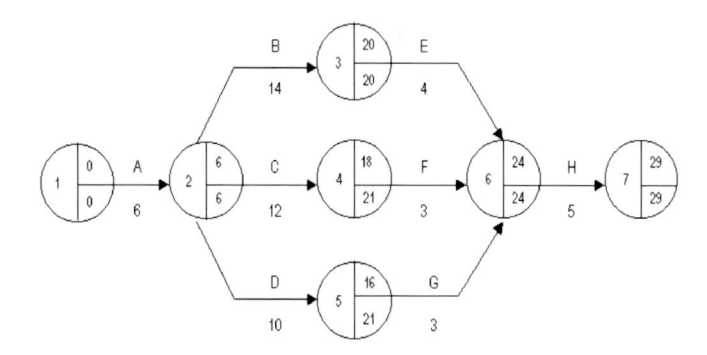

```
                    B  [20|3|  ]  E
                 ┌─[14|  |20 ]─[ | |  ]─┐
                 │                    4 │
                 │                      ↓
[1|0|  ]  A  [2|6|6]  C  [ |18|4]  F  [ |24|6]  H  [7|29|  ]
[ |0|6]─────[ | |6]─[ |12| ]─[ |21|3]─[ |24|5]─────[ |29|  ]
                 │                    ↑
                 │                    │
                 └─[ |16|  ]─[ | | ]──┘
                    D  [ |21|3]  G
                      [ |10|5]
```

Calculating Total Float and Identifying the Critical Path / Activities

Having filled in the nodes, this allows the business to identify the activities for which there can be no delay. If there is delay, then the project will go beyond 29 days. To do this, total float must be calculated.

Total Float represents the amount of delay available on any single activity which does not delay the project duration i.e. how long an activity can be extended / postponed so that the project is still finished within the minimum duration time. It is calculated by:

Latest Finish Time (LFT) – Duration – Earliest Start Time (of an individual activity)

Refer to Table 2 below:

Table 2: Calculating Total Float

Activity	LFT	Duration	EST	Total Float
A	6	6	0	0
B	20	14	6	0
C	21	12	6	3
D	21	10	6	5
E	24	4	20	0
F	24	3	18	3
G	24	3	16	5
H	29	5	24	0

Activities with a total float of zero represent those activities that cannot be delayed without delaying the entire project. Such activities (in our example A,B,E,H) represent **the critical path**. If C, for example, is delayed by 2 days, this will still enable the project to be finished on time, although it will reduce the total float of C to 1 day and the total float of F to 1 day (because F is dependent on C). On our network diagram, the critical path is where the EST's are equal to the EFT's. The critical path is usually shown by two parallel lines drawn through the critical activity arrows. Refer to Figure 7 on the next page.

Figure 7

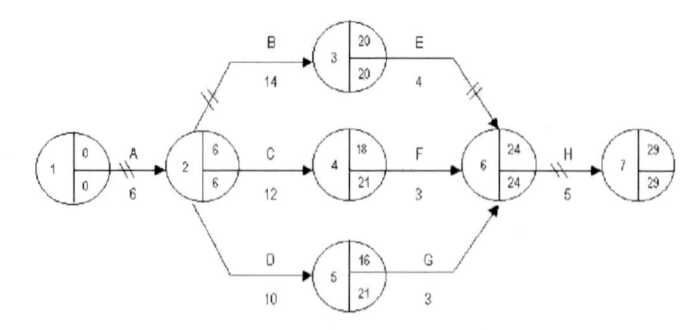

Role, Purpose and Benefits

Estimating and Minimising Project Completion Time

CPA allows a business to estimate the shortest possible time in which a project can be completed. It encourages an organisation to identify where activities can be carried out simultaneously, as opposed to one after the other, thus, minimising the time it takes to complete a project. The quicker the project can be completed, the sooner the business will get paid, thereby improving cash flow and liquidity. It also keeps costs to a minimum.

Costing and Selecting Projects to Undertake

CPA can be used in costing a job as it helps to identify all the resources required to complete a project including the time required to complete it. This can also help a business to decide whether or not to go ahead with a particular project. For example, calculation of the minimum duration time may indicate that a business has insufficient time (using existing resources) to complete a 'special' order, and that if they take the order it will actually delay previous deadlines agreed with other customers.

Planning and Organising Resources

CPA can help a business to make day to day operational decisions such as when to start specific activities that make up a project, when to order any materials required and when to schedule staff, thus helping to ensure labour, materials, etc are in the right place, at the right time, and there are no delays. It facilitates just in time operations to ensure materials, labour and other resources are only employed as and when required. This keeps costs (eg wages and salaries, stockholding) to a minimum and maximises cash flow and liquidity.

Prioritising Resources

CPA enables a business to Identify and distinguish between critical activities ie those that must be completed to avoid delaying an entire project, and non-critical activities ie those that may be delayed up to a certain point without delaying the completion of an entire project.

Identifying the critical activities ie those where there can be no delay, enables emphasis to be placed on ensuring these are completed on time (and / or exploring ways of reducing the length of these critical activities in order to reduce the time it takes to complete the entire project). Knowledge of critical and non-critical activities essentially enables a business to take better decisions when prioritising resources.

Motivating Staff

Communicating the expected finish times of each activity to employees can help managers to motivate staff as people can monitor their performance and assess how they are doing against the targets set.

Monitoring and Controlling Activities

CPA allows a business to monitor progress on individual tasks and enables timely and corrective action to be taken where required. In particular, by distinguishing between critical and non critical activities managers can make use of float on non-critical activities to transfer resources to critical activities to avoid delaying completion of the whole project wherever possible and, in some cases avoid late penalty payments that would otherwise reduce, or even eliminate, profit from a particular project.

Closing Comments

There are criticisms of critical path analysis, for example:

1. It relies on estimates of how long each task with take. Inaccurate estimation of time undermines the usefulness of the technique.

2. It requires a significant amount of planning and time.

3. It can lead to tight deadlines and may encourage employees to cut corners in the rush to meet these deadlines. Hence, it might lead to on-time completion at the expense of quality.

Overall, however, CPA can help to:

1. Minimise wastage of resources and maximise profitability.

2. Ensure customers are satisfied and provide a competitive edge through the effective management of time.

The Effective Management of Other Resources through Methods of Lean Production

Objectives

By the end of this topic you should be able to:

1. Define the terms just-in-time production, kaizen and cell production.
2. Outline the general requirements, potential benefits and potential drawbacks of each of these methods of lean production.

Key Terms

Just-in-time (JIT) production is a philosophy of producing products, whereby materials and components arrive at the workplace in such a way that the time lag between their arrival and work taking place is minimised and very little, if any (buffer) stock is kept in case of problems with delivery or work in progress, etc. It also applies to the finished product, because once the product has been made it is despatched immediately to the customer.

Cell production involves dividing the production process amongst small teams or 'cells'. Workers within each cell may operate on one or a group of functions of the production process, and are given responsibility for every part of the product and production process during the time that the work-in-progress passes through the cell. Responsibility may include task allocation, quality control, health and safety, purchasing of supplies, and stock control.

Kaizen is a Japanese word that means continuous improvement. It usually involves groups of workers that meet regularly to discuss how work-related tasks can be completed more efficiently. Because workers are involved in the detailed operation of the business, they are considered to be sufficiently well qualified to be able to identify any problematic areas and suggest improvements.

Just-in-time Production

Definition / Explanation

Just in time (JIT) production is a philosophy of producing products, whereby materials and components arrive at the workplace in such a way that the time lag between their arrival and work taking place is minimised and very little, if any (buffer) stock is kept in case of problems with delivery or work in progress, etc. It also applies to the finished product, because once the product has been made it is despatched immediately to the customer.

Potential Benefits

The idea behind JIT is that the business should hold the minimum amount of stock at any point in time. Reducing stock levels reduces costs associated with the following:

- **Cost of storage** – The cost involved in purchasing or renting additional storage capacity, heating and lighting, labour (monitoring and security), insurance (against fire and theft).

- **Costs of finance** – A business may have to borrow money to purchase stock, via an overdraft for example, (despite credit offered by suppliers). This is because it takes time to convert materials into finished goods, sell them, and receive the money from customers.
- **Opportunity cost** – Money tied up in stocks cannot be released until that stock has been sold and paid for. Opportunity cost is, for example, the interest that could be earned on this money. Alternatively, the money could be used to buy fixed assets to increase capacity.
- **Stock deterioration or obsolescence** – If too much stock is carried stock may become obsolete ie outdated.

Just-in-Time also helps to:

- **maximise quality** and **minimise waste and associated costs** – JIT puts pressure on employees to work together and check their work thoroughly in order to get 'perfect quality first time' as there is no surplus stock to fall back on if mistakes are made.
- **highlight inefficiencies and allow improvements to be made** – Reducing the buffer stock makes any problems in delivery, quality, machinery, workmanship more obvious, which is likely to result in a business making the effort to eliminate such problems.

There are also other benefits, including:

- **improved cash flow** – as less money is tied up in stock.
- **freed up storage space for more productive use** (linked to opportunity costs above) – helping to maximise the number of customers that could be served at any one time, and thus, maximising sales and profits.
- **increased motivation of workers** – as they tend to be given more responsibility, for example, in terms of ensuring products are right first time.

Potential Problems / Drawbacks

There are, however, potential problems / drawbacks associated with a JIT approach. JIT can:

- leave a business highly **vulnerable** to changes in **supply** as well as **problems with equipment and machinery**.
- increase the risk of **production halting** and **customer orders not being met** on time.
- restrict a firm's ability to meet **a sudden increase in demand** and, thus, restrict sales.

To be implemented and work successfully JIT requires:

- **careful planning** including **accurate sales forecasting**.
- **flexible and reliable suppliers** – able to deliver more frequently and in smaller quantities.
- **reliable machinery** – to ensure mistakes are not made and customers' orders can be met. This has implications for maintenance and capital investment.
- **staff with the right ability, motivation and commitment** to ensure quality is right first time. This has implications for training, working conditions, pay and other benefits.

In addition to the potential problems and drawbacks listed above, the implementation of a just-in-time approach may result in a business **losing out on bulk buying discounts** offered by suppliers, as well as **incurring greater administration / ordering and handling costs** from dealing with a greater number of smaller deliveries. Before implementing any JIT techniques a business would, therefore, be wise to research whether **the lower stockholding** (including storage, financing and opportunity costs), and **reduction in waste** stemming from the pressure to get quality right first time, were sufficient to compensate for any **loss in discounts** and would outweigh the **extra administration and labour costs** involved with handling a greater number of smaller deliveries.

Cell Production

Definition / Explanation

Cell production involves dividing the production process amongst small teams or 'cells'. Workers within each cell may operate on one or a group of functions of the production process, and are given responsibility for every part of the product and production process during the time that the work-in-progress passes through the cell. Responsibility may include task allocation, quality control, health and safety. It might even extend to the purchasing of materials and supplies and stock control.

Employees are usually trained in preventative maintenance. They are trained to spot a fault and correct it, without needing the help of a specialist engineer. If a mistake is spotted, the fault is not simply laid at the feet of the person who made the error, but at the feet of all those within the cell who failed to spot it! Cell members are also usually trained to do each other's jobs so that they can fill in for other members of the team if they are absent – providing some job variety.

The concept of the internal customer is significant to cell production. Individuals within cells should regard themselves as both customers and suppliers. Cells that pass work on to other cells must ensure the quality of their work meets the exact specifications required by the next cell. They should regard themselves as suppliers and the next cell as their customer, and do everything possible to meet their requirements.

Potential Benefits

The fact that cell production often involves making staff responsible for checking all their own work, **reduces the need for close supervision and associated costs.**

Other benefits arising from organising works on a cell production basis include:

- **less waste and costs associated with poor quality** – as workers are better trained and made to be more responsible for their actions, resulting in fewer mistakes / defects.
- **enhanced motivation and lower labour turnover and associated costs** – because employees are likely to gain greater job satisfaction from the increased job variety and responsibility (Herzberg's 'motivators') which may in turn, help to reduce labour turnover and associated costs. Dividing the workforce into small **teams** can also enhance motivation – helping to satisfy **social / love and belonging needs** (Maslow), as highlighted in the work of several motivational theorists, in particular, Mayo and his Hawthorne experiments.

There are also a number of other advantages associated with allowing staff to work in teams:

- People can draw upon the knowledge and skills of others, resulting in **better decisions.**
- People may be **more willing to be innovative** as responsibility is shared.
- There is **less disruption to the workplace** as team members generally have the ability to perform other members' jobs.

Potential Drawbacks

The drawbacks concern the potential costs, which mainly include:

- **training** – to increase the range of skills of cell members.
- **pay increases** – staff may expect pay to increase in line with the additional skills learned and increased responsibility.

Kaizen

Definition / Explanation

Kaizen is a Japanese word that means continuous improvement. It usually involves groups of workers that meet regularly to discuss how work-related tasks can be completed more efficiently. Because workers are involved in the detailed operation of the business, they are considered to be sufficiently well qualified to be able to identify any problematic areas and suggest improvements.

The results of kaizen groups are aimed at gradual change as opposed to major rethinks. Consequently, kaizen groups meet regularly, with the same objective, ie to improve the business.

Potential Benefits and Drawbacks

There are obvious advantages through access to **innovative ideas** that **reduce costs** and **improve quality**. There are also **motivational benefits** that can help the business to be **more productive**. Providing staff with a mechanism to express their opinion about improvements (which are acted upon), can help employees feel valued and more fulfilled – helping to satisfy people's esteem and self-actualisation needs (Maslow). In terms of Herzberg's theory, it provides staff with some level of responsibility, which can increase motivation (Herzberg's motivators). It is likely to result in more positive relationships between management and staff – aiding the satisfaction of social needs.

In addition to the above, employee participation can provide **easier implementation of decisions over improvements** as the more input an employee has in planning and carrying out a decision, the more motivated he / she is likely to be towards carrying it through to completion. It can also result in **better quality decisions** about improvements for two reasons:

1. Firstly, employees usually know more about their jobs then anybody else and are, therefore, the most qualified to make decisions over improvements.

2. Secondly, having a variety of opinions / viewpoints is more likely to lead to the identification of faulty assumptions, possible errors or omissions, and the timely correction of these.

There is, of course, the need for **well-qualified staff to organise and initiate the kaizen groups**. But, the process of general discussion leading towards improvement on a continual basis should actually help to increase the quality of all the staff who take part.

Overall, allowing employees to participate can not only help to **improve the quality of working life** and **satisfaction staff gain from work**, but also the **quality, efficiency** and **productivity** of the business.

Closing Comments

There may be cost implications associated with the introduction of lean production techniques which can be significant - for example - investment in training to change attitudes and ensure successful implementation. These costs are, however, generally short-term and outweighed by the significant savings and efficiencies gained from the adoption of lean production techniques in the longer-term.

5

HUMAN RESOURCE STRATEGIES

5.1

UNDERSTANDING HR OBJECTIVES AND STRATEGIES

HR Objectives

Objectives

By the end of this topic you should be able to:

1. Define the term human resource objectives.
2. State at least 4 examples of human resource objectives.

Key Terms

Human resource objectives are goals or targets that must be achieved by the human resource function to achieve the corporate objectives.

Matching Workforce Skills, Size and Location to Business Needs

A key objective of the human resource function is to ensure that there is the right number of employees, of the right quality (ie skills, qualifications, experience, etc), in the right place, at the right time. This is essential in order to meet the needs of customers and maximise sales.

Getting the right 'match' between labour requirements and business needs is also important from a cost perspective – helping to ensure staff are not being paid when they are not fully employed.

Achieving the right match can be a challenging task. It involves:

- taking into account corporate objectives and strategies and plans for their achievement
- making predictions about the future demand and supply of internal and external labour.
- devising strategies to deal with shortages and surpluses.

Dealing with labour surpluses can be a particularly challenging task when it involves redundancies, as these can negatively affect staff morale and motivation, as well as the business's reputation as an employer, and so need to be planned very carefully and handled sensitively.

For businesses that suffer from seasonal demand, matching workforce skills, size and location to meet the needs of the business is an ongoing concern and key objective.

Making Full Use of the Workforce's Potential

A key function of human resource management concerns planning how to get the best out of employees and how to maximise their potential within the business. This is likely to involve investment in training and development and providing opportunities for promotion.

Enabling staff to utilise more of their skills may help to satisfy higher order needs of self-actualisation (Maslow). Investing in training and development of staff can make employees feel valued, thereby helping to satisfy esteem needs. In addition, providing opportunities for promotion is also recognised as an important motivator by Herzberg.

Setting objectives relating to making full use of the workforce's potential can, therefore, help to:

- maximise job satisfaction.
- enhance the motivation and commitment of staff.
- increase staff retention.
- reduce labour turnover and associated costs (see below).

Minimising Labour Cost

Minimising labour costs should be a key objective of any business to eliminate waste of resources and maximise profit. It is particularly relevant to labour intensive industries where labour costs are high in relation to other costs and so have a significant effect on profitability. It might concern targets relating to:

- improving punctuality.
- reducing unauthorised absence.
- increasing staff retention / reducing labour turnover.

For example, high levels of absenteeism can result in overtime payments and / or payments to agency staff to cover for absent employees, as well as higher sick pay. Labour turnover, in particular, incurs significant costs which include the costs associated with advertising, interviewing, inducting and training new staff. Both also involve management time spent re-organising operations (arranging cover, extending deadlines) to cope with fluctuating staffing levels.

Maintaining Good Employer / Employee Relations

Maintaining good employer / employee relations is good business practice for the following reasons. It can:

- help to satisfy employees' social needs at work and help them to feel more valued (esteem needs). This can result in more motivated and committed employees and, thus, reduced absence, labour turnover and associated costs.
- encourage employees to air any grievances and enable these to be resolved at an early stage and so it can minimise the chance of industrial action eg strikes taking place and the damaging affect these can have on a business (discussed in detail in a subsequent section).
- encourage employees to put forward ideas / suggestions that may help to improve the performance of the business.
- result in staff being more willing to accept changes in the workplace.
- create a positive corporate image which can not only help to attract good quality staff but help to attract customers and, thus, help maximise sales.

Closing Comments

As with all other functional objectives, human resource objectives must be supportive of the overall corporate objective, and consistent with the objectives of other functional areas.

It should also be appreciated that Human Resource Management and the setting and achievement of HR objectives is part of every manager's job, irrespective of the function in which the managers operate. If a separate HR department exists within an organisation, then it is their job to act largely in a coordinating and advisory role for operational managers.

Assessing Internal and External Influences on HR Objectives

Objectives

By the end of this topic you should be able to:

1. Outline at least 4 internal influences on human resource objectives.
2. Outline at least 4 external influences on human resource objectives.

Key Terms

Internal influences on human resource objectives are factors coming from inside the business that can affect decisions over, or success in achieving, human resource objectives – for example – corporate objectives and strategy, corporate culture, other functional objectives and strategies, the business's financial position, size and strength of worker representation, and the nature of the product and the workforce.

External influences on human resource objectives are factors stemming from outside the business that can affect decisions over, or success in achieving, human resource objectives – for example – the state of the market, level and nature of demand, competitor activities, as well as political, legal, social, economic and technological factors.

Internal Influences

Corporate Objectives

As has been explained in several previous sections, a business's corporate objective(s) provide the boundaries for setting functional objectives and so corporate objectives will influence a business's financial, marketing, operational <u>and</u> human resource objectives. As with all functional objectives, human resource objectives must be consistent with and support the achievement of the business's overall objective(s).

Corporate Strategy

Human resource objectives will also be affected by the strategy decided upon to achieve the business's overall objectives. For example, growth in sales might be a key corporate objective and diversification into new markets the strategy decided upon to achieve this growth. This might involve the development of new products / services in new locations and, thus, the prioritisation of objectives relating to matching workforce skills, size and location to business needs.

Corporate Culture

Corporate culture can simply be defined as 'the way things are done round here'. A more structured definition is:

'a set of values, beliefs and assumptions shared by members (or the majority of members) within an organisation, that influence their behaviour and the decisions they take, and shape their expectations'.

The culture of an organisation can influence many aspects but especially the extent to which people are valued and the way in which they are treated. It largely stems from the attitude of senior managers. Some organisations regard people as the most important asset and so making full use of the workforce's potential through investment in training and development as well as ensuring good employee / employer relations may be important ongoing objectives. Others regard employees simply as a means to an end - another resource to be managed as efficiently as possible in order to achieve the prime objective and maximise profits. In which case, emphasis will be placed on matching workforce skills, size and location to business needs and minimising labour costs.

Marketing and Operational Objectives and Strategies

Human resource objectives need to be consistent with the objectives of other functional areas, in particular marketing and operations. For example:

- Objectives relating to increasing sales and market share will directly influence the demand for staff and influence targets relating to recruitment.
- Innovation may necessitate the need to hire additional staff with additional skills by a certain date to ensure new products or processes are implemented successfully.
- The need to cut production costs may lead to a drive to cut labour costs and, thus, human resource targets relating to these.

In addition, strategies implemented to achieve functional objectives can have a direct affect on objectives in other functional areas and may at times conflict with these. For example, investment in automation as a means to cut production costs could result in redundancies and affect employer / employee relations.

Financial Position

Recruitment and selection, training and development, and devising appropriate pay structures and other benefits to attract and motivate staff all have cost implications. Targets relating to any of these will, therefore, be constrained by the amount of finance a business has available.

Size and Strength of Worker Representation

Targets to cut labour costs may involve redundancies and / or changes in working practices which can be disruptive and unsettling for the workforce. They may, therefore, be opposed and resisted and difficult to achieve. If the workforce has the backing of a strong union such targets may have to be moderated / revised.

The Nature of the Product / Service and Workforce

The nature of the product and service directly influences the type and level of skills required. Where high levels of skill, qualification and experience are required, greater emphasis is likely to be placed on making full use of the workforce's potential - as a means of increasing staff retention rates. This is because highly skilled staff are more difficult and costly to replace.

External Influences

The State of the Market and Level and Nature of Demand

The size and growth of the market and, ultimately, the level of demand for a business's product will influence objectives relating to matching workforce size and skills to business needs. If the market for a business's product is growing then the focus may be on targets for recruitment and retention. In a saturated or declining market where competition tends to be more aggressive, emphasis may need to be placed on cutting labour costs.

In addition, as stated previously, when a business suffers from seasonal demand, matching workforce size to business needs is likely to be an ongoing concern and, thus, a key objective.

Competitor Activities and Competition for Labour from other Businesses

The activities of competitors may result in reduced demand for a business's product / service and, thus, influence targets relating to the size of the workforce.

The recruitment drives and employment packages of other business may also affect the ability of a business to secure the labour it requires to fulfil its objectives.

Economic Factors

Changes in interest rates, exchange rates, inflation and employment may affect a business's cost structure and the amount of disposable income people have to spend on goods and services and, ultimately, the level of demand for its products / services. These may force a business to focus on cutting costs including labour costs.

With regard to inflation unions tend to become more active during periods of inflation to ensure members achieve an increase in real wages which can, obviously, impact upon objectives relating to labour costs.

The rate of unemployment is also a key factor affecting the business's ability to match workforce skills, size and location to business needs, as well as objectives relating to labour costs. For example, when unemployment is high a business may find it easier and cheaper to recruit, as employees may actually approach them rather than vice versa, saving in recruitment costs. Objectives relating to labour costs may also be more easily achieved as unions generally have less bargaining power when there is a surplus pool of labour available for work, leading to fewer demands for pay rises.

Political and Legal Factors

Changes in government policy and changes in legislation can have a significant impact on a business's approach to the management of its human resources.

Recent governments have made use of supply-side policies to stimulate economic growth. For example, direct investment by the government in education and training initiatives, or providing tax or other incentives (Investors in People Scheme) for firms to invest in training, in order to increase skill levels and occupational mobility. Such investment and incentives may make it easier for a business to match workforce skills, size and location to business needs. On the other hand, employment protection legislation prevents people from being dismissed at will and, thus, limits a business's freedom to respond quickly to adapt workforce size to changing business needs.

Minimum wage legislation has also had an inflationary impact on labour costs in those businesses employing large numbers of unskilled labour. In addition, EU membership has brought limitations to the number of hours that can be worked by individual employees in any given week, which has implications for recruitment and labour costs.

Social and Demographic Factors

Partly due to legislation but also changes in social attitudes (and assisted by developments in technology – see below), more and more employees are expecting to be able to secure flexible working arrangements in order to fit in with family and other commitments. Although it can make the task of management more difficult, it can help a business to match workforce skills, size and location to business needs and minimise labour costs. (Flexible working practices are considered in a subsequent section below).

Changes in demography (ie the size and structure of the population) have a direct affect on the **supply** of labour and so will also affect a business's ability to match workforce size and skills to business needs. For example, there is currently an **ageing population,** a situation where a smaller working population is now supporting a non-working population that is greater than ever before. This is due to:

a) **a decline in the birth rate.** The main reasons for this are: couples delaying having children until a much later age - partly because more women are pursuing a career first; and increased use and reliability of modern methods of contraception.
b) **a fall in the death rate,** due to improved education and health awareness and technological breakthroughs in medical care.
c) **less school leavers** – due to above, and access to higher education.
d) **people taking earlier retirement.**

A business may, therefore, find it difficult to attract young people and suffer higher labour costs as labour may become more expensive due to the laws of supply and demand.

Other social factors include the fact that improvements in **education** have made employees much less prepared to accept orders handed down to them, and more likely to want to have a say in any major decisions which affect their working lives. Maintaining good employer / employee relations – for example – by providing opportunities for staff to have a say on decisions which affect them is, therefore, becoming increasingly important.

Technological Developments

Technological advances enable businesses to invest in labour saving equipment and so may make it easier for a business to achieve targets relating to labour costs.

The emergence of e-mail and mobile phone technology has also enabled much more flexible working practices such as homeworking or teleworking (considered further below) which, on the one hand, can significantly reduce fixed costs but, on the other hand, can make maintaining good employee / employer relations more difficult.

Trade Unions

If part of a business's workforce are members of a national union, then the business will be affected by decisions taken at a national level. Although a substantial amount of legislation was passed under the conservative government during the 1970's and 1980's to reduce the power of unions, a nationally recognised trade union can generate negative publicity and put pressure on a business to modify its behaviour with regard to the treatment of employees.

HR Strategies

Objectives

By the end of this topic you should be able to:

1. Define HR strategies.
2. Explain the difference between 'hard' HR strategies and 'soft' HR strategies.
3. Outline 2 general strengths and 2 general weaknesses associated with each approach.
4. Identify and comment on the appropriateness of the HR strategy used in a given situation.
5. Select and justify the most appropriate HR strategy to adopt in a given scenario.

Key Terms

HR strategies are plans or courses of action decided upon to achieve the business's human resource objectives.

Hard HR strategies focus on the tight control of employees in the pursuit of organisational objectives. They involve a systematic, rational approach to HR management – where quantitative factors take precedence over qualitative factors. The job to be done is seen to be far more important than the person doing it.

Soft HR strategies seek to fulfil the needs of the individual as well as fulfil organisational goals. They focus on nurturing and developing employees in order to maximise their potential. They take into account qualitative factors ie the feelings, needs and emotions of individual employees when making decisions, in order to gain the trust and long-term commitment of employees.

'Hard' Strategies

Explanation

Hard HR strategies focus on the tight control of employees in the pursuit of organisational objectives. They are based on the notion that employees are an expendable resource to be managed as effectively and efficiently as possible. They involve a systematic, rational approach to HR management – where quantitative factors take precedence over qualitative factors.

Hard strategies focus on the job to be done and deadlines to be met. The job to be done is seen to be far more important than the person doing it. Employees are likely to be highly directed ie issued guidelines on how tasks should be carried out and rarely consulted on work related issues. They are also likely to be closely monitored and supervised to ensure tasks are carried out to the standard required.

The Link with Taylor's Scientific Management, McGregor's Theory X and an Authoritarian / Autocratic Leadership Style

Hard HR Strategies can be linked to Taylor and the principles of Scientific Management, McGregor's Theory X and authoritarian / autocratic leadership styles.

Taylor (1856-1917) was a trained engineer who acted as a very early management consultant. He conducted numerous experiments into labour productivity at an American steel company. He was highly concerned with efficiency in the workplace and evolved the concept of **Scientific Management.** This involved the application of scientific principles to the process of management. His approach to maximising efficiency was based on careful measurement of tasks, and the monitoring and control of workers.

McGregor's **Theory X** Approach to Management is where the manager believes:

- People are inherently lazy, dislike work and try to avoid it.
- People must be coerced and controlled in order to work hard.
- The average person wants to avoid responsibility, prefers to be directed.
- People are not generally ambitious, take no initiative, have security as their greatest need.

If workers are perceived by managers as Theory X then a more **autocratic / authoritarian management style** may be considered appropriate in order to ensure worker co-operation and productivity. This is where the leader/manager:

- makes all the decisions and insists on obedience – he / she sets the objectives, policies, standards of performance, and plans the work activities - allocating roles, tasks, timing and work groups. Communication, therefore, tends to be one way, ie downwards.

- distances himself / herself from the group and rarely assists / participates in tasks assigned to the group except when explaining / demonstrating.

Strengths

A 'hard' HR approach may:

- make it easy to maintain effective control and get the job done to a high standard – as employees are given instruction and closely monitored / supervised.
- make it easier to implement measures (eg redundancies) that match workforce size to meet changing business requirements.
- result in lower labour costs due to minimum investment in training and development.
- be essential in times of crisis and when tight deadlines need to be met.

Weaknesses

However, such an approach may:

- alienate employees and not encourage them to foster commitment towards organisational goals.
- de-motivate employees – as they may feel oppressed and frustrated by the lack of responsibility or participation in decisions. This can make them feel under-valued, unfulfilled – affecting the satisfaction of esteem and self-actualisation needs.
- result in high labour turnover and associated costs ie advertising, selecting, inducting, training, loss in productivity while new staff are being trained.

'Soft' Strategies

Explanation

Soft HR strategies seek to fulfil the needs of the individual as well as fulfil organisational goals. They focus on nurturing and developing employees in order to maximise their potential and are based on the notion that employees are a highly valuable asset that can help to provide a competitive advantage. They take into account qualitative factors ie the feelings, needs and emotions of individual employees when making decisions over strategy in order to gain the trust and long-term commitment of employees. The job to be done and the person doing it are both seen as important and staff are likely to be regularly consulted about how they feel, allowed to make decisions about how to do their work, and work at a pace that is suitable to them rather than being forced to follow pre-set guidelines.

Soft HR strategies, therefore, include:

- keeping employees informed about business related issues and the reasons behind key decisions. This is considered vital in developing trust and gaining the commitment of employees.
- providing opportunities for employees to put forward their ideas, be consulted and participate in decisions.
- empowering employees / providing employees with greater autonomy over aspects relating to their work.
- making jobs as meaningful, interesting and varied as possible eg through job enrichment, enlargement and rotation.
- providing opportunities for development and promotion.
- identifying and implementing individual strategies to motivate individual employees.
- redeploying employees wherever possible rather than making them redundant.

The Link with the Work of Herzberg, MacGregor's Theory Y and a Democratic / Participative Leadership Style

Soft HR strategies can be linked to the work of Herzberg, McGregor's Theory Y and associated with a democratic / participative leadership style.

Herzberg in his 'Two Factor' Theory suggested that providing employees with meaningful, interesting work, responsibility, growth and advancement, as well as recognition for and opportunities for achievement, could encourage employees to work harder and give rise to satisfaction.

McGregor's 'Theory Y Approach to Management is where the manager believes that:

- people are able to exercise self control and direction over their work.
- the average person learns to accept and seek responsibility.

If workers are perceived by managers to demonstrate aspects of theory Y, then a more **participative / democratic style** may be required. Democratic leaders tend to:

- **consult** with staff and encourage them to participate in decision making, listen to their ideas, act upon advice, and explain the reasons behind decisions.
- **delegate** a great deal and may even give members the freedom to work with whomsoever they choose, and decide how tasks should be divided between the group.

Strengths

Strengths associated with a 'soft' approach include the following:

- morale, job satisfaction and motivation may be higher as workers may value the attention they are given and input they are allowed to have, resulting in…
- greater commitment to organisational goals and deadlines, increased productivity, reduced absence, lower labour turnover and associated costs.
- the business may gain a reputation as a good employer which can help to attract good quality employees.
- a more creative, multi-skilled and, thus, flexible workforce - able to respond appropriately to changing business needs.
- better quality decisions – the consultation and participation can lead to the identification of a range of alternatives, and the timely correction of faulty assumptions which could lead to errors or omissions.
- easier implementation of decisions – the more input a person has in planning and in carrying out a decision, the more motivated he / she is likely to be towards carrying it out to its completion.

Weaknesses

Weaknesses include the following:

- Slower decision making arising from the process of consultation and participation.
- Greater potential for conflict and loss of control as staff are encouraged to air their views and are provided with greater autonomy.
- If too much emphasis is placed on a 'soft' approach deadlines may be over-run and productivity may suffer.
- The cost of investment in ongoing training and development.
- Greater risk of staff being poached by competitors.
- More difficult to adapt the size of the workforce to meet changing market conditions and business needs.

The Appropriateness of the Two Approaches

In general employees are better educated and have higher expectations about their working life which includes being kept informed, consulted and provided with opportunities to participate in decisions, as well as having some degree of autonomy over their work, for example. It might be argued, therefore, that all businesses should lean towards a 'soft' approach. The most appropriate approach, however, will depend upon a range of factors, most notably:

- The nature of the business and task to be performed.
- The nature of the workforce.
- The business situation.

For example:

- If the task employees are expected to perform is complex and requires highly skilled employees then a soft approach may be more appropriate. This is because such staff may be difficult and costly to replace and are, therefore, less expendable. They may also have higher expectations about their working lives.

- Some people may prefer to be directed, and / or do not have the knowledge or the interest to make effective contributions to decisions, and / or are not interested in additional responsibility or promotion. In which case, a hard approach can be more effective and efficient.

- When the business's very survival is threatened and a fast decision is essential in order to ensure its survival, then a hard approach may be the only option.

Closing Comments

It should be appreciated that the two approaches are not incompatible and that in the majority of circumstances a balance between hard and soft strategies is what is required. This may involve the following:

- Making individuals / team members aware of organisational goals / targets and how their work contributes towards the achievement of such targets.
- Giving people guidelines / parameters within which to work whilst still allowing them to have a say on exactly how things should be done.
- Knowing each individual's talents / skills and matching them to project needs.
- Making sure staff have the necessary resources to get the job done.
- Monitoring staff but not every activity.
- Listening to concerns and letting staff air their grievances but where these cannot be resolved, explaining why, so that they can understand.
- Identifying individual needs and goals, designing rewards that help to meet these and encouraging commitment to organisational goals.

5.2
DEVELOPING AND IMPLEMENTING WORKFORCE PLANS

Components of Workforce Plans

Objectives

By the end of this topic you should be able to:

1. Define the terms workforce plan and workforce planning.
2. Outline the workforce planning process.
3. Describe common components of a workforce plan.

Key Terms

A **workforce plan** is a report detailing a business's labour requirements over a certain period of time, and the action required to ensure the right number and type of people are in the right place at the right time to enable a business to carry out its planned activities and fulfil its objectives.

Workforce planning involves determining the number and type of employees required, where and by when, to enable an organisation to carry out its planned activities and fulfil its objectives.

Overview

The workforce plan forms part of a business's overall corporate plan. It is a report detailing a business's labour requirements over a certain period of time, usually at least a year, and the action required to ensure the right number and type of people are in the right place at the right time to enable the business to carry out its planned activities and fulfil its objectives.

The process of identifying the organisation's human resource requirements and how to secure these requirements is known as workforce planning. It involves a number of key stages.

The Key Stages Involved in Workforce Planning

Supply Analysis

This involves examining the supply of labour and includes the following:

- **Analysing the current supply of labour.** This involves establishing / calculating the current number of employees in certain jobs / departments by skills, qualifications, age, length of service, productivity and performance results. In large, modern organisations such information is likely to be kept on a computerised staff database and, thus, easily obtained.

- **Forecasting internal supply.** This concerns predicting how the supply of employees is likely to change over time, and involves calculating the rate of labour turnover (to estimate those likely to leave in the future), as well as taking into account impending promotions, retirements, parental leave, or planned changes to working arrangements / practices. For instance, if new technology is expected to increase productivity (output per person) by 5%, then additional employees will only be required if output is planned to rise by 5% or more.

- **Assessing external supply.** This is influenced by the following factors:
    - Demographic – The age structure of the local population and the number of school and college leavers able and willing to work.
    - Local unemployment levels – The higher the unemployment the larger the pool of labour, though not necessarily with people having the skills and qualifications required by the business.
    - Local education and training schemes – These affect the availability of younger ages and skills and qualifications offered.
    - Competition from other employers.
    - Housing and transport developments – Both of these may help to attract potential employees into the area.

Demand Analysis

This involves estimating the number and type of employees likely to be needed in the future, taking into account the firm's objectives, plans and projected demand. Information on the latter could be obtained from the following:

a) Judgement of experienced managers and / or employees.
b) The use of statistical techniques such as time series analysis (which forecasts future requirements using past figures).
c) Carrying out a work study (identifying how long it will take to complete tasks, in order to assess the total hours required at the projected level of activity).

Undertaking Gap Analysis

This stage of the planning process compares the supply of labour with the demand for labour to identify any surpluses or shortages.

Solution Analysis

This involves the identification, consideration and selection of the most appropriate strategies to deal with any surpluses and / or shortages in order to match workforce size, skills and location to business needs.

Implementation of Solutions

This stage obviously involves implementing the strategies selected to deal with any surpluses / shortages (considered in components of workforce plans below).

Evaluation – Monitoring & Review

As with any plan, the implementation of the plan should be regularly monitored and corrective action taken where required. In this case, the forecasts of labour requirements should be compared to actual requirements, and the strategies selected to deal with any surpluses / shortfalls should be assessed to determine whether or not they are proving appropriate in securing the business's human resources requirements.

Components of Workforce Plans

The Workforce Size, Skills and Location Required to Match Business Needs

This very first section should detail the number and type (skills, qualities, qualifications, experience, etc) of employees required in each part of the organisation and when they are required. It should outline any surpluses and shortfalls following the supply, demand and gap analysis outlined above, which should take into account the business's objectives, plans and projected demand for its products / services.

Strategies

This part of the plan details the strategies required to close the gap between the supply of labour and the business's demand for labour, so that the firm has the correct numbers of workers (and with the right skills in the right location) to achieve its various objectives.

The strategies a business might adopt in the case of a shortfall include:

- The **use of overtime** – This might be appropriate in the case of a temporary / short-term shortfall. In the medium to longer-term this can prove costly.
- **Action to increase productivity** ie output per worker eg through job re-design, training.
- **External recruitment** and **more attractive / competitive packages**. If there is a shortage in the external supply of labour, a business may have to review the current package offered to employees in relation to competitors and make improvements, accordingly, in terms of rates of pay, bonuses, pension schemes and other fringe benefits. Where geographical mobility is an issue, a business may include relocation expenses in the terms and conditions of employment.
- **Investment in long-term training programmes**. When faced with a skill shortage a firm may take employees on with very few skills appropriate to a specific job and train them to perform a wide variety of jobs. This applies equally to both white-collar and blue-collar employees. An advantage of this is that it engenders significant levels of loyalty to the business.
- **Internal promotion.** A business may promote from within to fulfil any managerial / supervisory roles. Providing opportunities for promotion can help to increase motivation (self-esteem and self-actualisation) and staff retention rates, but may incur significant training costs.
- **Transfers in.** A business might be able to transfer employees working within the business to units / departments / sections facing shortages, if those being transferred are surplus to requirements in their current areas.
- **Outsourcing manufacturing or other business processes** (either in the short, medium or longer-term) to another business. (This strategy, including potential advantages and disadvantages, is considered in more detail in a subsequent section).
- **Mechanisation / automation** – to reduce the need for labour.

Strategies a business might use when the workforce is surplus to requirements include:

- **Reducing overtime.**
- **Short-time working** eg reducing the working week from 5 days to 4.
- **Reducing the amount of work subcontracted out** in order to make use of the spare labour.

- **Redeploying and retraining and transfers out to another part of the business.** If a business has a stated policy of investing heavily in human capital (people), then it might feel honour-bound to provide the maximum opportunities for all employees.
- **Downsizing** ie reducing the size of the workforce.
- **Delayering** ie removing a complete layer of management.

Removing opportunities for over-time and short-time working obviously affects employees' pay and can be a sensitive issue. In addition, the latter two strategies may not only prove costly in the short term with redundancy payments, but may negatively affect the morale of those employees who remain. This could indirectly have a negative affect on productivity. Consequently such policies need to be carefully considered and well managed. Looking for the least difficult route is almost impossible but if redeployment is not an option, then the following may be considered:

a **Firing the casual labour first.** It will be easier to fire casual workers with little or no compensation, because of the lack of legal repercussions.

b **Natural wastage.** This is where a business does not replace individuals when they leave, so it will normally have the desired effect of reducing employment costs in the long term. Although natural wastage provides the least conflict, apart from requiring the remaining employees to increase their responsibility at no extra salary / wage, the impact will not be felt immediately.

c **Voluntary redundancies / early retirement.** This is where employees are offered a package and invited to offer themselves for redundancy or early retirement. Such an offer can be more generous than the compulsory redundancy package, but it still causes ill feeling and lowers morale.

d **Compulsory redundancies.** This is the deepest cut of all, whereby the business pursues its stated policy on redundancy eg last in first out. Agreements within the contract, in terms of notice and payment, will need to be honoured and the business will have to ensure it does not employ someone else to do the same job if the business's labour requirements suddenly improve.

Costings / Budgets

This section of the plan details the costs involved in its implementation. These costs are expressed in terms of budgets which provide an important means of control. Targets for expenditure on activities may include targets for expenditure on advertising for recruitment, training and development, promotions and redundancies, for example.

Timing – Implementation Schedule

The final section of the plan should outline who is responsible for doing what by when. This is an important control mechanism, enabling progress to be monitored at regular intervals and corrective action taken as appropriate.

Closing Comments

The best plans will also include contingency plans. These should take into account possible problems and challenges the business may face in implementing the plan – for example – the unanticipated poaching of staff by competitors. They should outline the action to overcome these if they do arise, to ensure the business obtains the human resources it requires to meet its needs.

Assessing Internal and External Influences on Workforce Plans

Objectives

By the end of this topic you should be able to:

1. Outline at least 4 internal influences on workforce plans.
2. Outline at least 4 external influences on workforce plans.

Key Terms

Internal influences on workforce plans are factors coming from inside the business that can affect decisions over, or success in implementing, workforce plans – for example – the nature of the product / service, corporate objectives and strategy, objectives and strategy of other functional areas, the amount of finance available, improvements in labour productivity or the rate of absenteeism and labour turnover, and the size and strength of worker representation.

External influences on workforce plans are factors stemming from outside the business that can affect decisions over, or success in implementing, workforce plans – for example – customer demand, market and economic factors, competitor packages, technological change, demographic and social change, wage rates, government policy and employment legislation.

Internal Influences

The Nature of the Product / Service to be Provided

As previously outlined in the section on internal influences affecting HR objectives, the nature of the product and service will, obviously, directly influence the type and level of skills required.

Corporate Objectives and Strategy

The starting point in a workforce plan is corporate objectives, and the plan concerns the acquisition of human resources necessary to achieve those objectives. Forecasting demand for employees for a particular trading period will, therefore, require detailed knowledge of corporate objectives and plans for achieving these. For example:

- Expansion through diversification into new markets may require the recruitment of additional employees with different skills.
- Consolidation to ensure survival may necessitate downsizing and redundancies.

Objectives and Strategy of Other Functional Areas

Forecasting demand for employees for a particular future trading period also requires detailed knowledge of marketing and production plans. For example:

- Plans to increase market share through innovation and the launch of new products may require additional employees / employees with different skills.
- New technology to reduce running costs may require fewer employees with fewer skills.

Finance Available

Finance is required to implement the plan and this requirement may be significant when it involves plans for growth. It costs money to advertise, interview, select, induct, train and develop new staff. Even when the workforce plan involves downsizing there may be a cost in terms of redundancy payments. Close liaison with the finance department is, therefore, clearly required when drawing up the plan to ensure sufficient funds are available to implement it.

Labour productivity, Rates of absenteeism and Labour Turnover

If productivity per employee increases, or the rate of absenteeism and labour turnover reduces, this may negate or, at least, reduce the need for additional staff to be recruited.

Size and Strength of Worker Representation

Short-time working and redundancies can be disruptive and unsettling for the workforce. Any changes to employment practices will need to be discussed with workers and their representatives. This has implications for the timing of the plan and, if the workforce has the backing of a strong union, may result in strategies to cope with a surplus being moderated or revised.

External Influences

Customer Demand, Market and Economic Factors

The level and nature of customer demand for a business's product or service will determine the level and nature of staff required. A rise in demand for a business's product will increase the demand for labour. A fall in demand will reduce the demand for labour. This, in turn, is affected by market and economic factors. For example:

- Changes in interest or taxation rates may affect the amount of disposable income people have available to spend on the business's product or service and result in lower demand and, thus, lower demand for labour.
- A new competitor may reduce demand for a business's products and, thus, the demand for labour. Closure of a competitor may have the reverse affect.

Employment Packages Offered by Other Businesses

Strategies laid down in the plan to secure a business's HR requirements should also take into account the activities of other businesses. It will be vital to offer competitive packages in case of a labour shortage.

Technological Developments

Technological developments are leading to changes in distribution (e-retailers) patterns, working patterns, and changes in the skills required in the workforce. For example:

- The advent of the internet and VoIP technology has enabled employees to be based from home ie homeworking / teleworking (discussed in a subsequent section below).
- Machines, computers and robots are increasingly replacing people in the workplace, thus reducing the demand for labour, particularly unskilled. However, this is increasing the demand for certain skills such as those possessed by machine designers, computer operators and electrical engineers, etc.

Demographic and Social Change

Demographic factors affect the total supply of labour in an economy. They concern the size and structure of the population, in particular the number of people of working age (ie between 16 and 65), who are willing and able to work. This, in turn, is affected by birth and death rates (thus contraception, medical / health care); and migration ie the movement of people from one geographical area to another. As the previous section on HR objectives has highlighted, there is currently an ageing population. A business may, therefore, find it difficult to attract young people and suffer higher labour costs as labour may become more expensive due to the laws of supply and demand.

The level of education and training will, of course, affect the supply of labour in terms of skill levels. There has been much public criticism over the general standard of education, particularly with regard to the basic skills of reading and writing.

Another social factor affecting workforce plans is that more and more employees are expecting to be able to secure flexible working arrangements in order to fit in with family and other commitments.

Wage Rates

In general, the higher the level of skill required to perform a particular job, the higher the rate of pay. The higher the real wage rate (ie after inflation has been taken into account) between one occupation / profession and another, the more attractive the occupation / profession. This, in turn, is affected by the availability of labour. If a shortage exists then rates of pay are likely to rise in order to attract sufficient numbers to meet demand, and vice versa. However, if shortages exist for a particular skill, the average wage rate is pushed up, and vice versa. Where surpluses exist, the average wage rate is pushed down.

If wage rates are expected to rise then the fewer staff a firm will be willing to take on, and vice versa. In the case of the former, a business may investigate whether or not any processes can be mechanised which could result in redundancies.

Government Policy and Legislation

Government policy and legislation can affect the demand and supply of labour. Refer to the following examples:

- The minimum wage may have encouraged firms to invest in capital rather than labour intensive processes and reduced demand for labour.
- Government incentives for people to join a particular market where there are shortages, eg education, health and the police, make these areas more attractive and help to reduce skills shortages.
- Money to encourage employers to take people on and train them. The New Deal (introduced by Labour in 1997) was designed to achieve this.
- The EU Working Time Directive has limited the standard working week and increased the demand for labour, or technology to replace labour.

In addition to the above, the law requires that redundancies are preceded by consultation with representatives of the workforce with agreement on the criteria for selection of people for redundancy. From a management point of view the criteria should focus on people with the skills and potential to cope with the changes in working practices, but agreement with unions is a legal requirement and needs to be taken into account when drawing up the workforce plan.

Trade Unions

As stated above - in the section on internal factors and size and strength of worker representation, unions may be able to influence strategies decided upon to deal with a surplus or shortfall.

Closing Comments

The value of workforce plan is very much depend on accuracy of forecasts and research into internal and external factors and assumptions made about these factors during the time period in which the plan is to be implemented. Changes in external factors (and, in some case, internal factors) can, however, be difficult to predict. Hence, flexibility needs to be built into the plan to ensure timely response to any changes affecting its implementation, and its appropriateness to meeting the business's needs.

Issues in Implementing Workforce Plans

Objectives

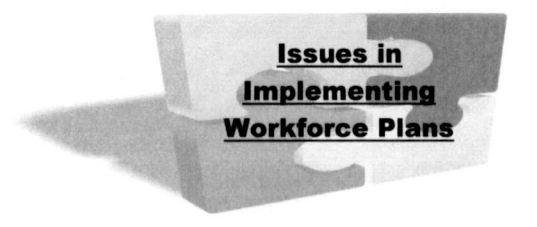

By the end of this topic you should be able to:

1. Describe at least 4 issues in implementing workforce plans.

Key Terms

Issues in implementing workforce plans include the effect on employer / employee relations and corporate image, cost and training requirements, as well as the danger of treating the plan as a rigid document.

Issues in Implementing Workforce Plans

Employer / Employee Relations

Any potential negative changes to the workforce such as short-time working and, in particular redundancies can affect employer / employee relations. Redundancies cause ill feeling and lower morale, especially if there has been a strong sense of teamwork within the workforce, as it disrupts social relationships. Lower morale can negatively affect motivation and productivity.

Consultation with the workforce over redundancies and other changes to employment practices is a legal requirement. But, besides avoiding financial penalties, communication and consultation with the workforce about redundancies can help employees to appreciate the reasons behind them and ensure the selection criteria is considered to be fair ie based on objective criteria such as length of service, experience, competency and qualifications or attendance, disciplinary and performance history. This should help to minimise any potential ill feeling amongst those staff who are leaving and those who are staying behind – helping to minimise any negative effect on motivation and productivity and long-term damage on employee / employer relations.

Minimising the need for compulsory redundancies eg through natural wastage, involuntary redundancies and / or retraining and redeployment should also help minimise the damaging effect on employee / employer relations.

Corporate Image

Layoffs and redundancies can lead to negative publicity which may negatively affect the reputation of the business as an employer - at least in the short-term, and may also affect customers' perceptions which, in turn, may negatively affect sales.

Likewise, the creation of new jobs can enhance a business's corporate image and have the reverse affect to that outlined above.

Training

If the workforce plan involves the recruitment of new staff there will need to be some induction training at the very least in order to familiarise new 'recruits' with the workplace and help them settle into their jobs as quickly as possible with the minimum amount of disruption.

The induction programme should not be rushed. Sufficient time must be allowed for individuals to settle in and fulfil their roles properly. Not only do such programmes enable a firm to maximise the productivity of new workers, but, from a legal point of view, they are an important vehicle for familiarising staff with health and safety procedures (including fire), which should be outlined immediately, from day one. Employees who do not undergo a formal induction process may feel insecure, unhappy, and in the worst case scenario, leave the business within the first few weeks of arriving, resulting in the recruitment process having to start all over again - adding to labour costs.

New products / processes and / or the redeployment of staff surplus from one area to an area where there is a shortage may also require new skills involving the re-training of staff.

Cost

As stated above, recruitment and selection, induction and training, re-deployment (necessitating re-location and re-training), and redundancy payments can all incur significant costs. These all need to be budgeted for. Close liaison with the finance department is required to ensure sufficient funds are available to implement the plan.

Danger of Treating the Plan as a Rigid Document

One final point to bear in mind is that numerous factors outside the control of the business can affect the implementation of the plan and / or its appropriateness in meeting the needs of the business. The plan should, therefore, not be treated as a rigid document that must be followed, resulting in slow reaction to changes in the business environment (and internal factors) and, ultimately, failure of the plan to meet business needs.

Closing Comments

Predicting the behaviour of people (employees and customers) and / or external events is not an easy task. It requires constant monitoring. Figures on the type and skills of employees required must be checked, revised and updated regularly as factors change. Any changes must be well thought out, particularly those requiring redundancies, as this could lead to industrial relations problems, affect morale and motivation and, ultimately, the business's performance.

The Value of Using Workforce Plans

Objectives

By the end of this topic you should be able to:

1. Outline the value and limitations of workforce plans.
2. Explain why the workforce planning process may be considered Justas imported as the completed plan.

Key Terms

The value of using workforce plans concerns their support in enabling the business to meet customer requirements and fulfil planned activities, as well as minimise labour costs. Their value is, however, limited by factors outside the business's control.

The Value and Limitations of Using Workforce Plans

Value

Although a plan is the end result of the planning process, many would argue that the planning process itself is just as important as the finished document. This is because the planning process forces the decision makers in a business to think, to research, to consult and to discuss. In the case of a workforce plan, it should ensure staffing requirements are thoroughly researched and that strategies to achieve these requirements are properly thought through and that nothing is overlooked.

More specifically, workforce planning can help to predict / anticipate labour shortfalls and labour surpluses before they actually occur and allow time to plan and implement appropriate strategies - for example - recruitment drives and training initiatives in the case of a predicted shortfall, and redeployment or even redundancies in the case of a predicted surplus to ensure the business needs are met.

The completed workforce plan provides a comprehensive framework which guides operations and decision making. It helps to prioritise and allocate resources and responsibilities to ensure that the right number and type of people are in the right place, at the right time in order to meet customer requirements, and minimise the damaging effect that labour shortages can have on a business. For example, in addition to customer dissatisfaction, lost orders and sales, a shortage can result in work overload and, thus, stress, absenteeism and, ultimately, labour turnover and associated costs.

The completed plan should also help to maximise productivity and profitability by eliminating surpluses which unnecessarily add to costs.

The completed plan also provides targets which can be used to monitor performance and activities, and enable timely and appropriate action to be taken as required.

Limitations

The value of the plan is, however, dependent on the accuracy of the forecasts and, even if the forecasts were based on an in-depth analysis, unpredictable changes in external factors eg a new competitor can affect the demand for a business's products / services and the demand for labour and, thus, the appropriateness of the original plan.

There are also numerous factors outside a business's control that may affect its ability to secure the labour it requires to meet business needs. For instance, skill shortages may be regional, or national, making it difficult to recruit staff even when there is a need. Competition may also make it difficult to recruit. With regard to the latter, workforce planning on its own will not help to attract and retain good staff in times of a predicted labour shortfall. Ensuring competitive pay and other conditions of employment would be essential but might not be possible if competition is larger and able to benefit from greater economies of scale and, thus, able to afford more attractive employment packages.

Closing Comments

Workforce planning is designed to ensure that the company has the human resources to achieve its functional and corporate objectives. Without a workforce of the right size and skills the company will not achieve its objectives. But, if the workforce exceeds the company's needs, it will add to costs and result in a failure to achieve profit targets. For these reasons, effective workforce planning is essential if the firm is to achieve its corporate objectives.

Although the construction of the plan does not guarantee success – due to the numerous factors outside a business's control that can impinge upon its performance, failure to plan, can greatly increases the chance of failure.

5.3

COMPETITIVE ORGANISATIONAL STRUCTURES

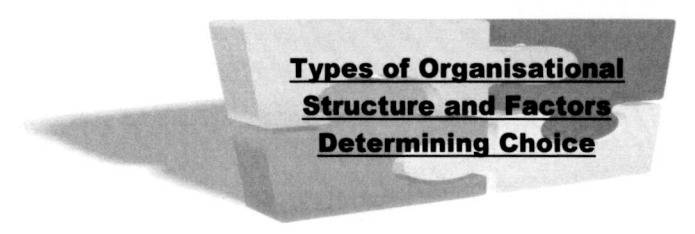

Types of Organisational Structure and Factors Determining Choice

Objectives

By the end of this topic you should be able to:

1. Define the terms organisational structure, departmentalisation, hierarchy, span of control, formalisation; functional, divisional and matrix organisational structures; mechanistic and organic organisational structures; technology.
2. Outline at least 3 advantages and 2 disadvantages associated with functional organisational structures.
3. Outline at least 2 advantages associated with divisional organisational structures.
4. Outline at least 2 advantages and 1 disadvantage associated with matrix organisational structures.
5. Outline at least 2 advantages and 1 disadvantage associated with mechanistic organisational structures.
6. Outline at least 1 advantages associated with organic organisational structures.
7. Explain at least 4 factors determining choice of organisational structure.

Key Terms

Organisational structure refers to the way in which an organisation's activities are grouped together and coordinated to ensure members work together to achieve organisational goals.

Departmentalisation is dividing and grouping an organisation's activities into distinct tasks or sets of tasks.

Hierarchy is the order of levels of management or supervisors within a business, from the lowest to the highest.

Span of control is the number of people reporting directly to a particular manager or supervisor (or the number of people for whom a manager or supervisor is directly responsible).

Formalisation is the drawing up of written policies, rules, regulations, job descriptions and standing orders, etc which prescribe the correct or expected action of members of an organisation.

A **functional organisational structure** is where staff are grouped into different departments / functional areas which perform a common set of activities eg Marketing, Operations, and Finance.

A **divisional organisational structure** is where staff are grouped around product / service lines, or customers groups, or geographical locations.

A **matrix organisational structure** combines both functional and product or market structures. For example, staff are organised into project teams that consist of people involved in a particular function, as well as people involved in a particular product or customer group. Each employee reports to both a functional or divisional manager and to a project manager.

A **mechanistic organisational structure** has a high degree of formalisation, many layers in the hierarchy, narrow spans of control, and highly centralised decision making.

An **organic organisational structure** has few rigid rules and regulations, few hierarchical levels, wide spans of control, and low centralisation, with people generally being allowed to use their own initiative.

Technology refers to the combination of skills, knowledge, tools, equipment, machines and computers used to carry out a business's planned activities.

Defining and Classifying Organisational Structure

Organisational structure refers to the way in which an organisation's activities are grouped together and coordinated to ensure the effort and activities of members fulfil the organisation's mission, aims and objectives.

Dividing and grouping an organisation's activities into distinct tasks or sets of tasks is known as departmentalisation.

Coordinating members' efforts to achieve organisational goals essentially occurs through any one, some, or all of the following:

- **informal communication** channels (the grapevine).
- the development of a **formal hierarchy** ie layers of supervisors and managers with the authority and responsibility to issue instructions to, and monitor and control the activities of people under their span of control.
- **formalisation** and **standardisation** - including clearly defined, communicated goals; written policies, rules and regulations; job descriptions; careful selection of staff; and training staff where applicable to ensure tasks are completed to the required and expected standard.

Organisations can be classified according to:

- how tasks are grouped together ie departmentalised.
- the degree of formalisation.
- the number of layers in the hierarchy and width of span of control.
- the extent to which the authority and responsibility for decision making is shared amongst members.

Before looking at specific types of organisational structure let us just consider each of the above factors in a little more detail:

- **Departmentalisation** results in specialisation. Specialisation helps to maximise productivity and profitability because employees become expert in carrying out a particular task, ie they become quicker and make fewer mistakes, thereby helping to minimise the number of labour hours required as well as the costs associated with poor quality work.

- **Formalisation** ie the drawing up of written policies, rules, regulations, job descriptions and standing orders, etc which prescribe the correct or expected action, serves to establish a framework where decision making can be delegated with reasonably predictable results, and logical outcomes such as the smooth running of the organisation, heightened efficiency and productivity can be expected.

- **Hierarchy and span of control** are terms that you should be familiar with from Unit 2. Hierarchy is the order of levels of management or supervisors within a business, from the lowest to the highest. Span of control refers to the number of people reporting directly to a particular manager or supervisor. In general, the fewer the levels of hierarchy, the more effective the communication, as there are fewer levels through which information has to pass. This can lead to faster decision making and faster response to change. These potential benefits will, however, be outweighed if the span of control, is too wide.

- **The terms centralisation and decentralisation** refer to the extent to which the organisation as a whole, passes authority and responsibility for decision making down into its divisions, departments and sections. (These terms are considered in much greater detail in the subsequent section on adapting organisational structures to improve competitiveness).

Types of Organisational Structure

Functional, Divisional and Matrix Structures

Organisational structures can be classified according to whether activities are grouped:

- into functional areas.
- around product / service lines or markets (customers, locations) served.
- or a mixture of both the above.

Functional organisational structures are where staff are grouped into different departments / functional areas which perform a common set of activities eg Marketing, Operations, and Finance. Such structures can help to:

- maximise efficiency as a result of specialisation – people become expert at carrying out their individual function.
- minimise duplication of effort / resources – there are clearly defined roles / responsibilities.
- simplify training – staff are only trained to do jobs within their functional areas.
- provide (potentially) a more comfortable working atmosphere – as people with the same interests (at least in terms of job roles) work together.

Potential drawbacks associated with functional structures include the fact that they:

- result in people having a narrow perspective – with functional managers and employees focusing so much on their own area that they lose sight of the overall business goals.
- make co-ordination across units difficult – due to the diverse interests / perspectives.
- limit the experience of people, and thus, fail to develop top management generalists.

These disadvantages can, however, be minimised through **regular communication** between the functional departments.

A **divisional organisational structure** is where staff are grouped around product / service lines, or customers groups, or geographical locations. Such structures can also help to maximise efficiency as a result of specialisation. Staff become expert in the product / service they are involved in providing, or customer group or geographical location they are involved in serving and therefore, become quicker at their job and make fewer mistakes. This can lead to a better quality product / service being provided to customers and may mean the business is more able to meet and respond quickly to customer needs.

A **matrix structure** combines both functional and product or market structures. Staff are organised into project teams that consist of people involved in a particular function, as well as people involved in a particular product or customer group, for example. Each employee reports to both a functional or divisional manager and to a project manager. Such structures can be highly beneficial as they:

- enable both lateral and vertical (upwards and downwards) communication to take place and the free flow of ideas that might be constrained in a traditional organisational structure – resulting in greater idea generation.

- consist of teams of people looking at the project from different angles. This is likely to ensure all the potential problems and essential requirements to produce a particular product / service are identified.

Furthermore, because people have had an input (who might not have had such input under the normal organisational structure), it is also likely to lead to better understanding and greater commitment to any changes required to produce new products and / or enter new markets, ultimately, helping to make diversification into new products / markets a success.

Potential disadvantages associated with matrix structures include:

- overlapping authority. Individuals working within a matrix organisation will have two or more superiors, and individuals may suffer if both parties make heavy demands upon them. To minimise this potential problem, it is essential that one person only is given full authority for a job / project during the life of the job / project, and that this authority is made clear to all those concerned.
- the fact that they are more complex to manage. This has implications for management recruitment and training.

Formal, Mechanistic versus Informal, Organic Structures

As stated above, structures can also be classified according to the degree of formalisation, number of levels in the hierarchy and width of span of control and the extent to which decision making is centralised.

A **mechanistic** (or bureaucratic) organisational structure, for example, has:

- a high degree of formalisation.
- many layers in the hierarchy and narrow spans of control.
- highly centralised decision making.

Such formal organisational structures can:

- aid the co-ordination and efficiency of members.
- reduce the potential for conflict.
- minimise the risk of things going wrong through the rigid rules and regulations its members must follow.

However, they can lead to:

- demotivation and impersonal relationships as the job is seen more important than the person and the rules, regulations and procedures limit personal freedom and spontaneity.
- slow response to changing business and environmental circumstances.

In contrast, **organic** organisational structures have:

- shared tasks.
- few rigid rules and regulations.
- few hierarchical levels and wide spans of control.
- low centralisation with people generally being allowed to use their own initiative.

Such informal organisational structures can:

- respond much more quickly to the environment – as people have more freedom to make decisions without having to adhere to rules and regulations and strict procedures.
- aid motivation – as people can use their own initiative.

Factors Influencing Choice of Organisational Structure

Size of the Business

In general, the larger the organisation, the more formal and the more complicated its structure. Growth puts pressure on an organisation, its management and its structure, forcing it to change and adapt in order to cope with the co-ordination and control problems that growth brings.

When a business is small consisting of a few employees a 'hands-on' approach is possible. Any formal arrangement for defining and grouping activities is unnecessary and tasks are allocated face to face. The owner / manager can regularly liaise with the workforce and oversee almost every decision, meeting, problem, etc.

As a business grows in size, it becomes increasingly difficult for the owner / manager to communicate with individual employees, oversee their activities, and ultimately, coordinate staff and maintain the tight level of control possible within a small business. Initially, with two or three extra staff employed in the business, the manager may accept a wider span of control, ie a greater number of people for whom he is directly responsible and who report directly to him or her. There will come a point, however, where the span of control becomes too wide and results in: work overload – leading to stress or inefficiency and loss of control; reduction in personal contact with subordinates – leading to workers feeling isolated / not receiving sufficient advice / feedback and, ultimately, affecting morale, motivation and performance. Consequently, another supervisory / managerial layer is needed in order to control the use of resources and, ultimately, help maximise productivity and efficiency.

In larger businesses there is also a natural tendency for people to be grouped into separate departments and those departments allocated different tasks. This is the process of internal specialisation, which develops hand in hand with the growth in the overall size and complexity of the organisation.

As the spread of separate groups and departments across an organisation increases with growth, additional procedures are required for the co-ordination and communication between these differing units and, it is generally accepted that as an organisation increases in size, it becomes more formalised, with written policies, rules, regulations, job descriptions and standing orders, etc, which prescribe the correct or expected action in order to coordinate and control member activities.

Business Environment

The business environment consists of factors external to the business over which it has no control. It includes social, legal, economic, political and technological factors, as well as competitor activities.

The business environment is often described as being **stable** (ie fairly static and predictable) or **dynamic** (ie forever changing, and more uncertain). If the environment is constantly changing, (for example, the electronics industry where technological advances lead to new demands from customers), a more informal, organic, decentralised structure may be required in order to be able to respond quickly to changes. For an organisation operating within a stable business environment, there is less need for an organic organisational structure.

Where there is a high degree of **competition** - for both customers and resources - then an informal, organic structure might be more appropriate in order to allow fast response to competitor activities. Where competition is low, there is less need for an organic structure.

If there are lots of stakeholder interests to take into account and lots of external variables to monitor, then a more decentralised approach may also be more appropriate.

© APT Initiatives Limited, 2009

Nature of the Business Activities and Technology Used

Technology refers to the combination of skills, knowledge, tools, equipment, machines and computers used to carry out a business's planned activities. The more complicated the technology and un-routine the task to be performed, the more difficult to draw up a set of procedures to account for every eventuality as the more unexpected events can arise. Thus, there is a greater need for a more flexible, less formal structure - to enable people to respond to unexpected situations. The less complex the technology and the more routine the task (such as the mass production of a standardised product time after time), the more appropriate a formal, mechanistic structure.

It should also be pointed out that a business selling a variety of different products and operating in a wide range of locations is likely to adopt a divisional rather than functional organisational structure. In addition, the more diverse and unrelated its activities and geographically spread out the organisation, the more appropriate a decentralised approach, and vice versa. If there is much similarity between a business's activities / operations, then centralisation might be more appropriate as policies made centrally are likely to be relevant to each of the business's operations, and economies are likely to be gained from such an approach.

Nature and Expectations of the Workforce

The more highly skilled, better educated and professional the workforce, the more likely they will expect freedom and autonomy in decision making and dislike close supervision. In which case, a more flexible, decentralised structure will be more appropriate.

Corporate Objectives and Strategy

Different structures suit different business strategies. For example:

- A differentiation strategy requires fast response to changing customer needs and so a less formal, flexible structure.
- A more formal, mechanistic structure might be appropriate for a low cost strategy in order to maximise efficiency.
- Companies that strive to be the market leader and the first to bring out new products or services may require a flexible, organic structure.

Beliefs and Preferences of Owners / Senior Managers

The beliefs and preferences of the owner / entrepreneur / senior managers employed within a business will also determine the degree of delegation that takes place ie the extent to which authority and responsibility for decisions and tasks are passed down to others in the organisation. An autocratic owner / manager – for example – may insist on a formalised structure and centralised decision making, to ensure tight control over member activities.

Closing Comments

Many people believe that growth is likely to lead to a mechanistic, bureaucratic structure. However, it is formalisation not bureaucracy that is an inevitable by-product of organisational growth and there are many structures existing in large scale organisations which better suit the size, technology and environment in which they operate. Indeed individuals have some control over the type of structure an organisation has, and it can be said that what is inevitable is that the continued growth of an organisation, perhaps rests on the ability of the individuals who hold the power base to adopt the type of structure that best suits the organisation and its surrounding environment.

Adapting Organisational Structures to Improve Competitiveness

Objectives

By the end of this topic you should be able to:

1. Define the terms centralisation, decentralisation, delayering, core and periphery workforce, annual hours contracts, zero hours contracts and outsourcing.
2. Outline factors to take into account when assessing the appropriateness of a centralised or decentralised approach.
3. Outline at least 3 advantages and 4 disadvantages associated with a centralised approach.
4. Outline at least 5 advantages and 3 disadvantages associated with a decentralised approach.
5. Comment on the appropriateness of centralisation or decentralisation in a given situation.
6. Outline the potential problems of introducing a more decentralised approach and ways in which these might be overcome.
7. Outline at least 2 potential advantages arising from a decision to delayer and 1 potential disadvantage.
8. Outline the potential problems that may be encountered with a decision to delayer and how these might be minimised.
9. Outline benefits and drawbacks associated with flexible working arrangements to both the employee and the employer.
10. Explain the difference between core and periphery workers.
11. Outline at least 3 benefits and drawbacks associated with home working.
12. Outline at least 4 potential benefits and 6 potential drawbacks associated with a decision to outsource.
13. Outline the main factors to take into account when making outsourcing decisions.
14. Comment on the appropriateness of outsourcing in a given situation.

Key Terms

Centralisation refers to the process of keeping the authority and responsibility for decision making in the upper levels of management.

Decentralisation refers to the process of passing authority and responsibility for decision making downwards from the upper levels of management to people at lower levels in the organisation.

Delayering is the removal of one or more managerial or supervisory layers.

Core and periphery workforce refers to the use of a core of permanent, full-time workers and a periphery of temporary, part-time workers in order to provide the flexibility required to cope with variations in demand. The core workers generally fill important roles ie roles considered to be essential to the firm's competitive advantage, and tend to be more trained and skilled. The periphery workers may not be as skilled or well trained, or may be skilled workers brought in for a specific purpose.

Annual hours contracts are where employees are required to work a certain number of hours each year. The hours worked each week will vary throughout the year according to the needs of the business.

Zero hours contracts are where people are expected to be available for work as and when required. There are no set hours or times.

Outsourcing is the process of employing outside contractors to perform tasks which although are not core activities of the organisation, were previously performed in-house; or the act of moving a firm's internal activities and decision making responsibilities to outside providers.

General Introduction

Organisational structure can affect:

- the motivation of staff.
- the efficiency of a business, its costs and profitability.
- the speed with which a business is able to respond to changes in the business environment.

In an increasingly competitive market place businesses are being forced to look at more and more ways in which they can improve their competitiveness and many have sought to adopt their organisational structure in order to improve their performance in this area.

Centralisation and Decentralisation

Explanation of the Two Terms and Factors Influencing Choice

The terms centralisation and decentralisation refer to the extent to which the organisation as a whole, passes authority and responsibility for decision making down into its divisions, departments and sections. In a highly centralised organisation power is concentrated in the upper levels of management. Key business decisions are taken by the most senior managers. In a decentralised organisation lower levels of management have the responsibility for many important decisions. Delegation is a key feature, ie the passing of responsibility and authority to make business decisions to people at lower levels in the organisation.

The previous section suggested that the appropriateness of centralisation (or decentralisation) will depend upon a range of factors including:

- the nature of the business and its activities.
- size and geographical spread of the organisation.
- the environment in which the organisation operates
- the ability of employees.

It will also depend upon the **risk** involved. The greater the risk involved, particularly with regard to financial decisions made within the organisation on a day to day basis, the greater the degree of centralisation likely. It should be noted, however, that a standardised approach ie centralisation or decentralisation may not be appropriate for all management functions. It depends upon the potential gains in terms of cost and efficiency. For example, if the majority of supplies are local, then it might be more efficient to decentralise the purchasing function. The decentralisation of personnel functions such as recruitment might also be more appropriate for similar reasons. On the other hand, a centralised approach might be more appropriate for Marketing in order to benefit from potential economies of scale, as well as for Finance, given the considerable risk often involved with financial decisions.

Potential Advantages & Disadvantages Associated with a Centralised Approach

In general, centralisation can provide the following advantages:

- **Greater control** – Senior management have a holistic viewpoint and, it is argued, are likely to be more experienced and skilful. Hence they may make better quality decisions than those further down the organisation.
- **Uniformity of decision making** – thus minimising potential conflict.
- **Economies of scale** – factors that lead to reduction in unit cost as a firm increases output / size and scale of operations.
- **Economies of staffing** – thus duplication of effort is eliminated.
- **Economies of specialisation** – Highly skilled personnel are available to the whole organisation, not just one unit.

Potential disadvantages associated with centralisation include the following:

- **Policy decisions made centrally might be too general** and not optimise decisions for specific areas of a business.
- **Overload / pressure on senior managers** – may lead to stress, resulting in poor job performance / low motivation, plus poor communication with lower level managers due to lack of time.
- **Too much power given to too few individuals** – Top managers may be more pre-occupied with status than the business, and may not be best placed to make decisions on a local scale.
- **Slower decision making** – requests have to be passed upwards and the decision awaited.
- **Poor motivation of lower level staff** – Lack of responsibility can be de-motivating and stifles personal development.
- **Loss of initiative of lower level staff** – People may not bother to put forward ideas if they are not part of the decision making process.

Potential Advantages & Disadvantages of a Decentralised Approach

Decentralisation may provide the following advantages:

- **Reduced workload / potential stress of senior managers** – freeing up their time to concentrate on major / strategic issues.
- **Power is dispersed** – senior managers are likely to be less pre-occupied with status / their position, and more concerned with the business.
- **Better quality decisions and managers** – more managers are involved who are likely to be better placed to make decisions over their sphere of operations, ensuring local conditions are taken into account, and better, more rounded managers are likely to develop as a result.
- **Faster decision making / faster response to change** – requests no longer have to be channelled upwards and the decision awaited, resulting in faster response to changes in market conditions.
- **Improved morale and motivation of lower level managers** – lower level managers are likely to feel valued and more self-fulfilled as a result of increased responsibility.
- **Increased respect from staff** – first line employees are likely to have more respect for their line managers if they feel decisions can be made locally, without referral to a higher authority.
- **Lower supervision costs** – as lower level managers become more responsible (and motivated).

A highly decentralised organisation may, however, experience the following:

- **Loss of direction and control.**
- **Lack of uniformity and consistency in decision making** – this may lead to workforce discontentment and can damage a business's image if standardised products / services are important to its success.
- **Loss of economies of scale, staffing & specialisation** – may lead to duplication of effort and best use not being made of the most skilled personnel.
- **Inter-unit conflict** – development of narrow departmental view.

Requirements of, and Potential Problems Associated with, Introducing a More Decentralised Approach

A more decentralised approach requires the following:

- managers to be **capable of doing more** than they have done in the past ie a different type of manager, ie one with entrepreneurial skills as opposed to one that just follows instructions / established procedures.
- a high degree of **trust**. Managers should be able to carry out these additional tasks without constant checking from head office / senior management.
- managers to feel **confident** in their own abilities to make important decisions.

One of the main barriers to implementing a more decentralised approach lies in managers' willingness to accept responsibility. **Unwillingness to accept responsibility** may be due to a number of reasons. For example, managers:

- may feel they have been given extra responsibilities without the associated remuneration.
- lack confidence in their own ability.
- be concerned about the greater accountability that there is for decision making.

The main way in which a business can change the existing culture and overcome any fears and insecurities existing employees might have is through **investment in training**. A business might also have considered the introduction of **financial rewards** to reward management for taking on board the additional responsibility.

In the longer-term, **recruitment and selection policies might need to be adapted** to ensure individuals are selected that fit in with a more 'empowered' organisational culture.

One final point to make is that feedback to the centre would still be a necessary feature in order to maintain effective control, allowing checks to be made as to whether the delegated authority is being used effectively.

Delayering

Explanation

As an organisation grows in size it develops supervisory or management levels. There are, however, a number of problems associated with tall hierarchical structures, namely:

- **Poor and / or slow communication** – the greater the number of levels, the longer it takes for messages to get passed through, and the greater the opportunity for information to get distorted.
- **Slower decision-making** – due to the number of levels through which information has to pass.
- **Slower response to change** – due to the potential weaknesses listed above (and the fact that hierarchical structures tend to have more rules, regulations and procedures).

Delayering is the removal of one or more managerial or supervisory layers. The argument is, however, the more flatter, leaner the organisation, the fitter and better able it is to cope with a rapidly changing environment. Delayering is often used when the business faces difficult times and, perhaps, needs to cut costs in order to survive eg increased competition, market saturation or recession.

Potential Advantages and Disadvantages of a Decision to Delayer

The removal of one or more managerial or supervisory layers can:

- **speed up communication and decision-making**.
- help a business to **respond more quickly** to changes in the marketplace.

Delayering also has the effect of increasing the span of control of lower level managers and there are a number of potential advantages and disadvantages associated with having a wider span of control:

- **improved motivation and morale** of the management and / or workforce – due to the increased responsibility (Herzberg's 'Motivators');
- **lower supervision costs**.

If too wide a span of control arises as a result, however, this can lead to **the over-burdening of managers** which may, in turn, result in inefficiency.

Potential Problems Associated with a Decision to Delayer

Delayering often leads to **redundancies** if staff cannot be redeployed elsewhere. This obviously increases costs in terms of redundancy payments, and can cause **ill feeling** and **lower morale,** not just amongst those employees made redundant, but also amongst those managers / supervisors and staff who are left behind, especially if there has been a strong sense of teamwork within the workforce – as it **disrupts social relationships**.

To eliminate the potential problems explaining the new strategy and its importance to a company's future success may help to minimise any ill-feeling arising from the redundancies, by helping staff to appreciate why they are necessary.

Flexible Workforces

Overview

Variable patterns of demand will result in variable fluctuations in the business's demand for human resources. The traditional pattern of employing only permanent, full-time staff can lead to inefficiency – for example - insufficient numbers of staff at peak times to meet customer orders on time and provide the right level of customer service, and too many staff at other times unnecessarily keeping fixed costs per unit high.

Variable patterns in demand, therefore, require flexible working arrangements in order to ensure sufficient numbers of staff to provide the right level of service to customers, whilst keeping fixed costs to a minimum.

A wide range of flexible working practices are emerging - some of which will be discussed in more detail below. These include:

- the employment of part-time workers instead of full-time. This may include job sharing and term-time contracts.

- the use of temporary contracts instead of permanent contracts.
- flexitime, self-rostering, compressed working weeks.
- annualised hours contracts.
- zero hours contracts.
- home working (or teleworking).
- outsourcing.

Many of the flexible working arrangements that are emerging provide a number of benefits. For the employees, they can help to:

- **alleviate the stress** involved in balancing home life and work commitments and encourage loyalty and commitment to the firm.

For the employer, they may help to:

- **increase productivity** – as a result of greater capacity utilisation, greater job satisfaction, lower absenteeism.
- **recruit staff more easily** – eg the availability of part-time work can attract skilled workers who are unable to work full-time and the availability of flexi-time to attract skilled staff who cannot work standard hours.
- **lower labour turnover and associated costs** – as a result of improved work-life balance for the employee – resulting in greater morale, loyalty and commitment.

On a negative side, where the use of part-time and temporary staff are concerned, there may be **increased costs for recruitment, training and administration**.

Let us now consider some of the ways in which businesses are securing a flexible workforce.

Core and Peripheral Workers

Businesses may employ a core of permanent, full-time workers and a periphery of temporary, part-time workers in order to provide the flexibility required to cope with variations in demand. The core workers generally fill important roles and tend to be more trained and skilled. They possess the skills that are essential to the firm's competitive advantages, and they provide the firm with functional flexibility. The periphery workers may not be as skilled or well trained, or may be skilled workers brought in for a specific purpose.

There are a wide number of part-time arrangements evident (ie arrangements whereby the employee works less than the standard 40 hour week). For example, working mornings, afternoons or evenings only, or working during school hours, certain days of the week, weekends, or alternate weeks. Term time contracts are popular for parents, more commonly mothers, who do not wish to work in the school holidays, possibly due to difficulties in finding someone to look after their children and / or the cost of child care.

Part-time work may also involve job-sharing where two (or more) people share what was traditionally a full-time job. This can provide a business with greater flexibility as both parties could be brought in at times of high demand. Greater continuity may be possible with regard to cover in case of absence, holiday, etc. In addition, different viewpoints can result in better quality decisions. On the other hand, it can lead to conflict and poor motivation as neither one person has complete ownership and accountability over the job. Regular communication is also essential to avoid duplication of effort.

Temporary work is where a person is employed for a short period of time, usually under a year. They may be directly employed by the employer or employed by an agency. They may involve **fixed term** contracts. This is where the term of employment is for a set period of time which is agreed in advance.

Such agreements, more often than not, do not require notice to be given by either party. Workers not on fixed term contracts, have the same rights to notice as permanent employees. To qualify for other employment rights (excluding equal opportunities), such as sick pay, holiday pay, etc temporary workers need to have worked for a minimum period of continuous employment with their employer.

The use of part-time and temporary workers can increase the flexibility of a business to **meet fluctuations in demand and help maximise capacity utilisation**. It may, however, prove more **expensive** than other methods used to cope with fluctuating demand such as overtime, as it incurs extra recruitment (unless agency staff are used), induction / training and administration costs. In addition, both part-time and temporary workers, by their very nature, tend to be **less motivated** and **committed** than permanent, full time members of staff.

The Use of Annual Hours or Zero Hours Contracts

A business might also make use of annual hours contracts or zero hours contracts, as follows:

- **Annualised hours contracts** are where employees are required to work a certain number of hours each year. The hours worked each week will vary throughout the year according to the needs of the business. Often some of the hours to be worked during certain weeks will be known and agreed beforehand – employees may even be able to have some say over the hours to be worked during these particular weeks. At the remaining times, the employee will be expected to be flexible to meet the needs of the business. Such a system is common, though not limited to, shift workers. It can help to minimise labour costs by cutting working hours and overtime, and provides flexibility for a business to meet fluctuating demand.

- **Zero hours contracts** are where people are expected to be available for work as and when required. There are no set hours or times. Legally if people are at their place of work while 'on call' or 'on stand-by' they must be paid the National Minimum Wage during this time, even though they are not actually working.

Home Working

Developments in ITC, notably telephones, mobile phones, faxes, computers, laptop computers and email, have enabled employees to work while travelling, or at a location other than their employer's workplace. A growing number of people in certain types of jobs such as sales and marketing, accounting, proof-reading and editing, are working on a permanent basis from home.

Home working or teleworking can save on office space and reduce fixed costs eg rent and rates. It can also reduce the cost of travel expenses (for the employer and / employee) and reduce the need to invest in social facilities. It can also have a positive effect on motivation as employees feel trusted to get on with the job which can boost their self esteem. It can also help to alleviate stress, especially the stress associated with commuting during rush hour traffic, for example. It may also be more productive as there are fewer interruptions and employees can spend more time working and less time travelling. From a social perspective the reduction in travel to and from work can cut down on air pollution.

On the negative side, however, it can be expensive to provide the employees with the necessary technology, difficult to monitor working hours, and lead to worker isolation with workers being out of touch with organisational goals. The lack of social interaction can also restrict the achievement of social needs and negatively affect motivation. The possibility of home working on a permanent basis is also, obviously, not possible if the job requires direct contact with customers.

Outsourcing

The outsourcing of some functions might ease the problem of demand fluctuations by, in a sense, passing it on to others. It can be defined as:

- The process of employing outside contractors to perform tasks which, although are not core activities of the organisation, were previously performed in-house.
- The act of moving a firm's internal activities and decision making responsibilities to outside providers.

Outsourcing manufacturing - for example - may be used:

- when there are parts of a product that the business is not able to produce efficiently, or it does not have the specialist knowledge or equipment.
- when a firm is already operating at maximum capacity.
- to cope with seasonal demand – saves the business having to expand.
- to cope with 'one-off' peaks in demand, take on extra orders.

When deciding whether or not to outsource or between activities that should or should not be outsourced, management guru Charles Coates advocates that business organisations should classify activities into critical (or core) activities, and non-critical activities. **Critical activities** are the key to a firm's **competitive advantage** and they must **remain in-house**. Non critical activities are support activities which are not the source of competitive advantage.

Coates advocates that the organisation focuses on the critical activities and, provided outside providers have a cost advantage, outsources the non critical ones. Obviously, if no outsider can perform the task more cheaply, then it should remain in house, but the organisation should always be ready to switch to outsourcing if a lower cost specialist emerges. The potential advantages and potential problems and disadvantages associated with outsourcing are summarised in the table below:

Potential Advantages	Potential Problems / Disadvantages
• Cost reduction – for example - the reduction in labour cost would include the reduction in wages, salaries, pension and national insurance contributions, training, holiday pay. • Improved efficiency. • Access to specialist expertise. • Enhanced flexibility. • Minimises inventories and materials handling. • Allows the firm to concentrate on performing internally those activities that are crucial for the firm's competitive advantage.	• Success depends upon a lower cost firm being available to undertake the work. • There are issues relating to quality of product and reliability of supply. • There are dangers in being tied in to an outside supplier. • There is a need to protect the firm's intellectual property. • Outsourcing involves a great deal of trust. • Increased danger of information leaks. • Less flexibility in responding to unexpected developments. • Possible loss of control. • The effect on the current workforce.

Out of the above disadvantages the question of quality is also a highly important one:

- Will the quality of the work outsourced be equal to that currently obtained?
- Will the organisation undertaking the work be as responsive as an operation in-house?

Ideally, the decision to outsource should follow the following steps:

Steps in Outsourcing Decisions

1. Distinguish between core activities that are a source of competitive advantage and non-core activities.
2. Be prepared to outsource non-core activities - but do not outsource if they are a source of competitive advantage.
3. Identify possible providers of services that can be outsourced.
4. Compare the cost when outsourcing with the in-house costs taking into account non quantifiable factors such as quality provides.
5. If an external firm can provide a service at a price that is lower with quality at least as high as in-house, then proceed with outsourcing the activity.
6. If no suitable external provider is available, then keep the activity in house but continue the search for a provider in the future.

From an HR perspective it is important to consider qualitative issues in more detail. Outsourcing will mean **redundancies** which, besides involving a cost, upset employees. If employees are members of a union and union density is high, this may maximise the redundancy packages offered and make the whole process far more time consuming to implement, which could increase costs quite significantly.

Closing Comments

Implementing any changes to the workplace is a sensitive issue and, if not managed well, can create conflicts with staff and negatively affect performance. Consequently, businesses should ensure that any changes:

- are fully discussed and agreed with employees and their representatives.
- comply with UK and EU legislation – notably the Working Time Directive and Sunday Trading Act 1994.

With regard to compliance with legislation, it is important to be aware of the fact that under the Protection of Employment (Part Time Work) Act 2001, the rights of full time workers have now been extended to part-time workers.

5.4

EFFECTIVE EMPLOYER / EMPLOYEE RELATIONS

Managing Communications with Employees

Objectives

By the end of this topic you should be able to:

1. Define the terms communication; formal and informal communication; vertical, lateral and diagrammatical communication; communication network; and barriers to communication.
2. Outline the key stages involved in the communication process.
3. Outline the importance of communication in ensuring tasks are completed to meet customer and business needs, motivating employees, and when devising and implementing strategy.
4. Explain the difference between formal and informal communication and outline their importance to the business.
5. Explain the difference between vertical, lateral and diagrammatical communication and provide an example of when each might be used.
6. Explain what is meant by the term communication network.
7. Describe the five types of communication network and their associated advantages and disadvantages.
8. State the different types of verbal and non-verbal communications, outline their advantages and disadvantages, and provide examples of when each might be used.
9. Outline at least 6 potential barriers to communication and ways in which these might be minimised.

Key Terms

Communication is the process of transferring information between people. It involves messages being sent and received, with confirmation of receipt, and interpretation of the message, being returned by the receiver to the sender. Effective communication is, therefore, a two-way process where information is passed from person to person in spoken, written or visual form.

Formal communication involves channels that have been approved by senior management and are officially recognised.

Informal communication refers to information shared outside official channels.

Vertical communication concerns information that flows from the upper hierarchical levels to the lower hierarchical levels (ie downwards communication) and vice versa (upwards communication).

Lateral (or horizontal) communication is communication which takes place across the organisation ie between people at the same level in the organisational hierarchy.

Diagonal communication takes place when employees report to managers within different departments.

Communication networks concern the way information flows between people in a particular work group.

Barriers to communication are factors that prevent a message from being received and / or correctly understood or interpreted. They include overload, intermediaries, lack of common language, lack of common sense of purpose, attitudes, low morale, environmental factors, time and position / status.

The Communication Process

Overview

Communication is the process of transferring information between people. The diagram below provides a simple model of the communication process, which essentially consists of six stages:

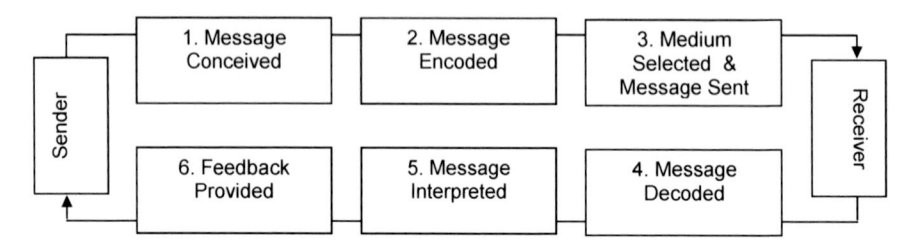

```
         ┌─────────────┐    ┌─────────────┐    ┌─────────────┐
         │ 1. Message  │───▶│ 2. Message  │───▶│ 3. Medium   │───┐
         │  Conceived  │    │   Encoded   │    │  Selected & │   │
         │             │    │             │    │Message Sent │   │
Sender   └─────────────┘    └─────────────┘    └─────────────┘   │ Receiver
         ┌─────────────┐    ┌─────────────┐    ┌─────────────┐   │
         │ 6. Feedback │◀───│ 5. Message  │◀───│ 4. Message  │◀──┘
         │  Provided   │    │ Interpreted │    │  Decoded    │
    ▲    └─────────────┘    └─────────────┘    └─────────────┘
    └──────────┘
```

The Individual Stages Explained

1. **Message Conceived.** The sender becomes aware that there is a message to communicate and decides on the outline content. *Eg: I must let Jim know about the time and place of the meeting tomorrow.*

2. **Message Encoded.** The sender selects an appropriate 'language' (verbal or non verbal) via which to communicate the message, and translates the message into words, symbols, diagrams, images or physical movement, ie body language.

3. **Medium Selected and Message Transmitted.** The sender selects a medium eg informal chat, written report, memorandum and a 'tool' for transmitting the message eg telephone, email attachment, notice board. (The various mediums and tools that can be used to transmit information are considered in more detail later below).

4. **Message Decoded.** The receiver 'reads' the message, which is hopefully in a 'language' that he / she recognises and is able to understand.

5. **Message Interpreted.** Having understood the 'language' of the message the receiver deciphers the true meaning.

6. **Feedback provided.** The receiver sends confirmation to the sender that the message has been received and (hopefully) correctly interpreted and understood eg via a nod, smile, written acceptance or telephone call, etc.

The Importance of Feedback

Feedback (ie a response to a message received) is perhaps the **most important** part of the communication process. It is essential in letting the sender know whether the message has been received, correctly interpreted and understood. The sender psychologically requires this feedback in order to satisfy his or her own safety / security and ego needs. He / she needs to know whether the task of communicating has been carried out correctly. More importantly, failure to provide feedback could be very costly to an organisation, resulting in, for example, incorrect deliveries which lead to delays in production, and ultimately, dissatisfied customers, lost sales and lower profits.

The Importance of Communication

Ensuring Customer and Business Needs are Met

Communication is vital to business success as it is essential in ensuring that:

- employees are clear on their roles, tasks and responsibilities, and work towards achieving the business aims and objectives.
- decisions made by management are carried through.
- potential problems are identified and discussed at an early stage, allowing timely and appropriate action to be taken.

From a business's point of view it can help to ensure that, (along with training and appropriate supervision), tasks are completed to the required standard and deadline set, so that customer expectations and, ultimately, the business objectives are met.

Motivating Employees

Communication is also extremely relevant to the motivation of employees:

- Providing an employee with information about what needs to be done, how to do it, by when, is important in relieving anxiety and thus fulfilling **safety** / security needs.
- Providing employees with information / feedback on how they are performing is important in satisfying their **esteem** needs.
- Communication requires the interaction of people and can help to satisfy employees' **social** needs.

Devising & Implementing Strategy

Two way communication is particularly important when planning and implementing strategy. For example:

- At the planning stage, customer research and feedback is essential in determining the most appropriate strategy(ies) to implement.
- Feedback from employees on any proposals is vital in identifying potential problems at the implementation stage.
- Communicating the reasons / potential benefits for any changes in strategy at the implementation stage, can also do much to lessen potential resistance.

Overview of Types of Communication / Ways of Classifying Communication

Communication can be classified according to:

- the media (channels or vehicles) used ie verbal (written and oral) and non-verbal (the use of images and illustrations, and body language).
- whether it takes place through officially recognised or unofficial channels ie formal and informal.
- the direction in which information flows in relation to the organisational hierarchy ie vertical, lateral and diagonal.
- The way it flows between people in a particular work group – communication networks.

Each of the above are discussed further below, including the advantages and disadvantages, where relevant.

Verbal and Non-Verbal Communication

Oral

Examples of oral communications are an informal chat, more formal interview or meeting. Oral communication may be carried out face to face, via video conferencing facilities, via telephone and, more recently, using Internet (VoIP / Skype) technology, as well as through loudspeaker and radio, for example.

The main advantages of oral communications are that they:

- are cheaper and more direct than other forms.
- allow for immediate exchange of views and instant feedback.
- provide opportunity for questions to check understanding.
- will expose attitudes.

The main disadvantage is that without a written or taped record important points may be missed or forgotten by sender and receiver. This could lead to disputes over what was agreed.

Oral communications are best used for personal matters, matters of great importance and 'unpleasant' matters. Effectiveness may depend upon tone of voice, pitch, volume, speed and clarity of expression.

Written

Examples of written communications are memorandum, letter, report, email, text. Tools used in written communications include notice board, post, computer / internet, fax and mobile phone.

The main advantages of written communications are that:

- they provide a permanent record that can be revisited and checked.
- responses do not have to be immediate.
- time can be taken to read and 'digest' the information to ensure understanding and develop appropriate responses.

However, they:

- can take time to produce.
- may be costly.
- are less personal.
- are open to misinterpretation.
- do not allow for an immediate exchange of ideas.

Lots of written paperwork can also be stressful.

Written communications are best used to clarify oral communication, for more complex matters, and to provide information for staff when they cannot all be there to receive it at the same time. Effectiveness may depend upon vocabulary, punctuation, grammar and clarity of expression.

Images and Illustrations

Examples of visual communications are table, chart, graph, diagram, map, drawing, painting and photograph. The main advantages of visual communications are that they:

- can reinforce written or oral.
- enable the simplification of written or spoken messages.
- need less words of explanation.

However:

- they are open to wider misinterpretation than oral or written forms.
- they may take a long time to prepare.

They are best used for open meetings, training sessions and conferences.

Body Language

Physical forms of communication may help or hinder the oral process. Body language may include facial expression, posture and gestures – for example – a smile, a wagging finger, a handshake, a hug. All these influence how a message may be received and understood.

Formal and Informal Communication

Formal

Formal communication involves channels that have been approved by senior management / the key decision makers, and are **officially recognised**. In order to maintain consistency and efficiency, set procedures are laid down in terms of the language and medium to be used. For example, standard application forms for use in the recruitment process, planned agendas for weekly meetings, purchase orders in finance for use with suppliers. Communication through the management hierarchy, ie vertical communication (see below) is usually classified as formal communication.

Informal

Informal communication refers to information communicated **outside official channels**. A great deal of information is communicated through such channels. For example, a member of staff may seek advice from someone other than his / her supervisor about work tasks, or pass on rumours to friends in other departments. This is often referred to as passing information 'through the grapevine'.

Too much informal communication can lower productivity. It may also lead to the untimely release of confidential information and result in conflict - for example - the threat of redundancies, resulting in unanticipated strike action or absenteeism. Communication through informal channels / the grapevine may also lead to information getting distorted.

Informal communication is, however, **important in satisfying people's social needs**. The grapevine can also be used effectively by management to disseminate information and, for example, judge employees' reactions to any planned changes, and make any necessary amendments before their implementation to ensure acceptance amongst employees.

Vertical, Lateral and Diagonal Communication

Vertical

Vertical communication concerns information that flows from the upper hierarchical levels to the lower hierarchical levels (ie downwards communication), and vice versa (upwards communication). **Downwards** communication is frequently used by management for giving instructions, assigning duties and responsibilities, and providing general information to employees. **Upwards** communication is generally used by employees to provide feedback on results achieved, make suggestions, seek clarification and air any grievances.

Lateral

Lateral (or horizontal) communication is communication which takes place <u>across</u> the organisation, ie between people at the same level in the organisational hierarchy. For example, the Research and Development department informing the Finance department of the costs of producing a new product. Lateral communication is usually used to share information and ideas, solve problems, and resolve conflict.

Diagonal

Diagonal communication may also take place, for example, on projects which involve several departments and there are no clear lines of authority and / or employees are required to report to several managers within different departments. This form of communication is common to matrix organisational structures.

Communication Networks

The Wheel

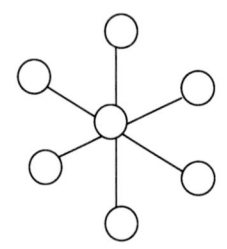

The wheel is where information is communicated to and from one central person, section or department. For example, a departmental head briefing individual members of staff, or head office communicating price changes to individual branches and receiving confirmation that these have been actioned. This can be associated with vertical communication and highly centralised organisations. Communication can be fast and efficient but only if there are not too many people involved. In addition, there is no interaction and the person at the centre has full control. Consequently, creativity may be stifled.

The Circle

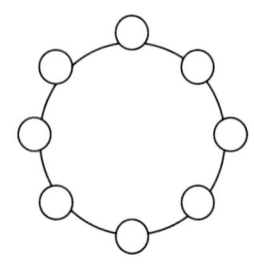

With the circle, individual people, sections or departments, only communicate with two other people, sections or departments. It is often associated with lateral communication.

Such a network provides more social interaction than the wheel, but can take a long time for messages to get through. Decision making is slower and it can be difficult to reach agreements as there is no-one coordinating the process.

The Chain and the Y Chain

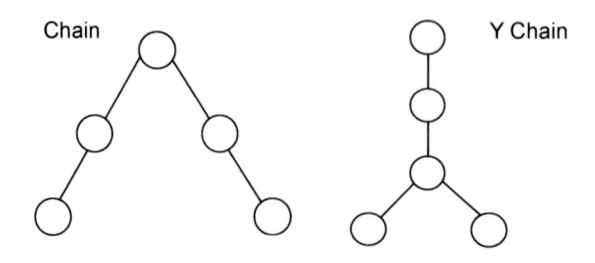

Chain

Y Chain

With the chain, information is communicated by one individual, section or department who then passes the information on to someone else. For example, in the formal organisational hierarchy, senior management passing information through middle to junior management.

In the chain, the person at the bottom only communicates with one other person. This can lead to feelings of isolation. In addition, decision making can be slow as intermediaries are involved.

All Channel

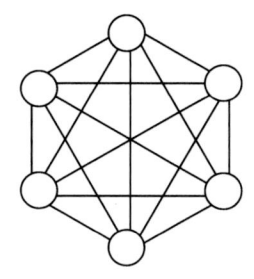

With the all channel network, there is no central figure. Each person (or section or department) communicates with any other person. This is only possible with smaller groups. It is common to decentralised organisations.

Because there is lots of interaction between individuals, it can be highly creative as individuals can bounce ideas off each other. Consequently, it is often used for brainstorming sessions. However, it can lead to conflict and, like the circle, decision making can be slow as there is no central figure co-ordinating the process.

Barriers to Effective Communication

Definition

Barriers to communication concern factors that prevent a message from being received and / or correctly understood or interpreted. The main barriers are considered below.

Overload

The Link with Size. In general, as an organisation increases in size the more formal it will become, ie the more written rules, regulations and official procedures it will have, such as job descriptions, recruitment and health and safety policies, disciplinary and grievance procedures, and codes of practice for dealing with customers, etc. Much emphasis is placed on the importance of keeping a permanent written record as this is considered essential in ensuring consistency and control. However, this can lead to people being swamped with paperwork, and result in any or all of the following:

- difficulty in finding key documentation when required.
- difficulty in prioritising.
- key information being missed as there is only a limited time to read and respond.
- failure to respond to urgent requests.

Too much communication can lead the receiver to feel stressed, resulting in low productivity and / or absenteeism for example, and associated costs, as they are unable to cope.

The Link with IT. Information technologies can help improve communications (see below) but because it is so much easier and quicker to generate and send large amounts of data, this can result in information / communication overload – with the receiver being unable to process all the information sent.

Intermediaries

Intermediaries concern the people involved in helping to transmit a message from the sender to the receiver. If lots of intermediaries are used to send a message then this could result in any of the following:

- excessive or long delays.
- the original message becoming distorted.
- the message never being passed on.

The latter may occur by accident or on purpose because of:

- power struggles – status clash between sender and receiver.
- nervousness, embarrassment, anger, resentment, prejudice or bias.
- uncertainty over accuracy - lack of understanding.
- lack of open-mindedness - receiver unwilling to consider new ideas.
- fear of how the receiver may react (eg if it is bad news).
- intermediaries who do not consider the message to be important /relevant.

The above generally happens as a business increases in size in terms of number of people employed. As a business increases in size, the more supervisory and management levels it develops and the more hierarchical it becomes. These develop in order to control the use of resources and ultimately, maximise productivity and efficiency. However, too many layers can lead to communication problems. This is because the greater the number of levels through which information has to flow:

- the greater the opportunity for information to get distorted or even lost, creating conflict and operational problems.
- the longer it takes for the process to take place, resulting in slower decision making.

To help ease communication problems resulting from size, a business could consider decentralising its operations. This can help to:

- speed up the communication and decision-making processes, as requests no longer have to be channelled upwards and decisions awaited.
- reduce the chance of communication overload occurring and the subsequent stress on senior managers.

Lack of Common Language

It may be that the sender is an expert in his / her field and makes excessive use of jargon, ie technical or specialist terms. If the sentence structure or general use of English is different to that of the receiver, then decoding problems may arise which make it difficult for the receiver to understand and interpret the message correctly. A sender may also use over-simplified language which the receiver finds condescending, (see 'Attitudes' below), resulting in a failure to act upon the message or provide adequate feedback.

Lack of Common Sense of Purpose

If receivers feel alienated and feel no commitment towards the achievement of organisational goals and / or their personal goals conflict with those of the sender, ie they share no 'common sense of purpose', then they are unlikely to be willing to receive or listen to new ideas. Alternatively, they may be willing to listen but do not give the message their full attention as they lack interest in the subject matter / believe it bears little relevance to them.

Attitudes

An attitude can be defined as a mental view / opinion held by an individual or group of individuals which influences their behaviour.

Attitudes concern our likes and dislikes and as such, can help or hinder the process of communication. For example, if a sender dislikes the receiver, he / she may deliberately make it difficult for a particular message to be understood - for example - by using complex terminology that the receiver does not understand. He / she may also use sarcasm or innuendo or over simplified language that the receiver is likely to find condescending. Any of these can cause resentment and could lead to the message being completely ignored and / or incorrectly acted upon. The receiver may also read what he / she expects and not what is actually there, resulting in incorrect action being taken.

Likewise, if the receivers of a message dislike the sender, they are likely to put less effort into decoding the message to ensure it is clearly understood and may even deliberately misinterpret the message as a way of 'getting to' the sender. They may also deliberately limit their feedback resulting in the sender not being certain that the message has been correctly understood / interpreted.

Furthermore, if the subject of the message concerns something the receiver dislikes, they may be unwilling to listen to the message and fail to act upon it.

Low Morale

Morale concerns the mental or emotional condition of an individual or group of individuals. One dictionary definition of morale is 'the state of an individual or group of individuals' spirits and confidence'. It may be said that if a person's morale is low, he / she is not likely to be motivated to work hard towards achieving organisational goals.

Low morale can cause communication problems, as follows:

If the sender suffers from low morale then he/she may not take the time to:

- compose a message carefully, resulting in vagueness and ambiguity.
- consider the receiver's abilities / limitations and thus, choose inappropriate language, resulting in the receiver not being able to understand.
- select an appropriate medium, eg tell someone bad news over the phone, when telling him or her face to face would have been more appropriate.

If the receiver suffers from low morale then he/she may:

- choose to completely ignore the message received.
- be easily sidetracked or distracted, and thus, fail to give the message his/her full attention.
- not take the time to understand the message eg by looking up words or concepts or asking for further explanation / clarification from the sender.
- not take the time to interpret it correctly, or deliberately misinterpret it.
- fail to provide the sender with feedback to reassure him / her that the message has been received and correctly understood / interpreted.

Environmental

Environmental barriers concern the place where the message is transmitted. A hot stuffy atmosphere, or room with inadequate heating, causing discomfort may lead to lack of concentration. A noisy workplace, such as a factory or busy office, may hinder hearing and concentration. Lack of privacy may cause discomfort or embarrassment and distract the receiver.

Time

Barriers relating to time, include: the time of day, length of communication, and how long the sender and receiver have available to deal with the communication.

Choosing the right time and place are very important because:

a) If both parties are in a hurry important points may be missed so communication may be ineffective.
b) If it is late, at the end of a hard day's work, tiredness may become a barrier to receiving information.
c) If the document or conversation is lengthy the receiver may find it hard to concentrate and important points may be missed.

Position / Status

Constraints will be placed on the communication process when the sender and receiver come from different levels of the organisational hierarchy. Communication with a superior may be rather more formal and restrained than it would be with an equal. For example, when an employee is consulted by the managing director the employee may only provide the answers that he / she thinks the MD would like to hear. **Age** and **status** may also adversely affect the process of communication - for example - if an older employee resents having to take orders from a young, newly appointed supervisor.

Ensuring Effective Communication

For the **sender** ensuring effective communication involves:

Thinking carefully before communicating

This will enable good decisions about what is to be said and ensure clarity of expression - the right choice of words.

Being direct, honest and prepared to listen to other viewpoints

This will help to encourage trust and the desire to respond well.

Considering time factors

Choosing a day when there are few other important issues to be dealt with and there is sufficient time available for both parties will ensure that the message is conveyed in a relaxed atmosphere and not rushed.

Keeping the message as brief as possible without detracting from important detail will aid concentration.

Selecting an appropriate environment

This will help to ensure the message is heard and given full concentration. For example:

- If communication is to be done on a one to one basis – a meeting or interview – then a private setting may be crucial to its success.
- For a meeting or conference where a large number of people may be involved it is important to ensure that there is ample space, seating, ventilation etc.

Choosing the most appropriate method and style of communication

This involves giving careful consideration to:

- what he / she hopes to achieve.
- the relationship that exists between him / herself and the receiver.
- current attitudes towards the subject under discussion.
- the skills and ability of the receiver and the nature of the message.

Being aware of physical responses

These provide important information for the sender (about the receiver), about attitudes, interpretation and commitment. For example:

- Eye contact between parties is essential for effective oral communication.
- Positive body language and tone of voice will convey interest, and enthusiasm.
- Impatience, boredom, arrogance, nervousness, are easily transmitted and are often difficult to hide.

The Use of Information Technology

As already stated, information technologies can help speed up the communication process and thus, the decision making process. Although there is the initial capital, installation and training cost, as well as running cost, involved in the introduction of new technologies, in the long run they can also help to reduce costs. For example, email saves on printing, stationery and postage costs, and video-conferencing on travel costs.

With regard to communication, however, the use of IT is not without its problems, as follows:

- Information transmitted electronically is subject to mechanical faults and breakdowns, which can result in a complete loss of information.
- Because it is so much easier and quicker to generate and send large amounts of data, this can result in information / communication overload – with the receiver being unable to process all the information sent.
- There is a potential problem with security and confidentiality. Information sent via e-mail or fax, for example, can often be easily accessed / viewed by others.
- Many office e-mails are also being used for non-business use, which are affecting staff productivity.
- Staff are also often resistant to the change new technologies bring in terms of working practices, routines and work groups.

Closing Comments

The emphasis placed in the AQA Unit 3 specification is on the importance of communication in employee / employer relations. Communication is, however, also essential in maintaining effective relationships between the firm and its external stakeholders, ie suppliers, customers, creditors, shareholders and the wider community, and plays an important part in creating a good public image. For example, effective communication with suppliers is required to ensure the right materials arrive, in the right quantity, at the right time; and in order to maximise sales, customers need to be well informed about the various aspects relating to the marketing mix, ie product, price, promotion and place. Furthermore, the business needs to know exactly what the customer wants so that they can provide it. Consequently, two-way communication with the customer is essential in maximising business success.

Methods of Employee Representation

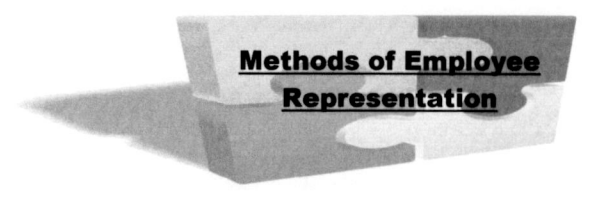

Objectives

By the end of this topic you should be able to:

1. Define the terms employee representation, consultation, trade union, collective bargaining and works council.
2. Outline 3 advantages and 2 disadvantages associated with employee representation.
3. Outline the role, objectives, functions of trade unions and the potential benefits and drawbacks of the process of collective bargaining.
4. Outline at least 2 benefits associated with works councils.
5. Outline at least 2 other forms of employee representation.

Key Terms

Employee representation involves providing workers with the opportunity to air their views on work related matters. It may take many forms including representation through trade union officials and the process of collective bargaining, works councils who meet regularly, or other ad hoc groups.

Consultation is where managers ask employees their views on work related matters, either directly or through representatives, before a decision is made.

A **works council** is where employee representatives form a permanent committee with the right to discuss / influence work related decisions, usually excluding pay and other terms and conditions of employment.

A **trade union** is an organisation of workers created to protect and advance the interests of its members by negotiating agreements on pay and conditions of work.

Collective bargaining is a process whereby the employer negotiates with employee representatives, usually one or more trade unions, who act on behalf of their members to get improvements on pay, and other terms and conditions of employment.

Introduction: The Legal Requirement for Representation & Consultation

Workers have a statutory right to be accompanied by a fellow worker or a trade union official when they are required to attend disciplinary and grievance hearings. This right can, and often is, voluntarily extended to representation over other work related issues, by agreements between the employer and employees or their trade union(s).

Legally, employers are required to consult employees or their representatives over:

- **planned collective redundancies** – under the Trade Union & Labour Relations (Consolidation) Act 1992 and Transfer of Undertakings (Protection of Employment Amendment) Regulations 1987.

- **health and safety in the workplace** – under the Safety Representatives and Safety Committees Regulations 1977 and The Health and Safety (Consultation with Employees) Regulations 1996.

Under The Information and Consultation of Employees Regulations 2004, employees within businesses of 50 or more employees, also have the right to be **informed and consulted** on matters relating to:

- the development of the business's activities and economic situation.
- changes to the level of employment within the business.
- substantial changes in work organisation and contracts of employment.

The right does not operate automatically. It is triggered by requests from employees.

Besides the legal requirement for representation at work, improvements in education have led people to expect to have a say in decisions that affect them, and more and more employers are recognising the benefits that this may bring in terms of the motivation and retention of staff.

Advantages and Disadvantages Associated with Employee Representation

Disadvantages

Allowing employees the opportunity to put forward their opinion over work related issues may mean that decisions are taken more slowly, and there is greater scope for conflict.

Advantages

Consulting and involving employees in decision making can, however, have a positive impact on motivation, improve decision making and assist in the effective management of change.

Firstly, with regard to motivation, asking workers for their views on work related issues may:

- help employees feel valued and more fulfilled (esteem and self-actualisation needs).
- result in more positive relationships between management and employees (social needs).

In addition, it can result in:

- **easier implementation of decisions**, as the more input an employee has in planning and carrying out a decision, the more motivated he / she is likely to be towards carrying it through to completion.
- **better quality decisions**, as having a variety of opinions / viewpoints is more likely to lead to the identification of any faulty assumptions, errors or omissions, and result in the timely correction of these. In addition, employees usually know more about their jobs than anybody else, thus management should utilise this knowledge and allow these viewpoints to be expressed.

Specifically, with regard to the **management of strategic change**, the consultation of all staff concerned as early as possible (well before the introduction of any changes) can be extremely beneficial. This:

- allows conflict to arise and be resolved at an early stage;
- enables improvements to be made to the original ideas regarding changes and how they should be implemented – by providing first hand information and expertise on the organisation;
- provides a better definition of the requirements of change;
- leads to fewer implementation problems.

The Main Methods of Employee Representation

Trade Unions and Collective Bargaining

A trade union is an organisation of workers, created to protect and advance the interests of its members by negotiating agreements on pay and conditions of work. Trade unions provide individual workers with an influential voice over decisions about various aspects of their job. On their own, individual workers would have little influence. There are several different types of union, though the distinction between them has been made more difficult in recent years due to mergers and amalgamations.

Under the Trade Union and Labour Relations (Consolidation) Act 1992 independent trade unions in organisations employing 21 or more workers have a statutory right to claim recognition for collective bargaining. Employers must allow workers to take a vote as to whether they want to have a trade union recognised by their employer, or not. If a ballot takes place, a vote of 40% will require an employer to recognise a union for negotiation purposes.

The main objectives of unions are to obtain the following for their members:

- good rates of pay.
- good working conditions.
- job security.
- influence over government policy (through sponsorship of MPs and financial contributions to political parties).

The main functions in terms of employee representation are:

1. **Individual Representation.** Unions represent individual employees who feel that their rights are being infringed upon, for example, in cases of unfair dismissal.
2. **Negotiation.** Unions assist members in resolving disputes with management by negotiating with management on their behalf ie the process of collective bargaining. These negotiations may concern issues relating to pay, work conditions such as hours worked and breaks, work facilities (heating, lighting, ventilation, work space, safety, noise etc), job descriptions and job specifications, grievance and disciplinary procedures, redundancy and dismissal.

For the **employee**, collective bargaining provides greater influence when negotiating with employers.

For the **employer**, this greater influence may result in increased labour costs, inflexible working practices, excessive disruptions to the workplace (resulting in lost orders / sales), and difficulties with implementing change. However, legislation in the 1980's has done much to quell the power of unions and restrict the above from happening. Furthermore, collective bargaining - particularly when it involves unions - can provide the following advantages:

- **Simpler and quicker negotiations.** It is likely to be easier and much less time consuming to negotiate and reach an agreement with one group representing a number of workers than each individual worker.
- **More realistic demands.** A union may take a more realistic view than individual workers who are heavily influenced by their own personal interests.
- **Support in implementing agreements.** Once a deal has been reached a union will help to see that it is supported by all the workers.

- **Expertise in solving problems.** Unions have built up many years of expertise and knowledge about a particular industry or organisation and may, therefore, be a highly useful source of advice to help solve problems and / or bring about change effectively.

- **Improvements in morale, motivation and, ultimately, organisational performance.** Improvements in pay and working conditions in response to employee requests will lead to a more satisfied, better motivated workforce and, therefore, improvements in productivity and / or levels of customer service.

- **Lower costs from failure to comply with legislation.** Unions encourage organisations to review and reflect on industrial practices and to comply with legal requirements.

The ability of unions to carry out negotiation and representative functions depends on the **strength** of the union in relation to management.

Union strength can be measured in terms of **union density**. Union density is calculated by dividing the number of workers who are members of a union into the total number of workers employed within the business, (ie the potential union membership), and multiplying by one hundred to obtain a percentage. Obviously, the higher the percentage, the higher the union density, and the greater the influence the union is likely to have (unless membership is spread across several unions, as these may have conflicting views).

Works Councils

A works council is where employee representatives form a permanent committee with the right to discuss / influence work related decisions, usually excluding pay and other terms and conditions of employment. They are known by many other names including joint consultative committees, staff or company councils, works or office committees, participation groups and joint panels.

Within Europe, (under the **Transnational Information and Consultation of Employees Regulations 1999),** works councils must be set up in multi-site companies that employ:

1. at least 1,000 workers in Europe.
2. at least 150 employees in each of at least two member states.

In the UK, part-time workers may be calculated as 'half' a person. Companies do not have to be 'European'. For example they could be American or Japanese yet still fulfil the above criteria.

Each work council consists of between 3 and 30 people made up of at least one representative from each country plus management representatives. Representatives discuss and negotiate a wide range of issues, such as, business performance, growth and development plans, changes in working practices, and collective redundancies.

Such forums can help to develop positive working relationships between management and employees. They can go a long way toward removing 'them and us' attitudes resulting from traditional hierarchical boundaries, (which create barriers to communication, can lead to poor morale and a lack of sense of common purpose).

Work councils are particularly useful in increasing employee awareness and appreciation of factors influencing management decisions (and vice versa). This may help employees (and managers) to be more 'reasonable' with their demands and expectations.

Other Forms of Employee Representation

Worker Directors

Worker directors are employees within a business who have been given a place on the board of directors to represent the interest of workers.

Quality Circles

Quality circles consist of groups of employees, usually between 3 and 12 who meet on a regular basis to discuss work related problems, identify solutions and present their ideas to management.

Employee Shareholders

This is where employees are given the opportunity to own shares within the business in which they work. As ordinary shareholders, they receive a variable dividend (a percentage of after tax profits according to how well the company has done) and have voting rights on important matters such as the election of directors and chairpersons.

Employee share ownership schemes may encourage employees to increase work effort in order to help a business develop and grow, and develop a common sense of purpose. They may also encourage employees to remain loyal to the firm for several years, minimising labour turnover and its associated costs. In practice, however, both managers and staff may sell their shares for cash at the first opportunity. Furthermore, with regard to participation in decision making, it is highly unlikely that employees (apart from senior management) will secure sufficient number of shares to have any significant influence on key business decisions.

Closing Comments

In the not so distant past many managers have been against allowing employees to have a say (and some still are), as they believe it to represent an erosion of their own 'right to manage' and of management control. They may fear loss of power, lack of discipline, that work may not get completed and, in general, that their management positions will become insecure.

In today's social environment, employees are much less prepared to accept orders handed down to them, and are more likely to want to have a say in any major decisions which affect their working lives. In any case, allowing employees to participate can not only help to improve the quality of working life and satisfaction gained from work but the efficiency and productivity of business organisations, as outlined above.

The above being said, there are times when allowing employees to express their opinion would not be appropriate. For example, when the employees involved lack the qualifications / expertise to make a meaningful contribution, or have only just joined the business (linked to the above), when the time to consult is limited, or when it involves trivial matters which would unnecessarily slow down decision making / productivity.

Methods of Avoiding and Resolving Industrial Disputes

Objectives

By the end of this topic you should be able to:

1. Define the terms work to rule, go slow, overtime ban, sit-in, work-in, strike, picketing, lockout, no strike deal, single union agreement, arbitration, conciliation, mediation, and industrial tribunal.
2. Outline the main sources of conflict between workers and their employers.
3. Outline 7 types of organised industrial action and 3 types of unorganised industrial action that employees may take against their employers.
4. Outline 4 types of industrial action employers may take against employees.
5. Outline the consequences of industrial disputes for the employer and the employee.
6. Outline 2 methods of avoiding conflict.
7. Outline 3 methods of resolving conflict.
8. Outline the role of ACAS in resolving conflict in the workplace.

Key Terms

No strike deals are agreements formed between employee and management representatives not to strike in return for something eg higher wages, improved working conditions, limited redundancies.

Single union agreements are agreements between employee and management representatives to recognise and negotiate pay and other terms and conditions of employment with one single union covering the whole of the workforce.

Arbitration is where an independent person or panel listens to both sides of a dispute and decides the outcome.

Pendulum arbitration is where an independent person or panel listens to both sides of a dispute and chooses between the two sides rather than tries to form a compromise between the two.

Conciliation is the act of bringing together the parties involved in a dispute and helping them to reach a mutually agreeable solution.

Mediation is where an independent person or panel acts as an intermediary in talking and making suggestions to both sides but the final outcome is left for the parties to decide.

An **industrial tribunal** is a body of people set up to settle disputes between employers and employees, usually consisting of a legally qualified chairperson and two lay persons who decide the outcome of the dispute.

ACAS is the advisory, conciliation and arbitration service set up in 1975 to help prevent and settle industrial disputes.

Overview

When agreements cannot be reached between workers and their employees industrial disputes arise. The main sources of conflict are:

- Rates of pay (including overtime arrangements).
- Working conditions eg hours, breaks, holiday entitlements.
- Flexible working eg irregular work to match demand.
- Introduction of new machinery / technologies eg resulting in different work tasks, work groups, or redundancies.

Where disputes do arise, these can either be resolved through industrial action or less aggressively through the use of intermediaries. Many businesses have also sought to implement agreements such as 'single union' or 'no strike' agreements to reduce or even eliminate the threat of industrial action.

Types of Industrial Action

Employees' Industrial Action

Industrial action may be classed as organised and unorganised. **Organised** action includes the following:

- **Work to rule** – Workers stick closely to the rules and regulations laid down in the job descriptions, contracts of employment and / or company manuals, much of which are only guidelines and are often disregarded.
- **Go slow** – Workers deliberately do their job more slowly.
- **Overtime ban** – Employees only work the hours they are contracted to work and refuse to do any overtime. This can result in loss of earnings for employees but can be very effective in getting management to listen to their views if carried out at a time when increased output is particularly important.
- **Sit-in** – Workers refuse to leave their workplace and do not allow any goods or workers to enter or leave.
- **Work-in** – Workers refuse to leave their workplace and continue working – usually following the threat of closure to prove the business is still a viable concern.
- **Strike** – Workers withdraw their labour and refuse to work. This can last anywhere between one hour to several weeks. (NB Under Collective Labour Law strikes must be agreed in a secret ballot).
- **Picketing** – Workers on strike try to persuade others to join in the dispute.

Less noticeable forms of **unorganised** action include lower work effort, lateness, absenteeism. These can be just as damaging to a firm in terms of lower output, lost orders, sales and profits.

Employers' Industrial Action

Employers' industrial action may take various forms, including:

- **Withdrawal of overtime and suspension** – The employer refuses to give extra pay/rates for overtime or withdraws the opportunity for employees to work overtime.
- **Lockout** – The employer temporarily closes the premises and may not pay wages to employees.
- **Changing standards and piecework rates** - for example - The employer may raise the standard of work required forcing employees to work harder to obtain the same amount of pay.
- **Closure** – Complete closure of the premises for the long-term.

The Consequences of Industrial Action

For the Employer

From an employer's perspective industrial action can result in:

- lost production.
- unfulfilled orders.
- lost revenue and profit.
- cash flow problems.
- loss of reputation and future custom.
- lower morale, labour turnover and difficulties recruiting staff.

For the Employee

From the employee's perspective industrial action can result in **loss of earnings** – particularly as a result of:

- withdrawal of overtime and suspension.
- closure (which obviously results in redundancies unless workers can be redeployed elsewhere).
- work-to-rule or go-slows - if workers are paid piece-rate.

Methods for Avoiding Conflict

No Strike Deals

To minimise the damaging effects that can result from strike action employers have sought to implement no strike agreements, ie: agreements formed between employee and management representatives not to strike in return for something eg higher wages, improved working conditions, limited redundancies, etc.

Single Union Agreements

In the not so distant past employers found themselves negotiating with several different unions within one workplace. To reduce the time, complexity, conflict and administration costs involved in dealing with several unions, employers have sought to implement single union agreements, ie where one union covering the whole of the workforce is recognised and negotiated with on pay and other terms and conditions of employment.

If both parties fail to reach an agreement, then a third party can be brought in to try and help them resolve their differences through conciliation, arbitration or mediation.

Methods for Resolving Conflict

Conciliation

Conciliation is the act of bringing together the parties involved in a dispute and helping them to reach a mutually agreeable solution. The conciliator listens to the views of both sides, and encourages both sides to look for common ground and reconcile their differences.

Conciliators have no power to impose, or even recommend settlements. They simply try to enable the parties in dispute to reach their own agreement.

Arbitration

Arbitration is when an independent person or panel listens to both sides of a dispute and decides the outcome. The arbitrator's decision (or arbiter's in Scotland) may or may not be binding in law. If both sides agree in advance then the decision can be binding. Otherwise either side can reject the decision.

Pendulum Arbitration

This is where an independent person or panel listens to both sides of a dispute and chooses between the two sides rather than tries to form a compromise between the two. As one side will ultimately lose out completely, this usually encourages both sides to act reasonably and try to get as close an agreement as they can before taking it to pendulum arbitration.

Mediation

Mediation is where an independent person or panel acts as an intermediary in talking and making suggestions to both sides but the final outcome is left for the parties to decide. This differs from conciliation in that, whilst the aim is for the parties to resolve the problem between themselves, the mediator will actually make suggestions along the way.

Industrial Tribunals

An industrial tribunal is a body of people set up to settle disputes between employers and employees, usually consisting of a legally qualified chairperson and two lay persons who decide the outcome of the dispute. They largely deal with disputes concerning equal opportunities and cases of unfair dismissal.

Where the employer is found to be at fault industrial tribunals can insist that compensation is awarded and, in the case of unfair dismissal, an employee is reinstated or re-engaged (though compensation is more common in such cases). NB They do not have the power to enforce their decisions. This has to be done via a separate application to a court.

The Role of ACAS

Definition

ACAS is an independent body set up by the Employment Protection Act 1975 with the aim of improving industrial relations. ACAS stands for the **A**dvisory, **C**onciliation and **A**rbitration **S**ervice. If management and employees or employee representatives cannot reach an agreement over a dispute then they may seek help from ACAS who provide conciliation, mediation, and arbitration services.

Funding

ACAS offers free services and impartial advice and is funded by public funds. Since 1993, however, under the Trade Union Reform and Employment Rights Act, ACAS has been allowed to charge a fee for a limited range of its services (as directed by the Secretary of State) including conferences, seminars and some of its advisory publications.

Organisation

ACAS is run by a chairperson (the only full-time member), and up to 15 members (limited to nine prior to 1989), who are appointed by the Secretary of State for a period of five years (and who can be reappointed).

Approximately one third of these members are appointed following consultation with the Trade Union Congress (TUC), one third are appointed after consultation with the Confederation of British Industry (CBI). The remaining members are regarded as 'independents' who, until recently, have been academics.

ACAS has over 600 employees, working in six regional offices in England, and its offices in Scotland and Wales.

Role and Function in Solving Industrial Disputes and Resolving Conflict

The precise role of ACAS with regard to industrial disputes and resolving conflict is to:

- give impartial and confidential information and advice on trade union disputes.
- help resolve disputes over trade union recognition by voluntary means.
- help resolve disputes when a union makes a claim for trade union recognition under the Employment Relations Act 1999.
- assist with membership checks and ballots to help resolve trade union recognition issues.
- assist employers and trade unions to draw up recognition and procedural agreements, and work together to solve problems.

(Source: ACAS)

Closing Comments

There has been a decline in the level of industrial disputes in recent years. This has led to greater emphasis being placed on the general advisory role of ACAS rather than its role in resolving conflict / settling disputes. ACAS provides advice (including codes of practice) to employees, Trade Unions and employers, over a wide range of employment matters, including:

- employment legislation.
- workforce planning.
- recruitment.
- health and safety.

INDEX

absorption costing 63, 65
ACAS 275, 278-279
accountancy norms 54
accounting equation 18
accruals 21
acid test ratio 43, 45
adaptation 131, 140
annual hours contract 250, 255
Ansoff's matrix 127-130
   defining 127-128
   market penetration 128
   market development 128
   product development 128
   diversification 129
arbitration 275, 278
asset turnover 43, 46-47
assets 17, 18
   and depreciation 25-26
authoritarian / autocratic leadership 225
average cost 166
average cyclical variation 109
average rate of return 79, 81, 92

balance sheets 17-22
   defining 17-18
   typical formats 18-19
   explanation of key terms 20-22
   strengths and weaknesses of 38-41
bank loan 59
barriers to communication 260, 265-268
   overload 265
   intermediaries 266
   lack of common language 266
   lack of common sense of purpose 266
   attitudes 267
   low morale 267
   environmental 267
   time 268
   position / status 268
barriers to trade 196-197
batch production 171, 173
brand valuations 41
break-even analysis and location 185, 190
budgets 147

CAD see Computer Aided Design
CAM see Computer Aided Manufacture
capacity 166
capacity utilisation 157
capital 17, 18
capital expenditure 74-75
   defining 74-75
   allocating 75

capital intensive
   defining 171
   strategies 171-173
   factors influencing 173-174
cash and cash equivalents
   defining 20
   and liquidity 23
cash flow 10-11
cash flows 79-80
cell production 212, 214
centralisation 249-251
centring 110
communication 259-269
   defining 259
   process 260
   formal and informal 263
   vertical, lateral and diagonal 263-265
   networks 259, 264-265
   barriers 265-268
   ensuring effective 268-269
competitive advantage 121
Computer Aided Design (CAD) 202, 203-204
Computer Aided Manufacture (CAM) 202, 204
conciliation 275, 277
consolidation 130
contribution costing 63, 66
core workforce 249, 254-255
corporate culture 220-221
corporate objectives 4-6
   defining 4
   relationship with functional objectives 5-6
   and strategies 7
corporate strategy 7
corporation tax 27
correlation 106, 111-113
   defining 106
   use in analysing markets 111-113
cost leadership 121, 122-123
cost minimisation 67-73
   defining 67
   to achieve financial and corporate objectives 67
   ways of minimising costs 68-73
   and liquidity 24
cost of sales 27, 29
costs 157
credit collection period 44, 49
creditors 21
   and liquidity 24
critical activities 205

critical path analysis 205-211
   defining 205
   drawing simple networks 206
   calculating EST's and LFT's 207-208
   calculating total float 209
   identifying the critical path 209
   role, purpose and benefits 210-211
current assets 17, 20, 23
current liabilities 17, 20-21, 23
current ratio 43, 44
customer loyalty 97

data analysis 116
data collection 116
data presentation 117
databases 116
debentures 21, 57, 60
debt collection period 44, 49-50
debtors 20
   and liquidity 23, 24
decentralisation 249-252
decision trees 86, 87-89
delayering 249, 252-253
delphi technique 114
democratic leadership style 226
departmentalisation 243, 244
depreciation 25-26
   defining 17
   purpose 25
   implications of 26
desk research 104
diagonal communication 259, 264
differentiation 121, 123-125
direct exporting 131, 138
diseconomies of scale 166, 167, 169-170
diversification 127, 129
dividend 31
   payable 21
   per share 44, 51-52
   yield 44, 52
   cover 52
divisional organisational structure 243, 245
downsizing 233
earnings per share 53
economies of scale 132-133
efficiency 158-159
employee representation 273-274
   defining 270
   legal requirements for 270-271
   advantages and disadvantages with 271
   methods of 272-274
employee shareholders 274
employer / employee relations 259-279
environmental targets 159-160
exceptional items 28, 30
exchange rates 135-136, 196
expenses 27, 30

external diseconomies of scale 166, 170
external economies of scale 166, 170
external influences
   on financial objectives 13, 14-15
   on marketing objectives 99, 100-101
   on marketing plans 149, 150-151
   on operational objectives 161, 162-164
   on HR objectives 220, 222-223
   on workforce plans 234, 235-237
extraordinary items 28, 30
extrapolation 106, 109-110

feedback 260
field research 104
finance costs 27, 30
finance income 27, 30
financial efficiency ratios 43, 46-50
financial objectives 10-15
   defining 5
   examples 10-12
   internal and external influences on 13-15
fixed assets 17, 20, 39
   and liquidity 23, 24
fixed costs 189
fixed term contract 254-255
flexible workforces 253-257
flow production 171
focus strategy 121, 125-126
foreign independent presence 131, 139
formal communication 259, 263
formal organisational structure 246
formalisation 243, 244
franchising 131, 139
full costing 63, 65
functional objectives 4-6
   defining 4
   relationship with corporate objectives 5-6
   relationship with strategies 7
functional organisational structure 243, 245
functional strategy 7
   defining 7
   relationship with functional objectives 7

gearing 35, 38, 41, 44, 50-51
globalisation 131, 140
go slow 276
government grants 58, 60
gross margin 36
gross profit 27, 30

hard HR strategies 224-225, 228
hierarchy 243, 244
hire purchase 57, 59
historical analysis 114
home working 255
horizontal analysis 33, 35
horizontal communication 259, 264

HR objectives 218-223
   defining 218
   examples of 218-219
   internal and external influences on 220-223
HR strategies 224-228
   defining 224
   hard 224-225
   soft 226-228
   appropriateness of 227-228
human resource objectives see HR objectives
human resource strategies see HR strategies

income statement (profit & loss) 27-31
   defining 27
   typical formats 28-29
   explanation of key terms 29-31
indirect costs 27
indirect exporting 131, 138-139
industrial disputes 275-279
industrial tribunal 275, 278
industry comparisons 33, 37, 54
inflation 40
informal communication 259, 263
informal organisational structure 246
information technology
   defining 115
   use in analysing markets 116-117
infrastructure 187
innovation 158
innovation 176-183
   defining 176
   types 176
   drivers of 177
   stages in 177-178
   implications of 180
   purpose, costs, benefits, risks of 181-183
intangible assets 20, 41
inter-firm comparisons 33, 37, 54
internal influences
   on financial objectives 13-14
   on marketing objectives 99-100
   on marketing plans 149-150
   on operational objectives 161-162
   on HR objectives 220-221
   on workforce plans 234-235
international location 195-198
   reasons for 195-196
   issues associated with 196-198
international markets 131-141
   definitions 131
   benefits of entering 132-133
   risks of entering 133-136
   minimising the risks of entering 137-138
   methods of entering 137-139
   standardisation or adaptation in 140

inventories 20
   and liquidity 23, 24
inventory turnover 43, 47-48
investment 77-78
   defining 77
   types of 77
   reasons for 77-78
investment appraisal 79-93
   defining 79
   quantitative techniques of 79-83, 91-92
   and location decisions 185, 191
investment criteria 84-85
   financial 84
   non-financial 85
investment decisions 86-93
   risk and uncertainty with 86
   assessing risk and uncertainty with 87
   managing risk and uncertainty with 87-89
   quantitative/qualitative influences on 90-93

job production 171, 173
joint venture 131, 139
just-in-time (JIT) production 212-213

kaizen 212, 215

labour intensive
   defining 171
   strategies 173
   factors influencing 173-174
labour shortfall strategies 232
labour surplus strategies 232-233
lateral communication 259, 264
lead time 202
lean production 200-215
   defining 200
   benefits and key requirements 201
leasing 57, 59
liabilities 17, 18
licensing 131, 139
lines of best fit 112-113
liquidity 10-11, 23-24
   defining 10-11
   the link with working capital 23
   implications of poor 23
   managing working capital to secure 24
   position 35
   level of 39
   and sale and leaseback 41
   ratios 43, 44-45
loan capital 57
localisation 131, 140

location decisions 185-198
    quantitative factors influencing 186-188
    qualitative factors influencing 188-189
    quantitative techniques used in 189-191
    benefits of optimal 192
    multi-site 193-194
    issues relating to international 195-198
lockouts 276
long-term liabilities 18, 21
low cost see cost leadership

marginal costing 63, 66
market analysis 103-119
    defining 103
    reasons for 104
    the value of 104
    use of information technology in 115-117
    difficulties in 118-119
market development 127, 128
market penetration 127, 128
market segmentation strategy 121
market share 97
market standing 97
marketing budgets 147-148
marketing mix 147
marketing objectives 5, 7, 96-98
    defining 96
    examples 96-98
    SMART 98
    and non-profit making organisations 98
    internal and external influences on 99-101
marketing planning 145-146
marketing plans 145-153
    defining 145
    components of 146-148
    internal and external influences on 149-151
    issues in implementing 152-153
marketing strategy
    defining 7
    assessing effectiveness of 142-143, 147
marketing tactics 145, 147
mass production 171
matrix organisational structure 243, 245
McGregor's Theory X and Y 225-226
mechanistic organisational structure 243, 246
mediation 275, 278
methods of finance 57-62
    defining 57-58
    advantages and disadvantages 59-60
    factors affecting choice over 61-62
morale 267
mortgage 57, 60
moving averages 106, 107-110
multi-site locations 193-194

net assets 18, 21
net book value 20
net current liabilities 17, 21
net present value 79, 81-83, 92
net profit 27, 30
net worth 19, 38
network analysis 205-211
no strike deals 275, 277
non-critical activities 205
non-current assets 17, 20
    and liquidity 23
non-current liabilities 18, 21
non-operating income 30

objectives 3
off-shoring 195
operating margin 36
operating profit 27, 30
operational objectives 156-164
    defining 156
    types of 156-160
    internal and external influences on 161-164
ordinary share capital 22
ordinary shareholders 22
organic organisational structure 243, 246
organisational structure 243-257
    defining and classifying 243-245
    types of 245-246
    factors influencing choice of 247-248
    adapting for competitiveness 249-257
outsourcing 251, 256-257
overdrafts 21, 57, 59
overtime ban 276

panel consensus 114
payables collection period 44, 49
payback 79, 80, 91
pendulum arbitration 275, 278
periphery workforce 249, 254-255
personal insight 114
personal sources of finance 57, 59
picketing 276
Porter's generic strategies 121-126
    defining 121
    low cost – cost leadership 122-123
    differentiation 123-125
    focus 125-126
preference share capital 22
preference shareholders 22
prepayments 20
price earnings ratio 53
primary marketing data
    limitations of 118
product development 127, 128-129
product differentiation 123-125

profit 28
   before tax 27, 30
   after tax 28, 30
   before interest and tax 30
   for the year 28, 30
   utilisation 28, 31
   quality 28, 32
profit and loss account see income statement
profit centres 63-66
   defining 63
   role, purpose and benefits 63-64
   establishing 64
   methods of allocating costs to 65-66
profitability ratios 43, 45-46
protectionism 195

qualitative influences
   on investment decisions 90, 92-93
   on sales forecasting techniques 107, 114
   on locations decisions 185, 188-189
quality 156-157
quality circles 274
quantitative influences
   on investment decisions 90-92
   on sales forecasting techniques 107-114
   on location decisions 185, 186-191
quotas 195

raising finance see methods of finance
ratio analysis 43-53
   defining 33, 36, 43
   types of ratios 43-53
   value and limitations of 54-55
receivables collection period 44, 49-50
redundancy 233
   voluntary 233
   compulsory 233
relocation 188
research and development 176, 177-178, 182
reserves 18,22
retained earnings 18,22
retained profit 22, 31, 57, 59
retrenchment 129
return on capital employed 11-12
   ratios 43, 45-46
return on equity 53
revaluations 18, 22
revenue 27, 29, 39
revenue expenditure 74-75
revenues 189
risk 86
ROCE see Return on capital employed
ROE see Return on equity

sale of assets 57, 59
sales forecasting 106
sales forecasts 106, 148
scale of production 166-170
scatter graphs 111-113
secondary marketing data
   limitations of 118
sensitivity analysis 86, 87
share capital 22, 58, 60
share premiums 18, 22
shareholder ratios 44, 51-53
shareholders' equity 18, 22
shareholders' funds 18, 22
shareholders' returns 12
simultaneous engineering 202, 203-204
single union agreement 277
single-site 193
site 193
sit-in 276
SMART objectives 98
soft HR strategies 224, 226-228
sources of finance see methods of finance
span of control 243, 244
spreadsheets 116
standardisation 131, 140, 244
stock 20
   and liquidity 23, 24
   turnover 43, 47-48
strategy, strategies 3
   and relationship with objectives 3
strike 276

tangible assets 20
tariffs 195
technology 243
test market 106
test marketing 106, 113-114
time series analysis 107-110
time-based management
   defining 202
   techniques 203-204
total assets less current liabilities 21
total equity 18, 22
trade and other payables 21
   and liquidity 23, 24
trade and other receivables 20
   and liquidity 24
trade credit 57, 59
trading profit 30
trend analysis 33, 36
trends 106-114
   defining 106
   establishing and extrapolating 107-110
turnover 27, 29, 39

uncertainty 86
unique selling point / proposition (USP) 121
unit cost 166

value analysis 176, 179
variable costs 189
venture capital 58, 60
vertical analysis 33, 35
vertical communication 259, 263

window dressing 38, 40-41
work to rule 276
worker directors 274
workforce planning 230-231
workforce plans 230-241
    defining 230
    stages involved in producing 230-231
    components of 232-233
    internal and external influences on 234-237
    issues in implementing 238-239
    value and limitations of using 240-241
work-in 276
working capital
    defining 17
    the importance of 22-23
    the link with liquidity 23
    managing 24
    manipulating 41
works councils 273

zero hours contract 250, 255